Newcastle United

POCKET ANNUAL
1994-95

Edited by
Jim Bluck

WORDS ON Sport

Newcastle United Pocket Annual 1994-95

Copyright © Jim Bluck – 1994

ISBN: 1-898351-11-2

Typeset by Bruce Smith Books Ltd

All photographs supplied by Empics Ltd.
Cover Photo: Peter Beardsley

Statistics supplied by Football Information Services.

First published in 1994 by
Words on Sport

Words on Sport Ltd
PO Box 382
St. Albans
Herts, AL2 3JD

Registration Number: 2917013

Registered Office:
Worplesdon Chase, Worplesdon, Guildford, Surrey, GU3 3LA

Printed and Bound in Great Britain by Ashford Colour Press Ltd, Gosport.

CONTENTS

Acknowledgements

Many thanks to all those people who, in one way or another, have contributed something to this first *Newcastle United Pocket Annual*. In particular, I would like to thank those friends, relatives and colleagues who have had to put up with endless tales of obscure Edwardian footballers while I was researching this book, as well as the players and management of Newcastle United for providing such fascinating material.

Disclaimer

In a book of this type it is inevitable that some errors will creep in. While every effort has been made to ensure that the details given in this annual are correct at the time of going to press, neither the editor nor the publishers can accept any responsibilities for errors within.

If you do notice any mistakes then please write in and we will try and rectify them for future issues. In addition, if there are other areas of information about Newcastle United Football Club that you feel should be included in future editions then please let us know of your choices.

Introduction

Welcome to the first ever Newcastle United Pocket Annual. In these pages you will find all you could ever wish to know about the club, as well as an in depth review of the events, high points, low points and controversies of the 1993/94 season.

It's been such a thrilling year for Magpies fans, with the return to the Premiership and storming performances taking the team to third place. Included are full statistics for the season's Premiership, FA Cup and Coca-Cola Cup campaigns as well as match reports from every game and details on every player who has made a first team appearance.

But that's not all. United have a long and proud history and we've also included historical records to put this season's achievements into perspective. There are details of every league and cup campaign since the days before United was formed from the merger of the Newcastle East End and West End clubs. We've also included United's European campaigns in the '60s and '70s as well as their record in the minor competitions, such as the Anglo Italian and ZDS Cups.

Complete career records of every player to have worn a United shirt are included and we have also recorded the international careers of every United player to have represented his country, be they English, Scottish, Irish, Welsh – or Chilean!

There are details of every other Premiership club, to help you find your way around the grounds next season, and a full round-up of the season's highlights, both on and off the field. Newcastle fans are renowned for their knowledge and appreciation of the game and we hope that this book will add a little more to your enjoyment, serving as a reminder of a glorious season and a guide to the team's future success.

1993-94 Season Reviewed

Back in August, most Newcastle supporters would have been happy with a respectable mid-table season. In the big time again for the first time since 1989, the Magpies could have been forgiven for a year of consolidation, building a team that could maybe challenge for honours in the near future. What actually happened, under the inspirational guidance of the almighty Kevin Keegan, was a near miracle.

Starting the season with much the same team that had run away with the First Division in 1993, United began a touch shakily. The only big summer signing, Peter Beardsley, missed the opening games, but a fine draw at Old Trafford showed that the team had what it takes. Slowly building to success, United ended the season as one of the leading teams in the land. At the time of writing, a UEFA Cup place has just been confirmed, due to the United Nations maintaining sanctions against the former Yugoslavian nations. Therefore third place in the Premiership represents unqualified success.

What's more, it's a very young side. Experience is there in the form of dependable Barry Venison in defence, Paul Bracewell in midfield and of course the fantastic Pedro, still going strong at the age of 33, but the number of youngsters who now have first team experience bodes well for the future. In defence, in addition to John Beresford, there's Steve Watson, who at just twenty has become a regular, Alan Neilson, now an established part of the Welsh international set-up and Robbie Elliott, filling in admirably wherever needed. Steve Howey is still a young man and hopefully will recover from his injury problems to reclaim his place in the side. Then of course there's record signing Darren Peacock, adding height and strength in the middle.

In midfield, Lee Clark, who had been so crucial to the promotion team was hampered by injury, but the likes of Scott Sellars, Ruel Fox and Robert Lee were the equal of any other partnership to be seen in the Premiership. Up front, the deadly duo of Cole and Beardsley were a phenomenon. Playing with a relish that defied his years, Pedro has re-established himself in the England team and of course Andy Cole has continued the incredible form of last year. Some people thought the young striker would be unable to transfer his form from the lower division into the top flight, but he surpassed even his own expectations by smashing the club's scoring record with 41 goals in the season.

Waiting in the wings there's Alex Mathie, a regular sub this season, Malcolm Allen with his attacking experience, Chris Holland, Mike Jeffrey, Matty Appleby, the new American 'keeper Brad Friedel – the list seems to go on forever.

On the field, highlights included two 7-1 wins against Notts County in the Coca-Cola Cup and Swindon in the league, doing the double over both of the Merseyside giants and smashing five past Aston Villa on the day that Andy Cole broke the scoring record. But perhaps the two best displays came against Norwich City. The East Anglian side's style of play complements Newcastle's passing, fluid football and both games against them this term were thrilling spectacles, United coming out on top both times.

The down side came in the cup competitions: dumped out of the Coca-Cola Cup by Wimbledon, in a week where team spirit was at a low, and then beaten by First Division Luton in the FA Cup, during another one of the season's troughs.

The league season started slowly but victories over Sheffield Wednesday and West Ham in September lifted the Magpies to the top half of the table and by Christmas, following the spectacular 3-0 win over Liverpool and the second draw against the Champions, United had reached the top five, where they were to stay.

A run of six successive wins followed by two draws, beginning in February, meant that Newcastle were certain of finishing in third place, above the likes of Arsenal, Leeds United and Liverpool, all Champions in the last few years.

The time will come when Peter Beardsley is no longer able to maintain his form at the highest level but for next season at least there can be little doubt that the strike pair will be at their best again. Cole and Beardsley scored 65 times between them in the 1993/94 season and United finished as the Premiership's leading scorers. With form like that it's no wonder that the crowds are flocking to St James' Park and, unless you have a season ticket, it's very difficult even to get in to the ground.

Keegan's achievement in turning round a side who, little more than two years ago, seemed doomed to the Second Division must not be underestimated, but it is the potential, the massive support and proud tradition that has enabled Newcastle to get back to the top. Keegan has said that United can become "the biggest club on earth, playing in a European league or perhaps the Inter-Planetary Cup." I'm not sure what the little green men of Mars would make of Beardsley and Cole, but I'm certain the fanatical Toon Army would give them something to think about!

With the ground full to capacity every week and United playing the exciting, attacking brand of football the loyal Geordie fans expect, Newcastle has become the team to watch for this season.

Newcastle Diary 1993/94

For a side just returning to the big time, it was perhaps surprising that the Newcastle squad saw so few changes over the summer. Gavin Peacock had gone to Chelsea, Kevin Sheedy was easing down his career with Blackpool and some other fringe players had left, but there were only three new signings – Nicky Papavasiliou, the Cypriot international from OFI Crete, Alex Mathie, the young forward from Morton and of course, the big signing – the return of Pedro. Many people thought Keegan had taken a big gamble by spending £1.4 million on a 32-year-old but Peter Beardsley turned out to be the buy of the season.

Still, it was not to be a good start, for either Beardsley or United as a whole. Key players such as Barry Venison and Scott Sellars picked up injuries through the pre-season warm ups and then, in the last of the friendlies, came the hammer blow. In a clash with Liverpool's Neil Ruddock, Peter Beardsley sustained a fractured cheekbone which was to keep him out until mid-September. With his plans in disarray, Keegan had to find a solution and on the Friday before the first game with Spurs, he signed striker Malcolm Allen, who was languishing in Millwall's reserves, and he was to prove an admirable stop-gap.

The season starts a week earlier than usual (optimistically to allow the England team time to prepare for the World Cup) and on 14th August, Newcastle play their first ever Premiership match against Tottenham Hotspur at St James' Park. They lose 1-0 and it begins to look as if it will have to be a season of consolidation, rather than a chase for glory. This feeling grows three days later when the Magpies go down 2-1 away to Coventry, with 'keeper Pavel Srnicek sent off in the process. On appeal, Srnicek's ban is reduced from three games to one, but it is still a blow. The injury list continues to grow, with Steve Howey suffering a groin strain against Spurs and, with a visit to the reigning Champions Manchester United next up, things are looking bleak. But a wonderful performance earns a 1-1 draw, Andy Cole getting his first goal of the season and young defender Steve Watson earning the plaudits. Four days later comes the first win, Malcolm Allen getting the only goal against Everton, then another 1-1 draw against one of the top sides, Alan Shearer getting Blackburn's equaliser after Andy Cole had scored. Off the field, the 23-year-old Yugoslav international Dragan Lukic begins trials with United, but nothing comes of them.

The last day of August sees yet another 1-1 draw, this time away to Ipswich.

September

A long gap without a game at the start of the month sees off-the-field concerns therefore taking centre stage. Peter Beardsley begins the process of taking legal action against Neil Ruddock for the incident that fractured his cheekbone, Nottingham Forest begin to show interest in reserve keeper Tommy Wright while United look at Reading defender Adrian Williams. Steve Howey has an operation on his groin and is later rushed back to hospital when the wound re-opens.

On the 13th, Newcastle make their debut on Sky's Monday night football slot and pull off a magnificent and thrilling 4-2 win over Sheffield Wednesday, Cole scoring twice along with Mathie and Allen, moving up to 13th position in the league. Liam O'Brien becomes another injury victim when he pulls a hamstring in training.

The following Saturday sees the return of Beardsley, recovered from his injury and showing some splendid touches, but United throw away a two goal lead to draw 2-2 at Swindon.

Keegan pays out £550,000 for the Liverpool reserve 'keeper Mike Hooper, the day before the Coca-Cola Cup 2nd round, 1st leg tie at home to Notts County. Although United win 4-1, Cole getting a hat-trick, County score first and the goal is put down to an error by Pavel Srnicek, so Hooper is set to make his debut in the next game against West Ham, keeping his place in the side until February. The massive Toon Army flag raised by fans is banned by the Fire Brigade as a fire risk.

United beat West Ham 2-0 on Hooper's debut, with both goals from Cole. On the day that a crowd of 8,000 saw the reserve game against Sunderland, Brian Kilcline turns down a move to Oxford United, despite not being able to get into the first team.

October

On the first of the month, Mike Jeffrey signs from Doncaster Rovers, in an exchange deal with David Roche. A 2-0 away win at Aston Villa moves United up to sixth place in the league. Midweek sees the return leg of the Coca-Cola Cup game against Notts County and United win 7-1, a magnificent performance capped by Andy Cole's hat-trick. Then another 11 day break from the field sees the team lose some of its momentum.

9

Kevin Keegan signs a new three year contract to keep him at St James' Park until 1997 and Lee Clark also signs a new contract. Keegan is refused permission to approach Crystal Palace striker Chris Armstrong and Newcastle are also linked with Manchester City's Keith Curle.

Back in action and United go down 2-1 at home to QPR, after Malcolm Allen misses a late penalty. Barry Venison and Paul Bracewell sign new contracts, before United go down to their second successive defeat at Southampton, with two wonder goals from Matt Le Tissier. Lee Clark is dropped for the Coca-Cola Cup tie at Wimbledon after a bust-up when he was substituted at the Dell and Andy Cole is also missing, suffering from 'home sickness'. Naturally, United lose 2-1 to Wimbledon but three days later it's Wimbledon at home in the league. The arguments have been settled, Clark and Cole are both in the team and United win 4-0.

November

Keegan introduces a new disciplinary code at the club, to prevent any more bust-ups. United give a trial to Ajax defender John Hansen, but he is not signed. A 3-1 win at Oldham is one of the most enjoyable games of the season, with Peter Beardsley in sparkling form. Lee Clark plays in the England Under 21s against San Marino, while Andy Cole is on the bench for the Senior squad in the last of the World Cup qualifiers.

Steve Howey is fit again, getting a run out in the reserves while teenager Robbie Elliott is back in the team for the Sunday game against Liverpool. Andy Cole destroys the Reds with a magnificent hat-trick in the first half hour.

The game against Sheffield United goes ahead despite the snow in Newcastle and the Magpies triumph 4-0, Beardsley scoring twice and Cole getting his 34th goal in just 30 games. Steve Howey comes on as a sub against Arsenal, but United go down 2-1.

December

Sir John Hall says Keegan is staying as speculation mounts that the Newcastle manager may be first choice for the England hot seat. Revenge for the defeat on the first day of the season on the 4th, as United win 2-1 at White Hart Lane, Beardsley getting the injury time winner. St James' Park succumbs to the weather and the Coventry City game on the 8th is called because of a waterlogged pitch. Kevin Keegan is named Manager of the Month for November. The pitch is still heavy for the visit of Manchester

United but the game goes ahead and Newcastle have the better of a 1-1 draw and are now established in the top five of the league.

Robert Lee signs a new three year contract and Mark Robinson comes through a reserve team outing after a long term injury. Cole and Beardsley score the goals that complete the 'double' over Everton in the 2-0 win at Goodison. Three days before Christmas, Leeds visit St James' Park in a vital game for European places, and draw 1-1. On the 28th a dismal display at Chelsea sees a 1-0 defeat the result. The only tickets available to Newcastle fans are priced at £25 and it's a less than merry Christmas all round. Keegan denies that he is going to sign Liverpool's Ian Rush.

January

Happy New Year with a 2-0 win over Manchester City on the 1st, but Paul Bracewell picks up a groin injury. Another win three days later, 2-1 away to Norwich City.

Barry Venison is out injured for the FA Cup 3rd round at home to Coventry, but Cole and Beardsley score to give United a 2-0 win. Norwich City's Ruel Fox becomes Kevin Keegan's next target in the transfer market, but he denies any interest in Les Ferdinand. Venison and Bracewell are fit again for the visit to QPR and a 2-1 win takes United to third in the table for the first time.

Keegan pays out £100,000 for Preston's Chris Holland, even though he has not started a league game for the Lancashire club. Andy Cole scores his 30th goal of the season at home to Southampton but United go down 2-1, with Le Tissier again in sparkling form for the opposition. There are increasing calls for Srnicek's return to the team as Mike Hooper is blamed for the Southampton goals.

First Division Luton Town are the visitors for the fourth round FA Cup tie and a disappointing performance sees United salvage a 1-1 draw with a second half penalty.

February

Kevin Scott is sold to Ossie Ardiles' Tottenham the day before Keegan finally secures the signature of Ruel Fox, paying out a record £2.25 million for the 26-year-old. A £2 million bid for defender Darren Peacock is turned down by Queens Park Rangers. Keegan is also chasing Dutch international Ulrich van Gobbel.

Paul Bracewell is out injured for the replay against Luton and a dire performance ends the Magpies' interest in the Cup, going down 2-0 with Hooper at fault again. Barry Venison and two other players are fined by the club after a wine bar incident. Andy Cole picks up an injury and is out for the Premiership game at Wimbledon. Fox makes his debut, but United lose 4-2 in another poor performance.

Despite the fact that van Gobbel wants to sign, United will not up their bid and the deal falls through. Srnicek replaces Hooper in goal for the trip to Blackburn Rovers but, despite an improved performance, United go down 1-0 and slip back to fifth in the table. The goals have dried up without Cole.

The rearranged home game against Coventry is nearly called off again but a snow-clearing operation allows the game to go ahead and with Cole back, United win 4-0, the returning striker getting three of the goals. Back to third in the league. Peter Beardsley is recalled to the England squad by new manager Terry Venables.

March

The first game of the month sees a lucky 1-0 win at Sheffield Wednesday but Steve Howey has a recurrence of the groin injury that has been troubling him all year and is out for the rest of the season. Beardsley wins his 50th cap for England in the 1-0 win over Denmark.

A massive 7-1 thumping of doomed Swindon Town sees Robert Lee get his first league goals of the season and, surprisingly, Andy Cole is not on the score sheet. A week later, Lee gets another two goals in a thrilling 4-2 win at West Ham. The rearranged game against Ipswich at home is won 2-0, as Chris Holland sets up both goals on his debut.

As transfer deadline day looms, Keegan takes Rangers defender Brian Reid on loan until the end of the season, but he is destined to be named just once as a sub. Then another record-breaking signing as Keegan pays £2.7 million for QPR centre back Darren Peacock. A £1.2 million bid fails to secure Coventry's Irish defender Phil Babb – the Midlands club demands £1.75 million.

Aston Villa win the Coca-Cola Cup, thus securing one of the two certain UEFA Cup places. With Newcastle unlikely to reach higher than third place, they will have to rely on getting an extra place at the expense of the former Yugoslavian teams if they are to get European football for next season. A sixth win in a row at home to Norwich, 3-0, with Cole, Lee and Beardsley scoring.

An early goal in the April Fool's day trip to Leeds and Newcastle desperately defend to hang on to the lead, but Leeds get a last gasp equaliser. Three days later and it's the first 0-0 of the season at home to Chelsea, in which John Beresford picks up an injury. With many of the team carrying slight injuries, the unbeaten run comes to an end against Manchester City, the relegation threatened team battling back to 2-1 after United took an early lead.

With the England game against Germany called off, Terry Venables organises a training session instead and Robert Lee is called up along with Cole and Beardsley.

On the anniversary of the Hillsborough disaster, United visit Anfield and, on an emotionally charged day, Peter Beardsley dominates his old team mates. Lee and Cole score in the 2-0 win. United have now completed the 'double' over both Merseyside teams for the first time ever. Lee Clark is told that his injury will keep him out of the game for the rest of the season. Alan Neilson makes his international debut for Wales and also signs a new three year contract to keep him at St James' Park.

United win 3-2 in a knife-edge game with struggling Oldham after which Brian Reid is recalled to Rangers. Three days later there's a night of records as United beat Aston Villa 5-1. Peter Beardsley plays his 600th league game while Andy Cole breaks the club's scoring record for a season. Next day the striker signs a new contract that will keep him at the club for another four seasons. Penultimate game of the season is at Bramall Lane where Sheffield United, fighting to avoid the drop, win 2-0. Elsewhere Arsenal also lose so United are virtually assured of third place and a potential UEFA Cup spot.

May

Peter Beardsley is named player of the season, Keegan signs a new three year contract and Arthur Cox comes back to the club. The final game is at home to Arsenal, the Londoners' one place behind United in the league and having just won the Cup-Winners' Cup. With nothing at stake there's a party atmosphere as United win 2-0. Peter Beardsley, but not Andy Cole, is in the England squad for the friendly against Greece.

Robert Lee on another telling run through the heart of the defence.

The Season

Match by Match

Ruel Fox

Newcastle United Results Summary 1993/94

Date	Type	Opponents		Scores	Scorers	Att.
14/08/93	FACP	Tottenham H	(h)	0-1		35,216
18/08/93	FACP	Coventry City	(a)	1-2	O'Brien	15,760
21/08/93	FACP	Manchester Utd	(a)	1-1	Cole	41,829
25/08/93	FACP	Everton	(h)	1-0	Allen	34,833
29/08/93	FACP	Blackburn Rovers	(h)	1-1	Cole	34,272
31/08/93	FACP	Ipswich Town	(a)	1-1	Cole	19,102
13/09/93	FACP	Sheffield Wed	(h)	4-2	Cole 2, Mathie, Allen	33,890
18/09/93	FACP	Swindon Town	(a)	2-2	Clark, Allen	15,015
22/09/93	CCC1R	Notts County	(h)	4-2	Cole 3, Bracewell	25,887
25/09/93	FACP	West Ham Utd	(h)	2-0	Cole 2	34,336
02/10/93	FACP	Aston Villa	(a)	2-0	Allen, Cole	37,336
05/10/93	CCC1R/2	Notts County	(a)	7-1	Allen 2, Beardsley, Cole 3, Lee	6,068
16/10/93	FACP	QPR	(h)	1-2	Allen	33,926
24/10/93	FACP	Southampton	(a)	1-2	Cole	13,804
27/10/93	CCC2R	Wimbledon	(a)	1-2	Sellars	11,531
30/10/93	FACP	Wimbledon	(h)	4-0	Beardsley 3, Cole	33,392
08/11/93	FACP	Oldham Athletic	(a)	3-1	Cole 2, Beardsley	13,821
21/11/93	FACP	Liverpool	(h)	3-0	Cole 3	36,374
24/11/93	FACP	Sheffield United	(h)	4-0	o.g., Beardsley 2, Cole	35,101
27/11/93	FACP	Arsenal	(a)	1-2	Beardsley	36,091
04/12/93	FACP	Tottenham H	(a)	2-1	Beardsley 2	30,780
11/12/93	FACP	Manchester Utd	(h)	1-1	Cole	36,388
18/12/93	FACP	Everton	(a)	2-0	Cole, Beardsley	25,189
22/12/93	FACP	Leeds United	(h)	1-1	Cole	36,388
28/12/93	FACP	Chelsea	(a)	0-1		23,133
01/01/94	FACP	Manchester City	(h)	2-0	Cole 2	35,658
04/01/94	FACP	Norwich City	(a)	2-1	Beardsley, Cole	19,564
08/01/94	FAC3R	Coventry City	(h)	2-0	Cole, Beardsley	35,444
16/01/94	FACP	QPR	(a)	2-1	Clark, Beardsley	15,774
22/01/94	FACP	Southampton	(h)	1-2	Cole	32,129
29/01/94	FAC4R	Luton Town	(h)	1-1	Beardsley	32,216
09/02/94	FAC4R/2	Luton Town	(a)	0-2		12,503

Date	Type	Opponents		Scores	Scorers	Att.
12/02/94	FACP	Wimbledon	(a)	2-4	Beardsley 2	13,358
19/02/94	FACP	Blackburn Rovers	(a)	0-1		21,269
23/02/94	FACP	Coventry City	(h)	4-0	Cole 3, Mathie	32,216
05/03/94	FACP	Sheffield Wed	(a)	1-0	Cole	33,224
12/03/94	FACP	Swindon Town	(h)	7-1	Beardsley 2, Lee 2, Watson 2, Fox	32,216
19/03/94	FACP	West Ham United	(a)	4-2	Lee 2, Cole, Mathie	23,132
23/03/94	FACP	Ipswich Town	(h)	2-0	Sellars, Cole	32,216
29/03/94	FACP	Norwich City	(h)	3-0	Cole, Lee, Beardsley	32,216
01/04/94	FACP	Leeds United	(a)	1-1	Cole	40,005
04/04/94	FACP	Chelsea	(h)	0-0		32,216
09/04/94	FACP	Manchester City	(a)	1-2	Sellars	33,774
16/04/94	FACP	Liverpool	(a)	2-0	Lee, Cole	44,601
23/04/94	FACP	Oldham Athletic	(h)	3-2	Fox, Beardsley, Lee	32,216
27/04/94	FACP	Aston Villa	(h)	5-1	Bracewell, Beardsley 2, Cole, Sellars	32,216
30/04/94	FACP	Sheffield United	(a)	0-2		29,013
07/05/94	FACP	Arsenal	(h)	2-0	Cole, Beardsley	32,216

Key: FACP = FA Carling Premiership
        FAC = FA Cup
        CCC = Coca-Cola Cup

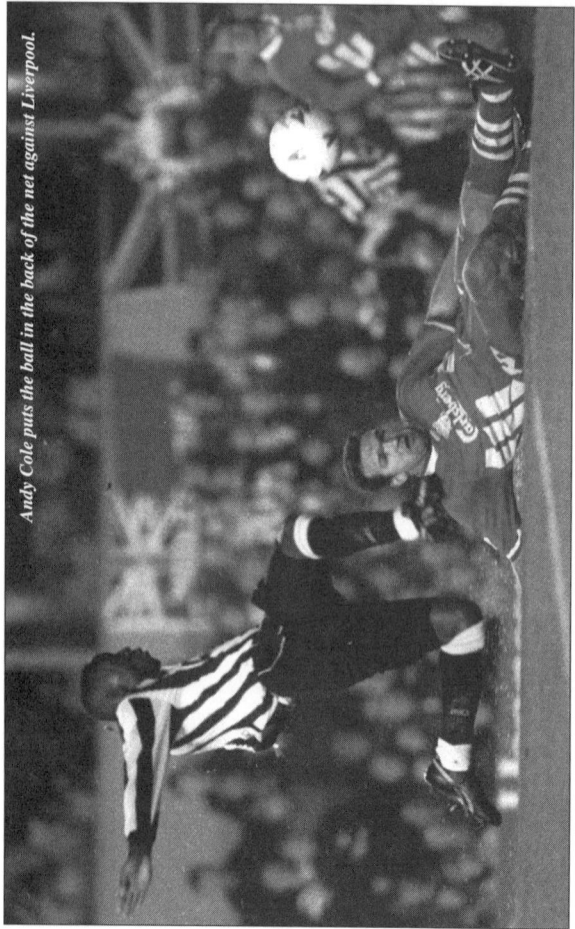

Andy Cole puts the ball in the back of the net against Liverpool.

Newcastle United   (0) 0
Tottenham Hotspur   (1) 1

Saturday, 14th August 1993, St James' Park   Att.: 35,216

NEWCASTLE UNITED

1	Pavel	SRNICEK
2	Barry	VENISON – *Booked*
5	Kevin	SCOTT
6	Steve	HOWEY
3	John	BERESFORD
7	Robert	LEE
4	Paul	BRACEWELL
10	Lee	CLARK
17	*Niki*	*PAPAVASILIOU (+75)*
9	Andy	COLE
21	*Malcolm*	*ALLEN (†61)*

Subs

13	Tommy	WRIGHT
16	*Liam*	*O'BRIEN (+75)*
19	*Steve*	*WATSON (†61)*

TOTTENHAM HOTSPUR

1	Erik	THORSTVEDT
2	Dean	AUSTIN
5	Colin	CALDERWOOD
6	Gary	MABBUTT
23	Sol	CAMPBELL
15	David	HOWELLS
4	Vinny	SAMWAYS
14	Steve	SEDGLEY
12	Jason	DOZZELL
8	*Gordon*	*DURIE (+73)*
10	Teddy	SHERINGHAM

13	Ian	WALKER
17	*Andy*	*TURNER (+73)*
20	Darren	CASKEY

Match Facts

- The first time Newcastle had lost their first home game of the season since 1987

Score Sheet

SHERINGHAM 36 min – 0-1

Referee:
Mr. D. Allison (Lancaster)

Result of this Season's Fixture

Newcastle Utd.
Tottenham H.

Caught Unawares

Not the best of starts to the Premiership campaign, but for several good reasons. It's not often that a team starts the season with a long injury list, you expect that to come later, but United were without several key players for the curtain raiser.

Brian Kilcline, Tommy Wright and Scott Sellars were all sidelined, having missed out on the friendly with Liverpool a week earlier but most importantly, the returning hero Peter Beardsley, who was later to prove so crucial to the smooth running of the team, was also missing. His fractured cheekbone was the result of a controversial challenge by Neil Ruddock in the Anfield game.

United took to the field with Malcolm Allen partnering Andy Cole up front, the striker having been signed from Millwall just the day before. It was a great opportunity for the former Norwich and Watford star, who had probably been expecting to play in the Lions' reserves, not in front of the 35,000 fans who expectantly filled St James' Park. The brand new £5.6 million Leazes End stand basked in the summer sunshine as the season got underway, but it was quickly clear that Newcastle were not quite ready for the big time.

The Spurs manager was returning to his old home and Ossie Ardiles' team was given plenty of hospitality as a hard working but predictable United saw plenty of possession but made little impact. For Spurs, the twin strikers Sheringham and Durie always looked likely to break through. Indeed Srnicek had to pull off a couple of good saves before Sheringham's decisive strike just before the break. The keeper came off his line to try and force Sheringham wide but the England international kept his head to slot the ball into the net.

For all their effort, the Premiership's new boys never looked like taking the points. Cole never really got into the game and Allen was stifled by a strong Spurs defence. At the back, Beresford and Scott in particular clearly had some work to do to adjust to the new level of play.

Liam O'Brien had settled his contractual difficulties with Keegan and came on as a sub, bringing a bit of spark to the side and almost getting an equaliser, but all in all, it was a disappointing start to the season. Spurs thoroughly deserved their win and Keegan knew that, if United were to establish themselves in the top flight, things would have to improve.

League Record

	Home					Away				
	P	W	D	L	F	A	W	D	L	F	A
FAPL 93/94	1	0	0	1	0	1	0	0	0	0	0
All Time FAPL	1	0	0	1	0	1	0	0	0	0	0
All Time FL/FAPL	3591	1026	384	386	3584	2039	446	440	909	2125	3148

	Home	Away	Total
Attendances	35,216	0	35,216

Coventry City
Newcastle United

(0) 2
(1) 1

Wednesday, 18th August 1993, Highfield Road   Att.: 15,760

COVENTRY CITY			NEWCASTLE UNITED		
23	Jon	GOULD	1	Pavel	SRNICEK *(+34) – Sent Off*
4	Peter	ATHERTON	19	Steve	WATSON
20	Phil	BABB	3	John	BERESFORD
6	David	RENNIE	4	Paul	BRACEWELL
3	*Steve*	*MORGAN (+74)*	2	Barry	VENISON – *Booked*
18	Sean	FLYNN	5	Kevin	SCOTT
19	*Tony*	*SHERIDAN (†74)*	7	Robert	LEE
12	Peter	NDLOVU	10	Lee	CLARK
17	Roy	WEGERLE	9	Andy	COLE – *Booked*
10	Mick	QUINN	17	*Niki*	*PAPAVASILIOU (+34)*
7	John	WILLIAMS	16	Liam	O'BRIEN

Subs

1	Steve	OGRIZOVIC	13	*Tommy*	*WRIGHT (+34)*
24	*Paul*	*WILLIAMS (+74)*	21	Malcolm	ALLEN
9	*Mick*	*HARFORD (†74)*	24	Matty	APPLEBY

Match Facts

- Srnicek's dismissal was to be the only red card shown to a Newcastle plaer all season.

Score Sheet

L. O'BRIEN 22 min – 0-1

P. NDLOVU 58 min – 1-1

M. HARFORD 85 min – 2-1

Referee:
Mr. I. Borrett (Norfolk)

Result of this Season's Fixture

Newcastle Utd.
Coventry City

Seeing Red

This was getting ridiculous. The Monday after the Spurs game, defender Steve Howey managed to injure himself in training, aggravating a groin strain that necessitated a trip to a London specialist. This meant that, with the season less than a week old, the Toon's injury list had stretched to eighteen!

United could have done without any more problems, but the bad luck was to continue, with the dismissal of Srnicek for a professional foul on Roy Wegerle, which led to a draconian three game ban for the Czech. The decision, according to the new laws of the game, could not be argued with but justice was clearly not done – that one incident probably costing Newcastle the game.

It was a bright start. Venison looked comfortable at centre back, having been moved from full back to cover for Howey and United were comfortably dominating the game when Liam O'Brien's free-kick was deflected into the Coventry net by Peter Atherton. Then came the sending off, with Tommy Wright coming on to cover for Srnicek and Niki Papavasiliou being sacrificed.

In the second half, the home team's one man advantage began to tell, although they never really got on top of the game, with Lee and Clark continuing to look dangerous for United. But in the 58th minute Coventry were level. The speedy Zimbabwean international Peter Ndlovu coming in from the left to smash a fine shot past Wright. The winner came just five minutes from time when substitute Mick Harford headed a cross, from beyond the far post, over Wright and into the net. United deserved at least a draw from this game and Harford later admitted that he had intended to nod the ball back into the area for someone else – so he actually scored by accident!

To add to United's woes, both Venison and Cole received yellow cards, Venison for the second match running. Still the game gave the first signs that the Toon had what it takes to make an impact in the top flight.

League Record

	Home						Away				
	P	W	D	L	F	A	W	D	L	F	A
FAPL 93/94	2	0	0	1	0	1	0	0	1	1	2
All Time FAPL	2	0	0	1	0	1	0	0	1	1	2
All Time FL/FAPL	3592	1026	384	386	3584	2039	446	440	910	2126	3150

	Home	Away	Total
Attendances	35,216	15,760	50,976

Manchester United (1) 1
Newcastle United (0) 1

Saturday, 21st August 1993, Old Trafford   Att.: 41,829

MANCHESTER UNITED

1	Peter	SCHMEICHEL
2	Paul	*PARKER (+85)*
4	Steve	BRUCE
6	Gary	PALLISTER
3	Denis	IRWIN
12	Bryan	ROBSON
16	Roy	KEANE
8	Paul	INCE
14	*Andrei*	*KANCHELSKIS (†70)*
10	Mark	HUGHES
11	Ryan	GIGGS

Subs

9	Brian	*McCLAIR (†70)*
5	*Lee*	*SHARPE (+85)*
13	Les	SEALEY

NEWCASTLE UNITED

1	Pavel	SRNICEK
2	Barry	VENISON
5	Kevin	SCOTT – *Booked*
19	Steve	WATSON
3	John	BERESFORD
7	Robert	LEE
10	Lee	CLARK
4	Paul	BRACEWELL
16	Liam	O'BRIEN
17	Niki	PAPAVASILIOU
9	Andy	COLE

13	Tommy	WRIGHT
21	Malcolm	ALLEN
24	Mattie	APPLEBY

Match Facts

• Newcastle have not won at Old Trafford since the 1971/72 season.

Score Sheet

R. GIGGS 40 min – 1-0

A. COLE 70 min – 1-1

Referee:

K. Morton (Bury St Edmunds)

FA Carling Premiership

		P	W	D	L	F	A	Pts
15	Queens Park Rangers	3	1	0	2	4	8	3
16	Chelsea	3	0	1	2	2	4	1
17	**Newcastle United**	**3**	**0**	**1**	**2**	**2**	**4**	**1**
18	Manchester City	3	0	1	2	1	3	1
19	West Ham United	3	0	1	2	1	4	1

Result of this Season's Fixture

Newcastle Utd.

Manchester Utd.

Life in the Fast Lane

This is what it's all about. This time last year the Toon were looking forward to visiting the likes of Barnsley and Peterborough. Now it was Old Trafford and the reigning champions. And Newcastle proved that they were up to the challenge.

The mercurial Frenchman Eric Cantona was missing from the Manchester line-up, but it was still a team of superstars and the less experienced in the Newcastle team could have been forgiven for being intimidated by the huge crowd and sparkling opposition, but they weren't. With Bracewell dominating the midfield, Steve Watson put a brake on the dashing Welshman, Giggs, and the threat of Cole seemed to cause more panic in the heart of Manchester's defence.

Lee Clark and Robert Lee were full of ideas coming out of midfield and Niki Papavasiliou gave probably his best performance of the season, all energy and passion – he was clearly inspired by the big stage. Sadly, though, it was the Cypriot's foul on Bryan Robson that led to Newcastle going a goal behind, just before the break. You can't allow Giggs the opportunity of a free-kick just outside the area and although Srnicek managed to get his hands to the shot, it was 1-0 to the home team.

It was an undeserved lead and Newcastle came out for the second half determined to get back into the game. It was a wonderful performance, full of grit and determination to complement the skill and the deserved equaliser came twenty minutes from the end. Cole had already just missed a chance, provided for him by Papavasiliou, but he wasn't going to let slip a second opportunity. O'Brien played the ball out to Papavasiliou and Cole sprinted forward, indicating just where he wanted the ball placed. The pass was inch perfect and Cole was through. Newcastle's first point of the season and Cole's first goal of the season – the first of many.

There was a chance to snatch the three points late on when Cole again went close after a Lee Clark run but nevertheless it was a splendid performance.

There was a booking for Kevin Scott but the game was generally played in good spirit and was a highly entertaining spectacle. Although Manchester had far more corners (9 to 2) and shots on target (11 to 5) than Newcastle, the Champions knew they had met a team well capable of matching their game.

League Record

	Home						Away				
	P	W	D	L	F	A	W	D	L	F	A
FAPL 93/94	3	0	0	1	0	1	0	1	1	2	3
All Time FAPL	3	0	0	1	0	1	0	1	1	2	3
All Time FL/FAPL	3593	1026	384	386	3584	2039	446	441	910	2127	3151

	Home	Away	Total
Attendances	35,216	57,589	92,805

Newcastle United   (1) 1
Everton   (0) 0

Match Four

Wednesday, 25th August 1993, St James' Park   Att.: 34,833

NEWCASTLE UNITED

1	Pavel	SRNICEK
19	Steve	WATSON
3	John	BERESFORD
2	Barry	VENISON – Booked
5	Kevin	SCOTT
4	Paul	BRACEWELL – Booked
16	Liam	O'BRIEN
17	Niki	PAPAVASILIOU
10	Lee	CLARK – Booked
9	Andy	COLE
21	Malcolm	ALLEN

Subs

13	Tommy	WRIGHT
20	Alan	NEILSON
24	Matty	APPLEBY

EVERTON

1	Neville	SOUTHALL
12	Paul	HOLMES (†76)
3	Andy	HINCHCLIFFE
2	Matthew	JACKSON
7	Mark	WARD
14	John	EBBRELL – Booked
8	Graham	STUART
11	Peter	BEAGRIE (+45)
15	Paul	RIDEOUT
9	Tony	COTTEE
6	Gary	ABLETT

Subs

13	Jason	KEARTON
16	Pedray	RADOSAVICEVIC (+45)
19	Stuart	BARLOW (†76)

Match Facts

- United's first win in the top flight for 13 games, dating back to March 1989.

Score Sheet

M. ALLEN 18 min – 1-0

Referee:
Mr. G. Ashby (Worcester)

FA Carling Premiership

		P	W	D	L	F	A	Pts
12	Wimbledon	4	1	2	1	6	5	5
13	Chelsea	4	1	1	2	4	4	4
14	**Newcastle United**	**4**	**1**	**1**	**2**	**3**	**4**	**4**
15	West Ham United	4	1	1	2	4	4	4
16	Oldham Athletic	4	1	1	2	4	7	4

Result of this Season's Fixture

Newcastle Utd.

Everton

Winning ways

A look at the form table before this game would have indicated an away win. United, with just one point from three games, were up against one of the Premiership's last 100% records, but this was to be the start of a disastrous decline for the Merseysiders that would soon see the loss of manager Howard Kendall and ultimately lead to a relegation battle.

Compared to the performance against Man Utd., this first win came from a slightly disappointing Newcastle performance, but a clean sheet and a first goal for Malcolm Allen, brought a three point haul to St James' Park.

Peter Beardsley was still injured, so missed out on the opportunity to show his former boss exactly why he shouldn't have sold him, but it was Beardsley's last minute stand-in who earned the points. United started brightly and it took just eighteen minutes for Allen to strike the decisive blow, his shot taking a wicked deflection off Everton's Matthew Jackson, looping over Southall and into the net. Everton created few chances throughout the game, although their striker Tony Cottee will feel he should have done better with two chances that he would normally have expected to put away.

For the Toon, Niki Papavasiliou again had an outstanding game while Watson and Venison dominated in defence. Andy Cole had one of his quieter nights, but Neville Southall did have to make one magnificent save from him, as well as another from Lee Clark, to prevent the winning margin becoming any larger.

A couple of silly bookings were picked up – Bracewell for encroachment and Clark for time-wasting – but, more worryingly, Venison collected his third yellow card in four games and a suspension came that bit nearer.

League Record

	P	W	D	L	F	A	W	D	L	F	A
			Home						**Away**		
FAPL 93/94	4	1	0	1	1	1	0	1	1	2	3
All Time FAPL	4	1	0	1	1	1	0	1	1	2	3
All Time FL/FAPL	3594	1027	384	386	3585	2039	446	441	910	2127	3151

	Home	Away	Total
Attendances	70,004	57,589	127,638

Newcastle United   (0) 1
Blackburn Rovers   (0) 1

Sunday, 29th August 1993, St James' Park   Att.: 34,272

NEWCASTLE UNITED

1	Pavel	SRNICEK
19	Steve	WATSON
2	Barry	VENISON
5	Kevin	SCOTT
3	John	BERESFORD
7	Robert	LEE
16	Liam	O'BRIEN
4	Paul	BRACEWELL
17	Niki	PAPAVASILIOU
10	Lee	CLARK
9	Andy	COLE

Subs

13	Tommy	WRIGHT
21	Malcolm	ALLEN
20	Alan	NEILSON

BLACKBURN ROVERS

1	Bobby	MIMMS
20	Henning	BERG
2	David	MAY
12	Nicky	MARKER
6	Graeme	Le SAUX
7	*Stuart*	*RIPLEY (+68)*
4	Tim	SHERWOOD
17	*Patrik*	*ANDERSSON (†62) – B'ked*
11	Jason	WILCOX
8	Kevin	GALLACHER
10	Mike	NEWELL

Subs

13	*Frank*	*TALIA*
22	*Mark*	*ATKINS (†62)*
9	*Alan*	*SHEARER (+68)*

Match Facts

• The first time United had gone four games without defeat in the top division since December 1988

Score Sheet

A. COLE 60 min – 1-0

A. SHEARER 76 min – 1-1

Referee:
Mr. S. Lodge (Barnsley)

FA Carling Premiership

		P	W	D	L	F	A	Pts
13	Queens Park Rangers	5	2	0	3	8	10	6
14	Chelsea	5	1	2	2	5	5	5
15	**Newcastle United**	**5**	**1**	**2**	**2**	**4**	**5**	**5**
16	Oldham Athletic	5	1	2	2	5	8	5
17	West Ham United	5	1	1	3	3	8	4

Result of this Season's Fixture

Newcastle Utd.

Blackburn Rvrs.

A tale of two strikers

The crowd's expectations for this match were high. Fresh from their fine draw at Old Trafford and the win over Everton, it was a chance for Newcastle to take on the team whose recent record represented the target for the season. Promoted in 1992, Blackburn have already established themselves as one of the leading Premiership teams and, for the Toon, equalling Blackburn's first season back in the top Division would represent great success.

The first half, however, didn't live up to expectations. The huge crowd were left disappointed as too many laborious runs and poor passes came to nothing, with only the in form Papavasiliou, with support from the solid Bracewell, bringing any spark of energy to the proceedings.

At half time, Keegan reorganised the team and this was the catalyst for a much better second period. Young Clark, who had been playing up front with Cole, was withdrawn to his more natural midfield role, with Lee going forward to partner the main striker. This had immediate effect and in the 51st minute, Lee turned smartly and put Cole through with a neat pass. The striker was blocked by Sherwood and might have won a penalty, but he persevered, shook off the defender and beat Mimms, only to see the ball bounce off the post. He deserved more and it wasn't long before he got it. Beresford put a good ball through the Rovers defence and Cole, beating the offside trap, coolly knocked it past the keeper.

Cole could have had another in the 69th minute but after getting in a good position he mis-hit his shot. By that time, however, Blackburn had made the substitution which was to change the course of the game. The England striker Alan Shearer was still in the process of recuperating from a long term injury and was far from fully fit, but his scoring instincts were enough to earn the visitors a point. He had only been on the pitch for seven minutes when Sherwood set him free with a through ball. Shearer waited to avoid being caught offside then drew Srnicek off his line, before side-footing home from 10 yards.

In the end, a draw was a fair result and the game rested on the actions of the two men who were to battle it out at the top of the Premiership goal scoring table for the rest of the season.

League Record

	Home						Away				
	P	W	D	L	F	A	W	D	L	F	A
FAPL 93/94	5	1	1	1	2	2	0	1	1	2	3
All Time FAPL	5	1	1	1	2	2	0	1	1	2	3
All Time FL/FAPL	3595	1027	385	386	3586	2040	446	441	910	2127	3151

	Home	Away	Total
Attendances	104,276	57,589	161,865

Ipswich Town
Newcastle United

(0) 1
(1) 1

Match Six

Tuesday, 31st August 1993, Portman Road   Att.: 19,102

IPSWICH TOWN

1	Craig	FORREST
2	Mick	STOCKWELL
5	John	WARK
6	David	LINIGHAN
3	Neil	THOMPSON – *B'ked*
14	Steve	WHITTON
18	*Steve*	*PALMER (+57)*
7	Geraint	WILLIAMS
17	Simon	MILTON
11	Chris	KIWOMYA
12	*Paul*	*GODDARD (†63)*

Subs

13	Clive	BAKER
19	*Frank*	*YALLOP (+57)*
9	*Bontcho*	*GUENTCHEV (†63)*

NEWCASTLE UNITED

1	Pavel	SRNICEK
19	Steve	WATSON
2	Barry	VENISON
5	Kevin	SCOTT
3	John	BERESFORD
7	Robert	LEE
4	Paul	BRACEWELL
10	*Lee*	*CLARK (+59)*
17	*Niki*	*PAPAVASILIOU (†86)*
9	Andy	COLE
21	Malcolm	ALLEN

13	Tommy	WRIGHT
16	*Liam*	*O'BRIEN (+59)*
20	*Alan*	*NEILSON (†86)*

Match Facts

• United have not won in the league at Portman road since the first game of the 1975/76 season

Score Sheet

L. CLARK 47 min – 1-0
C. KIWOMYA 78 min – 1-1

Referee:
Mr D. Gallagher (Banbury)

FA Carling Premiership

	P	W	D	L	F	A	Pts
12 Sheffield United	5	2	1	2	8	10	7
13 Leeds United	6	2	1	3	4	9	7
14 Newcastle United	**6**	**1**	**3**	**2**	**5**	**6**	**6**
15 Queens Park Rangers	5	2	0	3	8	10	6
16 Chelsea	5	1	2	2	5	5	5

Result of this Season's Fixture

Newcastle Utd.
Ipswich Town

One Sided but just One Point

Total domination of the match at Portman Road was not enough to earn United their second win of the season. A splendid attacking display was let down by some poor finishing, the linesman's flag and most importantly, bad luck.

Attack after attack in the first half led to nothing with Clark and Lee magnificent in midfield, forcing Ipswich to cram their defence. Even then they were always stretched by a rampant Cole, who definitely made up for his lacklustre display against Blackburn.

Linighan and Wark in the heart of the Ipswich defence had no answer to Cole's pace and, when he was put through by Lee, only a fingertip save from Forrest kept him out. He was again involved in creating two chances for Allen, the first being blocked by the keeper at close range, the second rebounding off a defender into Forrest's arms. The chances kept coming but Ipswich held out as Watson's shot was cleared off the line by Stockwell and Cole hit the back of the net only to see his effort disallowed for offside.

The goal finally came just two minutes after the break when Clark came in from the right, played a one-two with Lee then put the perfect pass in for Cole, who slotted home from twelve yards. The goal had been a long time in coming and this might have been the signal for the floodgates to open, but Forrest was on top form and the only other goal went Ipswich's way. A long, speculative ball upfield was met by Venison's head, but his control was poor and Kiwomya pounced on the loose ball to equalise. It could so easily have been seven or eight one, such was United's domination, but in the end it was case of hanging on for the point as Ipswich tried to make the most of their luck in the dying moments.

There was one disturbing incident when Kevin Keegan was struck on the head as a fan hit the top of the dug-out, but his anger was soon dissipated when the fan apologised.

League Record

	Home						Away				
	P	W	D	L	F	A	W	D	L	F	A
FAPL 93/94	6	1	1	1	2	2	0	2	1	3	4
All Time FAPL	6	1	1	1	2	2	0	2	1	3	4
All Time FL/FAPL	3596	1027	385	386	3586	2040	446	442	910	2128	3152

	Home	Away	Total
Attendances	104,276	76,691	180,967

Newcastle United (1) 4
Sheffield Wednesday (1) 2

Monday, 13th September 1993, St James' Park   Att.: 33,890

NEWCASTLE UNITED

13	Tommy	WRIGHT
19	Steve	WATSON
2	Barry	VENISON
5	Kevin	SCOTT
3	John	BERESFORD
7	Robert	LEE
10	Lee	CLARK
4	Paul	BRACEWELL
17	*Niki*	*PAPAVASILIOU (+62)*
9	Andy	COLE
21	Malcolm	ALLEN

Subs

29	John	BURRIDGE
14	*Alex*	*MATHIE (+62)*
16	Liam	O'BRIEN

SHEFFIELD WEDNESDAY

1	Chris	WOODS
2	Roland	NILSSON
5	Nigel	PEARSON
17	Des	WALKER
3	Nigel	WORTHINGTON
8	Chris	WADDLE
11	John	SHERIDAN
16	Graham	HYDE
15	Andy	SINTON
10	Mark	BRIGHT
14	*Chris*	*BART-WILLIAMS (+86)*

12	Andy	PEARCE
20	*Gordon*	*WATSON (+86)*
13	Kevin	PRESSMAN

Match Facts

• The last time United scored four against the Owls was in the 1985/86 season

Score Sheet

A. COLE 21 mins – 1-0
A. SINTON 26 mins – 1-1
A. SINTON 47 mins – 1-2
A. COLE 76 mins – 2-2
A. MATHIE 81 mins – 3-2
M. ALLEN 88 mins – 4-2

Referee:
Mr. L. Dilkes (Mossley)

FA Carling Premiership

		P	W	D	L	F	A	Pts
11	Ipswich Town	7	3	2	2	7	7	11
12	Leeds United	7	3	1	3	6	9	10
13	**Newcastle United**	**7**	**2**	**3**	**2**	**9**	**8**	**9**
14	Chelsea	7	2	3	2	7	6	9
15	Queens Park Rangers	7	3	0	4	10	14	9

Result of this Season's Fixture

Newcastle Utd.
Sheffield Wed.

Sky High

The first Monday night game of the season, in front of the Sky TV cameras, saw an absolute classic, as United's three late goals snatched victory from the jaws of defeat. With United keeper Srnicek suspended, the opposition featured former Tyneside favourite Chris Waddle and the back in form England stalwart Des Walker. While Andy Cole bagged a brace for the Toon, the real star of the show was an unheralded 23 year old substitute making his first Premierhsip appearance, Alex Mathie. The summer signing from Morton was to make his Newcastle debut a game to remember.

It was raining heavily at kick off, but this did nothing to dampen the players' spirits. After twenty minutes John Beresford put the ball through to Malcolm Allen but he saw his shot blocked by Chris Woods. Nevertheless, Andy Cole's predatory instincts saw him pounce on the opportunity to knock the ball home from close range.

A good start for United but Wednesday were soon level. Waddle, in the face of some barracking from the crowd, showed his old flair down the right hand side, gave a perfect pass to Sheridan who in turn crossed for Sinton to sweep it home. The little England man made it 2-1 to the visitors two minutes into the second half, with Waddle again the provider. He beat Beresford again down the right, before crossing for Sinton to head in at the far post.

It looked as though Wednesday might keep their advantage until Papavasiliou made way for Mathie just past the hour. It took him some time to get into the game and it was just about his first touch of the game when he put the cross in that would lead to Newcastle's equaliser. Robert Lee knocked it down and Cole turned and shot the ball past Woods.

There were just eight minutes to go when Mathie got a goal of his own. His first time volley from Allen's clip on was later described by Keegan as 'world class'. With three minutes to go, Robert Lee recovered a corner to put a searching cross in from the left, and Allen sealed a magnificent victory with a powerful header.

It was a thrilling match and heralded the arrival of a new star at St James' Park.

League Record

	P	W	D	L	F	A	W	D	L	F	A
			Home						Away		
FAPL 93/94	7	2	1	1	6	4	0	2	1	3	4
All Time FAPL	7	2	1	1	6	4	0	2	1	3	4
All Time FL/FAPL	3957	1028	385	386	3590	2042	446	442	910	2128	3152

	Home	Away	Total
Attendances	138,166	76,691	214,857

Swindon Town
Newcastle United

(0) 2
(2) 2

Saturday, 18th September 1993, The County Ground   Att.: 15,015

SWINDON TOWN

1	Fraser	DIGBY
14	Adrian	WHITBREAD
6	Shaun	TAYLOR
5	Luc	NIJHOLT
3	Paul	BODIN
4	Micky	HAZARD
10	Martin	*LING (+68)*
7	John	MONCUR
2	Nicky	SUMMERBEE
9	Jan-Aage	FJORTOFT
25	*Andy*	*MUTCH (†74)*

Subs

23	Nicky	HAMMOND
26	*Terry*	*FENWICK (+68)*
12	*Steve*	*WHITE (†74)*

NEWCASTLE UNITED

13	Tommy	WRIGHT
19	Steve	WATSON
2	Barry	VENISON
5	Kevin	SCOTT
3	John	BERESFORD
7	Robert	LEE
10	Lee	CLARK
4	Paul	BRACEWELL
8	Peter	BEARDSLEY
9	Andy	COLE
21	Malcolm	ALLEN

1	Pavel	SRNICEK
15	Brian	KILCLINE
14	Alex	MATHIE

Match Facts

• The last time United let go a 2-0 half time lead was against Nottingham Forest in the FA Cup 4th round of 1991. The game finished 2-2 and United lost the replay five days later.

Score Sheet

L. CLARK 37 min – 0-1

M. ALLEN (pen) 45 min – 0-2

M. LING 60 min – 1-2

A. MUTCH 62 min – 2-2

Referee:
Mr H. King (Merthyr Tydfil)

FA Carling Premiership

	P	W	D	L	F	A	Pts
11 Wimbledon	7	3	3	1	9	6	12
12 Ipswich Town	8	3	2	3	8	9	11
13 Newcastle United	**8**	**2**	**4**	**2**	**11**	**10**	**10**
14 Chelsea	8	2	4	2	8	7	10
15 Queens Park Rangers	8	3	1	4	12	16	10

Result of this Season's Fixture

No Fixture

Beardsley's Back

Despite Liam O'Brien being sidelined with a hamstring injury this was a day to celebrate as it saw the return of the wounded to the front-line. Killer was on the subs bench, but most importantly Pedro was in the team.

Peter Beardsley's injury had healed more quickly than expected and, given the option of making his return at the County Ground or putting it off for another game, he pounced on the chance, played the full ninety minutes and showed just what United had been missing.

Despite the boost of Beardsley's return, this was a case of what might have been, with the Toon throwing away a two goal lead against a team that was destined to struggle all season. Beardsley and Lee Clark provided the inspiration for a good first half performance, playing from behind the front two to create plenty of problems for the Swindon defence. For the first goal, eight minutes before the break, Cole passed to Clark, who slid the ball past Digby at the near post. Allen got the second from the spot after Lee was brought down just inside the area by John Moncur.

United were cruising but two points were thrown away in the space of two minutes. Ling got a lucky rebound from Steve Watson and ran on to take Swindon's first and the second came when Bodin's cross was met with a sharp header from Andy Mutch.

There was a touch of desperation after that, as the match became ill tempered, reflecting United's frustration at losing a well deserved lead. There were plenty of good things in this match, however and, despite not scoring, Andy Cole stood out. One particular run saw him twist and turn, twice slipping over and regaining his feet, before having a good shot well saved by Digby. Truly world class play.

League Record

	Home						Away				
	P	W	D	L	F	A	W	D	L	F	A
FAPL 93/94	8	2	1	1	6	4	0	3	1	5	6
All Time FAPL	8	2	1	1	6	4	0	3	1	5	6
All Time FL/FAPL	3598	1028	385	386	3590	2042	446	443	910	2130	3154

	Home	Away	Total
Attendances	138,166	91,706	229,872

Newcastle United (1) 4
Notts County (1) 1

Wednesday, 22nd September 1993, St James' Park   Att.: 25,887

NEWCASTLE UNITED			NOTTS. COUNTY	
1	Pavel	SRNICEK	Steve	CHERRY
19	Steve	WATSON	Craig	SHORT
15	Brian	KILCLINE	*Michael*	*JOHNSON (+67)*
2	Barry	VENISON	Dean	THOMAS
3	John	BERESFORD	Phil	TURNER
7	Robert	LEE	Richard	WALKER
4	Paul	BRACEWELL	*Michael*	*SIMPSON (†75)*
10	Lee	CLARK	Mark	DRAPER
8	Peter	BEARDSLEY	Gary	McSWEGAN
9	Andy	COLE	Gary	LUND
21	Malcolm	ALLEN	Kevin	WILSON

Subs

29	John	BURRIDGE	Bob	CATLIN
14	Alex	MATHIE	*John*	*DIJKSTRA (+67)*
17	Niki	PAPAVASILIOU	*Paul*	*DEVLIN (†75)*

Match Facts

• The Magpies biggest win in the competition since 1973 – only to be bettered in the next leg

Score Sheet

P. SRNICEK 16 min o.g. – 0-1

A. COLE 30 min – 1-1

A. COLE 54 min – 2-1

A. COLE 63 min – 3-1

P. BRACEWELL 72 min – 4-1

Referee:
Mr. J. Worrall (Warrington)

League Cup – First Round, First Leg

County Down

Given what was to come a fortnight later, perhaps this Coca-Cola Cup First Leg victory wasn't as good as all that, but it wasn't bad for starters.

It had looked a tricky tie, the inconsistent County side seemingly intent on reminding United of where they were last season and an early blunder by keeper Srnicek did not bode well for the Premiership side. Mark Draper lofted an indirect free-kick into the box and Srnicek came for it, only succeeding in knocking into his own net. Just a quarter of an hour gone and already one-nil down. The First Division side were playing with plenty of spirit, but Andy Cole is a Nottingham lad and County – he wasn't going to let his old boyhood enemies get one over on him!

The first instalment of his hat-trick came on the half hour, when Robert Lee pounced on a defensive error to win the ball and knock it into the danger zone, where Cole guided it over the line. It remained level until half time, but soon after the break United were in front, when County's keeper Steve Cherry could only parry a John Beresford shot and Cole was on hand to make it two. Just past the hour mark it was three and the game was sealed. The Notts County defence allowed a Robert Lee cross to elude them all, it got through to Cole and he turned, making no mistake with his right foot shot.

The striker may have got three goals, and Beardsley showed his class again but United's main inspiration was Paul Bracewell who dominated the midfield. He got his reward for a hard night's work, claiming the best goal of the game, when he exchanged passes with Lee Clark before curling a splendid left-foot shot past the keeper.

With the potential embarrassment of defeat by a lower division team and the dreadful start to the match, this was a very professional performance from United, giving the visitors no chance.

Cup Record

		Home					Away				
	P	W	D	L	F	A	W	D	L	F	A
League Cup	80	21	6	9	69	33	9	8	7	53	82

	Home	Away	Total
Cup Attendances	25,887	0	25,887

Newcastle United (0) 2
West Ham United (0) 0

Match Ten

Saturday, September 25th 1993, St James' Park   Att.: 34,336

NEWCASTLE UNITED

30	Mike	HOOPER
2	Barry	VENISON
3	John	BERESFORD
19	Steve	WATSON
5	Kevin	SCOTT
7	Robert	LEE
4	Paul	BRACEWELL
10	Lee	CLARK
21	Malcolm	ALLEN
8	Peter	BEARDSLEY
9	Andy	COLE

Subs

1	Pavel	SRNICEK
15	Brian	KILCLINE
14	Alex	MATHIE

WEST HAM UNITED

1	Ludek	MIKLOSKO
15	*Kenny*	*BROWN (+65)*
12	Tony	GALE
4	Steve	POTTS
33	David	BURROWS
11	Dale	GORDON
34	Mike	MARSH
14	Ian	BISHOP
16	Matt	HOLMES
9	*Trevor*	*MORLEY (†65)*
35	Lee	CHAPMAN

13	Gerry	PEYTON
6	Martin	ALLEN
**	*Jeroen*	*BOERE (†65) Sent Off*

Match Facts

• Andy Cole's twin strikes took his
Newcastle tally to 22 goals in just 21 games

Score Sheet

A. COLE 51 min – 1-0
A. COLE 84 min – 2-0

Referee:
Mr. M. Reed (Birmingham)

FA Carling Premiership

		P	W	D	L	F	A	Pts
9	Tottenham Hotspur	8	4	2	2	12	6	14
10	Coventry City	9	3	5	1	12	9	14
11	**Newcastle United**	**9**	**3**	**4**	**2**	**13**	**10**	**13**
12	Chelsea	9	3	4	2	9	7	13
13	Liverpool	9	4	0	5	13	8	12

**Result of this
Season's Fixture**

Newcastle Utd.
West Ham Utd.

Hammers Go Under

After Swindon the week before, it was time to face the other of last season's promoted teams, but the Londoners looked a much sterner proposition. After a shaky start, Billy Bonds had strengthened his side immeasurably, through the exchange deal that took Julian Dicks to Anfield, with Burrows and Marsh coming to Upton Park and the signing of Lee Chapman.

The Hammers came to this game with plenty of confidence after a couple of revitalised performances but it was to be the day that United finally proved to the rest of the country that they were to be more than just Premiership also-rans in their first season back at the top.

For Newcastle there was a major change between the posts. The day before the Notts County game, Keegan had snapped up Liverpool reserve keeper Mike Hooper for £550,000 and after Smicek's mistake in the Cup, he was given an early opportunity to make a name for himself. Hooper gave a good performance on this occasion, but it was to be the start of Newcastle's only real selection controversy of the season.

The first half demanded patience from both Newcastle's players and the vociferous crowd as, despite some delightful build-up play, the Hammers defence held firm, effectively stifling the home side. Indeed they could well have gone in front as Chapman had one effort disallowed and perhaps should have taken another. But come the second half the Toon finally found that they had what it takes.

Just six minutes after the break Malcolm Allen strode down the left wing, crossed and Beardsley's dummy fooled the West Ham defence. The ball came through to Cole on the edge of the area and he hammered past Miklosko. Number two came with six minutes left when Clark gave the perfect pass for Cole to run onto and he duly dispatched it from twenty yards.

League Record

	P	W	D	L	F	A	W	D	L	F	A
			Home						Away		
FAPL 93/94	9	3	1	1	8	4	0	3	1	5	6
All Time FAPL	9	3	1	1	8	4	0	3	1	5	6
All Time FL/FAPL	3599	1029	385	386	3594	2044	446	443	910	2130	3154

	Home	Away	Total
Attendances	172,502	91,706	264,208

Aston Villa (0) 0
Newcastle United (0) 2

Saturday, 2nd October 1993, Villa Park   Att.: 37,336

ASTON VILLA			NEWCASTLE UNITED		
1	Nigel	SPINK	30	Mike	HOOPER
7	Neil	COX	19	Steve	WATSON
5	Paul	McGRATH	3	Barry	VENISON
4	Shaun	TEALE	5	Kevin	SCOTT
3	Steve	STAUNTON	3	John	BERESFORD
6	Kevin	RICHARDSON	7	Robert	LEE
15	*Gordon*	*COWANS (+64)*	4	Paul	BRACEWELL
14	Andy	TOWNSEND	10	Lee	CLARK
9	Dean	SAUNDERS	21	Malcolm	ALLEN
10	Dalian	ATKINSON	9	Andy	COLE
22	*Guy*	*WHITTINGHAM (†56)*	8	Peter	BEARDSLEY

Subs					
13	Mark	BOSNICH	1	Pavel	SRNICEK
7	*Ray*	*HOUGHTON (+64)*	15	Brian	KILCLINE
11	*Tony*	*DALEY (†56)*	11	Scott	SELLARS

Match Facts

• The Magpies first win at Villa Park since 1985

Score Sheet

M. ALLEN 46 min Pen – 0-1

A. COLE 80 min – 0-2

Referee:
Mr P. Durkin (Dorset)

FA Carling Premiership

		P	W	D	L	F	A	Pts
4	Norwich City	10	5	3	2	19	11	18
5	Blackburn Rovers	10	5	3	2	14	10	18
6	**Newcastle United**	**10**	**4**	**4**	**2**	**15**	**10**	**16**
7	Aston Villa	10	4	4	2	12	11	16
8	Wimbledon	10	4	4	2	11	11	16

Result of this Season's Fixture

Aston Villa
Newcastle Utd.

Heroes and Villains

A place in the top ten for the first time was the reward for this magnificent victory, which stretched United's unbeaten run to nine games.

Villa were on a high after their mid-week win in Europe, so with home advantage and a big crowd, they had to start the game as favourites. The threat of Atkinson and Saunders looked on paper to be very dangerous and there was the pace of Tony Daley on the bench, but the United defence was magnificent and completely stifled Villa's attack. Indeed, Villa only managed one shot on target in the game. Venison was playing with a chest infection but he didn't let this affect him and he was superb, with able support from the rest of the back four.

Scott Sellars was on the bench after recovering from injury, but he wasn't needed. In midfield Robert Lee and Lee Clark were sharp and effective, using the ball with plenty of imagination while Peter Beardsley showed his sheer class yet again.

It wasn't a rout but Newcastle dominated, outplaying Villa in every area of the field. Whatever Villa tried was immediately countered, although Daley did cause a few problems late on.

No goals in the first half, but immediately after the break Staunton was forced into a clumsy challenge on Robert Lee in the penalty area and Malcolm Allen confidently converted. There were a lot of offside decisions, 12 against each team, but Newcastle's victory had a certain inevitability about it and it was Andy Cole who sealed it with ten minutes remaining. Beardsley collected a ball from Lee and pushed it through to the striker, who needed two goes before he hit the back of the net.

This was the most complete performance of the season so far and led to the first of the rumours of Keegan taking over the helm of the English national side. Villa boss Ron Atkinson was typically scathing of his team's performance in the after-match press conference, but it would have been fairer to point out that Newcastle were simply superb.

League Record

	Home						Away				
	P	W	D	L	F	A	W	D	L	F	A
FAPL 93/94	10	3	1	1	8	4	1	3	1	7	6
All Time FAPL	10	3	1	1	8	4	1	3	1	7	6
All Time FL/FAPL	3600	1029	385	386	3594	2044	447	443	910	2132	3154

	Home	Away	Total
Attendances	172,502	129,042	310,544

Notts. County (0) 1
Newcastle United (3) 7

Tuesday, 5th October 1993, Meadow Lane Att.: 6,068

NOTTS COUNTY

Steve	CHERRY	
Chris	*SHORT (+45)*	
Meindert	DIJKSTRA	
Phil	TURNER	
Richard	WALKER	
Paul	COX	
Paul	DEVLIN	
Mark	DRAPER	
Gary	McSWEGAN	
Tony	AGANA	
Andy	*LEGG (†80)*	

Subs

Bob	CATLIN	
Dean	*THOMAS (+45)*	
Gary	*LUND (†80)*	

NEWCASTLE UNITED

30	Mike	HOOPER
19	Steve	WATSON
3	John	BERESFORD
2	*Barry*	*VENISON (+69)*
5	Kevin	SCOTT
7	Robert	LEE
4	*Paul*	*BRACEWELL (†69)*
10	Lee	CLARK
8	Peter	BEARDSLEY
21	Malcolm	ALLEN
9	Andy	COLE

1	Pavel	SRNICEK
15	*Brian*	*KILCLINE (+69)*
11	*Scott*	*SELLARS (†69)*

Match Facts

• Not only was 7-1 United's biggest win in the competition, but the 11-2 aggregate was also a record.

Score Sheet

M. ALLEN 22 min – 0-1

M. ALLEN 35 min Pen – 0-2

P. BEARDSLEY 44 min – 0-3

G. McSWEGAN 51 min – 1-3

A. COLE 59 min – 1-4

A. COLE 62 min – 1-5

A. COLE 82 min – 1-6

R. LEE 85 min – 1-7

Referee:
Mr. A. Flood (Stockport)

League Cup – First Round, Second Leg

Seven up

With Newcastle already 4-1 up from the first leg, the tie was as good as over before kick-off, but this thrashing still represented a magnificent performance, and brought Andy Cole yet another hat-trick. Nevertheless, we had seen enough of Notts County in the first leg to realise that if they could get an early strike, they would be capable of putting United under severe pressure, so it was important to have the right attitude right from the start.

This is exactly what happened and the three goal lead at half time meant that United could enjoy themselves in the second half. Malcolm Allen was involved in all three goals. The first came from a Robert Lee cross. Beardsley picked the ball up from Lee Clark and his centre struck Andy Cole, the ball spinning off him straight to Allen who was on hand to score.

The second goal came from the penalty spot, Allen converting after himself being fouled by County's Meindert Dijkstra. The striker turned creater for the third goal, putting a perfect through ball for Peter Beardsley to push home the first goal of his second spell with United.

McSwegan gave the First Division side a bit of hope six minutes after the break when he hammered in a twenty yard shot, but Andy Cole, with most of his family in the crowd, was about to take the match by the scruff of the neck. In the 59th minute he slotted his first strike through keeper Cherry's legs. Three minutes later it was 5-1 as Cole nodded in Allen's cross from close range.

Keegan made a couple of substitution's with twenty minutes to go, and this saw Scott Sellars' first appearance of the season. United were relaxed now but it didn't stop the scoring as Beresford and Allen worked the ball between them, before Beresford unselfishly pulled the ball back for Cole to tap in. It was 7-1, 11-2 on aggregate, just five minutes from the end as Peter Beardsley's inventive over-head kick was picked up by Lee, who pounced on the chance to break his duck for the season.

With England just about to face their nemesis in Rotterdam, the calls were mounting for Andy Cole to break into the national side.

Cup Record

	Home						Away				
	P	W	D	L	F	A	W	D	L	F	A
League Cup	81	21	6	9	69	33	10	8	7	60	83

	Home	Away	Total
Cup Attendances	25,887	6,068	31,955

Newcastle United (0) 1
Queens Park Rangers (1) 2

Saturday, 16th October 1993, St James' Park   Att.: 33,926

NEWCASTLE UNITED

30	Mike	HOOPER
19	Steve	WATSON
2	Barry	VENISON
5	Kevin	SCOTT
3	John	BERESFORD
7	Robert	LEE
4	Paul	BRACEWELL
10	Lee	CLARK
21	Malcolm	ALLEN
9	Andy	COLE
8	Peter	BEARDSLEY

Subs

1	Pavel	SRNICEK
15	Brian	KILCLINE
11	Scott	SELLARS

QUEENS PARK RANGERS

13	Jan	STEJSKAL
2	David	BARDSLEY
6	Alan	McDONALD
5	Darren	PEACOCK
3	Clive	WILSON
7	Andrew	IMPEY
14	Simon	BARKER
4	Ray	WILKINS
11	Trevor	SINCLAIR
9	Les	FERDINAND
10	Bradley	ALLEN

24	Steve	YATES
1	Tony	ROBERTS
19	Devon	WHITE

Match Facts

• United have now failed to beat Ragners at home in the League for the last four attampts

Score Sheet

L. FERDINAND 10 min – 0-1

M. ALLEN 48 min – 1-1

B. ALLEN 50 min – 1-2

Referee:
Mr K.Hackett (Sheffield)

FA Carling Premiership

		P	W	D	L	F	A	Pts
9	Wimbledon	11	4	5	2	13	13	17
10	Liverpool	11	5	1	5	15	9	16
11	**Newcastle United**	**11**	**4**	**4**	**3**	**16**	**12**	**16**
12	Everton	11	5	1	5	14	15	16
13	Coventry City	11	3	6	2	13	11	15

Result of this Season's Fixture

Newcastle Utd.

QPR

The Bubble Bursts

The unbeaten run came to an end in the eleventh game, with United going down at home to an impressive Queens Park Rangers. For the visitors, England striker Les Ferdinand was dominant, the veteran Ray Wilkins superb and in fairness the Londoners thoroughly deserved their win, although United so nearly snatched an equaliser at the death.

Ferdinand had missed England's defeat in Holland just four days earlier through injury and showed how dearly he had been missed in that game. Despite not being entirely fit, he had a splendid game, making a major nuisance of himself in United's defence and winning just about everything in the air. It didn't take him long to give Rangers the lead. The ever alert Wilkins sliced through the Toon's defence with a great ball to the striker, who pushed it into the net in a roundabout way – he managed to strike both posts with his shot before the ball finally crossed the line!

It was a game where both sides showed some special touches but, especially for United, it never really caught fire, even when Malcolm Allen fired home the equaliser just after the break. The goal came from Steve Watson's searching cross, which was headed on by Lee, before Allen blasted a first time volley into the top of the net. Rangers never allowed United to take advantage of this come-back and it took them just two minutes to restore the lead. Wilkins was again the creator as his corner was won by Ferdinand in the air. He nodded the ball down and Bradley Allen was on hand to score.

The penalty came in the dying moments of the match when Alan McDonald was rather harshly judged to have handled. If the penalty had been awarded against Newcastle, the crowd would have been livid, but you can't look a gift horse in the mouth and it seemed as if United had been gifted a point. However, Malcolm Allen's soft shot was saved by Stejskal and, in all honesty, justice was seen to be done.

The unbeaten run was over and Newcastle now knew that they would have to be at their best for every game if they were to be a real success in the Premiership.

League Record

		Home					Away				
	P	W	D	L	F	A	W	D	L	F	A
FAPL 93/94	11	3	1	2	9	6	1	3	1	7	6
All Time FAPL	11	3	1	2	9	6	1	3	1	7	6
All Time FL/FAPL	3601	1029	385	387	3595	2046	447	443	910	2132	3154

	Home	Away	Total
Attendances	206,428	129,042	335,470

Southampton
Newcastle United

(0) 2
(0) 1

Sunday, 24th October 1993, The Dell   Att.: 13,804

SOUTHAMPTON		
1	Tim	FLOWERS
2	Jeff	KENNA
18	Steve	WOOD
17	*Kevin*	*MOORE (+82)*
11	Francis	BENALI
27	Paul	ALLEN
28	Peter	REID
10	Neil	MADDISON
3	Mick	ADAMS
7	Matthew	Le TISSIER
9	Iain	DOWIE

NEWCASTLE UNITED		
30	Mike	HOOPER
19	Steve	WATSON
2	Barry	VENISON
5	Kevin	SCOTT
3	John	BERESFORD
10	*Lee*	*CLARK (+70)*
4	Paul	BRACEWELL
21	*Malcolm*	*ALLEN (†70)*
8	Peter	BEARDSLEY
7	Robert	LEE
9	Andy	COLE

Subs

25	Neal	BARTLETT
20	*Paul*	*MOODY (†82)*
13	Ian	ANDREWS

1	Pavel	SRNICEK
14	Alex	MATHIE
11	Scott	SELLARS

Match Facts

• Matt Le Tissier was one of only two players to score against United in both League games this season. The other was Leeds United's Chris Fairclough.

Score Sheet

M. Le TISSIER 61 min – 1-0

A. COLE 72 min – 1-1

M. Le TISSIER 86 min – 2-1

Referee:

Mr P. Don (Middlesex)

FA Carling Premiership

		P	W	D	L	F	A	Pts
9	Liverpool	12	5	2	5	16	10	17
10	Wimbledon	11	4	5	2	13	13	17
11	**Newcastle United**	**12**	**4**	**4**	**4**	**17**	**14**	**16**
12	Everton	12	5	1	6	14	16	16
13	Coventry City	12	3	6	3	14	16	15

Result of this Season's Fixture

Southampton
Newcastle Utd.

Matt Walks Over United

Struggling Southampton clinched all three points against United thanks to two splendid goals by the mercurial Channel Islander Matt Le Tissier. It should have been a very different story, however, and United were made to pay for a string of wasted chances in the first half.

This game came at the height of the Saints' fans protests against manager Ian Branfoot and just before keeper Tim Flowers' expensive transfer to Blackburn Rovers. There was a demonstration before the match intended to delay the kick-off, but in the end the Saints fans went home with something to be happy about.

Keegan had denied that United were interested in signing QPR's Les Ferdinand for a reported £3.8 million fee, but perhaps he could have done with another deadly finisher as Andy Cole was to have one his off days. In the sixth minute, it was he who was caught offside to deny Robert Lee an early goal and he missed three other good chances before the break. Flowers also pulled off a good save from Lee Clark and really it was Southampton who were hanging on, until Le Tissier struck.

Just past the hour mark, Le Tissier was lurking on the left-hand side of the box to pick up a loose ball. From nowhere, he created a stunning goal, rounding Barry Venison, flicking the ball over Scott's head, switching feet, knocking the ball into the air again then putting a pin point low shot past the advancing Hooper. A brilliant goal.

Keegan responded with two substitutions but this brought an angry reaction from Lee Clark, one of the players to be pulled off, and he headed straight for the dressing room. Keegan chased after him and almost dragged him back to the bench – a nasty incident that could do no good for team morale.

However, the substitutions seemed to do the trick and an Alex Mathie cross provided Cole with the chance to atone for his earlier mistakes by nodding the ball past Flowers.

But, with just four minutes left, it was another piece of Le Tissier magic that decided the game. A loose ball came out of the Newcastle defence, Le Tissier caught it on his chest, controlled it with his thigh and then smashed a dipping 20 yard shot over Hooper. Two supreme quality goals and a string of wasted chances had turned a probable victory for United into defeat.

League Record

	P	W	D	L	F	A	W	D	L	F	A
		Home					**Away**				
FAPL 93/94	12	3	1	2	9	6	1	3	2	8	8
All Time FAPL	12	3	1	2	9	6	1	3	2	8	8
All Time FL/FAPL	3602	1029	385	387	3595	2046	447	443	911	2133	3156

	Home	Away	Total
Attendances	206,428	142,846	349,274

Wimbledon
Newcastle United

(1) 2
(1) 1

Wednesday, 27th October 1993, Selhurst Park   Att.: 11,531

WIMBLEDON

1	Hans	SEGERS
2	Warren	BARTON
3	Brian	McALLISTER
4	Vinny	JONES
6	Scott	FITZGERALD
7	*Andy*	*CLARKE (†73)*
8	Robbie	EARLE
9	John	FASHANU
10	Dean	HODSWORTH
24	Peter	FEAR
35	Alan	KIMBLE

Subs

26	*Neal*	*ARDLEY (†73)*
37	Perry	DIGWEED
36	Gary	BLISSETT

NEWCASTLE UNITED

30	Mike	HOOPER
19	Steve	WATSON
2	Barry	VENISON
5	Kevin	SCOTT
3	John	BERESFORD
4	Paul	BRACEWELL
8	Peter	BEARDSLEY
11	Scott	SELLARS
7	Robert	LEE
14	Alex	MATHIE
21	*Malcolm*	*ALLEN (+77)*

1	Pavel	SRNICEK
15	*Brian*	*KILCLINE (+77)*
20	Alan	NEILSON

Match Facts

• United have not been beyond the 3rd
Round of this competition since 1976/77

Score Sheet

W. BARTON 23 min – 1-0

S. SELLARS 28 min – 1-1

D. HOLDSWORTH 69 min – 2-1

Referee:
Mr. I. Hemley (Ampthill)

Undone by the Dons

With players of the quality of Warren Barton, Dean Holdsworth and Robbie Earle, Wimbledon are no longer the uncultured thugs that reputation would have and have been playing some stylish football this season. So this was no game for Newcastle to go into as unprepared as they were.

In fact, Wimbledon were also below par this night, but with off the field bust-ups meaning that United fielded an unsettled team, they were good enough to end Newcastle's Coca-Cola Cup campaign.

Lee Clark was left out of the team after the incident at the Dell and Andy Cole was also missing. At the time, his non-appearance was a mystery, but the whole notorious 'homesickness' incident was soon to come to light.

It was a scrappy but even first half, with the intimidating presence of Fashanu not really causing too many problems in United's defence, but it was the home team who took the lead on 23 minutes, following a Peter Beardsley error. His mis-timed clearance fell to Earle who promptly knocked it into the box for full-back Barton to score. Five minutes later and United were level, Sellars curling the ball past Segers after being fed by Beardsley.

1-1 was a fair half-time score and, given the circumstances, Newcastle would have been happy to take the tie back to Tyneside but it was not to be. On 69 minutes, Vinny Jones put a cross in from the right and as Scott and Fashanu both went for the ball, it broke clear for Holdsworth to head in.

It was a poor goal to decide a poor match. Without Cole, Newcastle's front line looked impotent with Mathie slowly drifting out of the game and Malcolm Allen again being substituted. Hooper had a shaky game and Venison picked up another yellow card. Wimbledon had only had three shots on target, compared to United's seven, but they made two of them count and it was the Londoners who went into the hat for the next round.

Cup Record

		Home					Away				
	P	*W*	*D*	*L*	*F*	*A*	*W*	*D*	*L*	*F*	*A*
League Cup	82	21	6	9	69	33	10	8	8	61	84

	Home	*Away*	*Total*
Cup Attendances	25,887	17,599	43,486

Newcastle United   (1) 4
Wimbledon   (0) 0

Saturday, 30th October 1993, St James' Park   Att.: 33,392

NEWCASTLE UNITED

30	Mike	HOOPER
19	Steve	WATSON
3	John	BERESFORD
2	Barry	VENISON
5	Kevin	SCOTT
4	Paul	BRACEWELL
7	Robert	LEE
10	Lee	CLARK
11	Scott	SELLARS
9	Andy	COLE
8	Peter	BEARDSLEY

Subs

1	Pavel	SRNICEK
14	Alex	MATHIE
15	Brian	KILCLINE

WIMBLEDON

1	Hans	SEGERS
2	Warren	BARTON
3	Brian	McALLISTER
6	Scott	FITZGERALD
35	Alan	KIMBLE
24	Peter	FEAR
7	*Andy*	*CLARKE (†57)*
8	Robbie	EARLE
9	John	FASHANU
10	Dean	HOLDSWORTH
4	Vinny	JONES

14	*Gerald*	*DOBBS (†57)*
37	Perry	DIGWEED
36	Gary	BLISSETT

Match Facts

• Andy Cole's strike took him to the top of the Premiership's scoring table, with 10 goals in 13 games

Score Sheet

BEARDSLEY 36 min Pen – 1-0

A. COLE 60 min – 2-0

P. BEARDSLEY 63 min – 3-0

P. BEARDSLEY 71 min – 4-0

Referee:
Mr. V. Callow (Solihull)

FA Carling Premiership

		P	W	D	L	F	A	Pts
7	Liverpool	13	6	2	5	20	12	20
8	Queens Park Rangers	13	6	2	5	24	21	20
9	**Newcastle United**	**13**	**5**	**4**	**4**	**21**	**14**	**19**
10	Tottenham Hotspur	13	5	4	4	21	14	19
11	Everton	13	6	1	6	16	16	19

Result of this Season's Fixture

Newcastle Utd.
Wimbledon

Revenge

Just three days after the defeat at Selhurst Park, United gained a truly satisfying revenge with this devastating return to form. After the incidents of the last week, it was good to see the two wayward stars patch up their differences with the club and return to the field. Although all the pre-match limelight was on Cole and Clark, by the end it had switched to Peter Beardsley, whose hat-trick stole the show.

Ordinarily, it would be hard to see how a team could reverse a result in quite such a thorough way in just three days, but it had been such a turbulent week that anything could have happened. Lee Clark, who had just turned 21 years of age, revealed that he had come close to packing in his football career altogether after the Southampton incident, but it was a good job he didn't because he was an inspiration in midfield and Andy Cole inevitably got another goal on his comeback.

The first goal, however, came from the penalty spot when Vinny Jones brought down Robert Lee in the box. Peter Beardsley was the new penalty taker, with Allen in the reserves and he made no mistake with his kick. It remained 1-0 until the second half when a devastating spell of three goals in eleven minutes destroyed the visitors.

On 60 minutes, the two 'bad boys' combined for the second goal. Lee Clark's powerful shot was only parried by Segers in the Don's goal and Cole was on hand for the rebound. Three minutes later and Beardsley was smashing in a free-kick from just outside the area.

He sealed his hat-trick after Cole had challenged in the box. Beardsley got onto the loose ball to skilfully chip Segers and send ten the St James' Park faithful wild.

It was a totally one-sided affair and the visitors managed just five shots in the whole match, only one on target. They won just three corners and Hooper had very little to do. Wimbledon also had Barton, Fear and Jones all booked for fouls and it was a sorry day for the Crazy Gang. They should have known better than to embarrass the Toon!

League Record

	Home					Away				
	P	W	D	L	F	A	W	D	L	F	A
FAPL 93/94	13	4	1	2	13	6	1	3	2	8	8
All Time FAPL	13	4	1	2	13	6	1	3	2	8	8
All Time FL/FAPL	3603	1030	385	387	3599	2046	447	443	911	2133	3156

	Home	Away	Total
Attendances	239,820	142,846	382,666

Oldham Athletic   (1) 1
Newcastle United   (0) 3

Monday, 8th November 1993, Boundary Park   Att.: 13,821

OLDHAM ATHLETIC

26	Lance	KEY
5	Richard	JOBSON
2	Craig	FLEMING
6	Steve	REDMOND
22	Chris	MAKIN
19	Roger	PALMER
10	Mike	MILLIGAN
11	Paul	BERNARD
20	Mark	BRENNAN
9	Ian	OLNEY (+64)
14	Graeme	SHARP

Subs

3	Neil	POINTON
12	Neil	ADAMS (+64)
13	Jon	HALLWORTH

NEWCASTLE UNITED

30	Mike	HOOPER
19	Steve	WATSON
2	Barry	VENISON
5	Kevin	SCOTT
26	Robbie	ELLIOTT
10	Lee	CLARK
4	Paul	BRACEWELL
11	Scott	SELLARS
7	Robert	LEE
8	Peter	BEARDSLEY
9	Andy	COLE

1	Pavel	SRNICEK
20	Alan	NEILSON
14	Alex	MATHIE

Match Facts

• United have not lost at Boundary Park since 1981

Score Sheet

R. JOBSON 35 min – 1-0
A. COLE 52 min – 1-1
P. BEARDSLEY 73 min – 1-2
A. COLE 81 min – 1-3

Referee:
Mr R. Gifford (Mid Glam.)

FA Carling Premiership

		P	W	D	L	F	A	Pts
7	Queens Park Rangers	14	7	2	5	25	21	23
8	Blackburn Rovers	14	6	5	3	18	14	23
9	**Newcastle United**	**14**	**6**	**4**	**4**	**24**	**15**	**22**
10	Wimbledon	14	5	5	4	16	19	20
11	Tottenham Hotspur	14	5	4	5	19	15	19

Result of this Season's Fixture

No Fixture

Party time

Newcastle's growing reputation as one of the most entertaining teams in the Premiership, not just one of the best, really came to the fore in this match. Of course, Oldham played their part and all through their time in the top flight they have always been enjoyable to watch, but with Beardsley and Cole on top form, Newcastle really turned on the style for Sky's TV cameras.

Eighteen shots compared to the home team's two shows just how much United dominated this game, but it was Oldham who held the half time lead, completely against the run of play. In the 35th minute, Hooper couldn't hold on to Brennan's free kick as he was challenged by Jobson and Olney, and it was the former who was on hand to score. United's play was superb, full of intricate passing and inventive runs, with Sellars and Clark making the most of the freedom given to them, but six good chances were not enough to hold Oldham.

"We were too elaborate", said Keegan of the first half performance so it was a slightly more direct approach which Newcastle employed in the second half and it didn't take long before it started to pay dividends.

It was a Wimbledonesque goal which brought about the equaliser. A long kick from Hooper was flicked on by Lee and Andy Cole was there to chip the ball into the net. The second goal was more Newcastle – Sellars set Beardsley free and he got past Jobson before hammering home a left foot shot. It was Sellars again who created the third goal, his ball allowing Cole to stumble a shot home from twelve yards.

Cole could have got his hat-trick late on, but he shot just wide, although the real reason Newcastle didn't win by more was a fine performance between the posts by Oldham's 'keeper Key, who was onloan from Sheffield Wednesday.

After the game, Kevin Keegan was full of praise for Peter Beardsley, who was now really showing himself to be one of the bargains of the season. His brilliant form was later to earn him his recall to the England team and his 50th international cap.

League Record

		Home					Away				
	P	W	D	L	F	A	W	D	L	F	A
FAPL 93/94	14	4	1	2	13	6	2	3	2	11	9
All Time FAPL	14	4	1	2	13	6	2	3	2	11	9
All Time FL/FAPL	3604	1030	385	387	3599	2046	448	443	911	2136	3157

	Home	Away	Total
Attendances	239,820	156,667	396,487

Newcastle United (3) 3
Liverpool (0) 0

Sunday, 21st November 1993, St James' Park   Att.: 36,374

NEWCASTLE UNITED

30	Mike	HOOPER
19	Steve	WATSON
2	Barry	VENISON
5	Kevin	SCOTT
26	Robbie	ELLIOTT
10	Lee	CLARK
4	Paul	BRACEWELL
11	Scott	SELLARS
7	Robert	LEE
8	Peter	BEARDSLEY
9	Andy	COLE

Subs

1	Pavel	SRNICEK
21	Malcolm	ALLEN
14	Alex	MATHIE

LIVERPOOL

1	Bruce	GROBBELAAR
4	Steve	NICOL
19	*Torben*	*PIECHNIK (+45)*
25	Neil	RUDDOCK
22	Steve	HARKNESS
15	Jamie	REDKNAPP
7	Nigel	CLOUGH
8	Paul	STEWART
21	Dominic	MATTEO
9	Ian	RUSH
23	Robbie	FOWLER

13	David	JAMES
10	*John*	*BARNES (+45)*
11	Mark	WALTERS

Match Facts

• The first victory over Liverpool at home since 1985, when George Reilly got the only goal

Score Sheet

A. COLE 4 min – 1-0
A. COLE 15 min – 2-0
A. COLE 30 min – 3-0

Referee:
Mr G. Ashby (Worcester)

FA Carling Premiership

		P	W	D	L	F	A	Pts
6	Arsenal	15	7	5	3	15	8	26
7	Blackburn Rovers	15	7	5	3	20	14	26
8	**Newcastle United**	**15**	**7**	**4**	**4**	**27**	**15**	**25**
9	Liverpool	15	7	2	6	24	15	23
10	Tottenham Hotspur	15	5	5	5	20	16	20

Result of this Season's Fixture

Newcastle Utd.
Liverpool

Reds Routed

So maybe it wasn't the strongest of Liverpool sides, but the satisfaction of thrashing one of the biggest clubs in the country was enormous, especially for Andy Cole, whose devastating first half hat-trick ripped the stuffing out of the opposition. This was quite simply a perfect performance, the Magpies completely dominating the game and it firmly established them as one of the leading teams in the land.

The signs were there right from the start as Paul Bracewell won a loose ball from Matteo with a deft flick that left the young Liverpool midfielder standing. It took just four minutes to start the scoring as Robbie Elliott set Robert Lee free on the left. His lightning pace was far too much for Nicol, and the cross was heading goalwards, even before Cole latched on to the ball to make certain.

Liverpool's defence was in disarray, having no idea of how to handle Cole, Beardsley and Lee. Piechnik and Nicol just looked confused, and what better way could there have been for Beardsley to repay Ruddock for a broken cheekbone than to run rings around him on the field?

The second strike came after a quarter of an hour as Beardsley jinked round Piechnik to put the perfect ball in to Sellars, who saw Cole free and laid the ball to him for an easy tap-in.

On half an hour, Lee and Sellars worked the ball down the left again and the latter's cross found Cole again free. It was a third goal for the striker as he sidefooted past Grobbelaar.

That was it really. The game was over after just thirty minutes. Liverpool put John Barnes on in the second half, the England player making his first appearance of the season after another bout of injury. He showed some of his class but didn't have the sharpness to make any real difference. Liverpool did have a good chance late on, but Jamie Redknapp, with the goal at his mercy, sliced the ball high and wide.

Cole's hat-trick had all come from simple tap-ins. It was his scoring instinct that provided the finishing touch to the spectacular work of the deeper players, Beardsley, Lee and Sellars. This was teamwork at its best.

League Record

| | Home | | | | | | Away | | | | |
	P	W	D	L	F	A	W	D	L	F	A
FAPL 93/94	15	5	1	2	16	6	2	3	2	11	9
All Time FAPL	15	5	1	2	16	6	2	3	2	11	9
All Time FL/FAPL	3605	1031	385	387	3602	2046	448	443	911	2136	3157

	Home	Away	Total
Attendances	276,194	156,667	432,861

Newcastle United (2) 4
Sheffield United (0) 0

Wednesday, 24th November 1993, St James' Park   Att.: 35,101

NEWCASTLE UNITED

30	Mike	HOOPER
19	Steve	WATSON
26	Robbie	ELLIOTT
4	*Paul*	*BRACEWELL (+75)*
5	Kevin	SCOTT
2	Barry	VENISON
7	Robert	LEE
8	Peter	BEARDSLEY
9	Andy	COLE
10	Lee	CLARK
11	Scott	SELLARS

Subs

1	Pavel	SRNICEK
14	*Alex*	*MATHIE (+75)*
15	Brian	KILCLINE

SHEFFIELD UNITED

1	Alan	KELLY
11	Mitch	WARD
15	Charlie	HARTFIELD
14	David	TUTTLE
26	Jamie	HOYLAND
33	Roger	NILSSON
10	Willie	FALCONER
8	*Paul*	*ROGERS (†75)*
18	Dane	WHITEHOUSE
17	Carl	BRADSHAW
27	*Bobby*	*DAVISON (+75)*

22	*Andy*	*SCOTT (†75)*
23	*Chris*	*KAMARA (+75)*
31	*Salvatore*	BIBBO

Match Facts

• Newcastle had not lost to the Blades since Decmber 1978. This was all to change later in the season.

Score Sheet

Sheff. Player 9 min o.g. – 1-0

BEARDSLEY 12 min Pen – 2-0

A. COLE 70 min – 3-0

P. BEARDSLEY 73 min – 4-0

Referee:

Mr J. Worrall (Warrington)

FA Carling Premiership

		P	W	D	L	F	A	Pts
1	Manchester United	16	13	2	1	33	13	41
2	Blackburn Rovers	16	8	5	3	22	15	29
3	Aston Villa	16	8	5	3	18	13	29
4	**Newcastle United**	**16**	**8**	**4**	**4**	**31**	**15**	**28**
5	Norwich City	15	7	6	2	24	14	27

Result of this Season's Fixture

No Fixture

Keep on Keeping on

With the Magpies in the sort of form they were, it seemed a bit unfair that the next visitors to St James' Park were poor, doomed Sheffield United and Dave Bassett's side took the inevitable battering. Moving to centre stage for United this evening was Scott Sellars, giving his finest performance of the season so far. Sellars is a Sheffield lad, a Wednesday fan as a boy and he was watched by most of his family as his new team demolished his boyhood rivals.

In fact, Sellars thought he had got the first goal after just nine minutes, when he and a Sheffield defender together went for a Peter Beardsley cross and the ball found its way over the line. The goal was originally credited to Sellars, but was later put down as an own goal. Just three minutes later and the hometown boy was again involved in a Newcastle goal. This time he was brought down in possession inside the penalty area and Peter Beardsley confidently struck the spot kick home.

Things went dead a little after this. Not surprisingly, the Yorkshire strugglers had come to Tyneside with an ultra-defensive set up and they successfully put the brake on until well into the second half. Despite a competent performance at the back, however, they created few chances and at 2-0 down, they had to try and open things up a bit. As soon as they did, Newcastle pounced with two more goals and the victory was complete.

In the 70th minute, the Magpies got a goal which cynics might say was straight out of the Dave Bassett playbook. Mike Hooper belted the ball from his area right up field to the waiting Beardsley. He controlled it, slipped it inside to Cole and it was 3-0. About as Route One as a goal can get. Number four was more typical Newcastle, Lee and Sellars exchanging passes before the latter played it to Beardsley, who twisted and turned before smacking home a crisp left-footer.

Not the strongest test of the season, but a four nil can never be easy and this was, yet again, a top notch performance.

League Record

	P	W	D	L	F	A	W	D	L	F	A
			Home						**Away**		
FAPL 93/94	16	6	1	2	20	6	2	3	2	11	9
All Time FAPL	16	6	1	2	20	6	2	3	2	11	9
All Time FL/FAPL	3606	1032	385	387	3606	2046	448	443	911	2136	3157

	Home	Away	Total
Attendances	311,295	156,669	467,962

Arsenal
Newcastle United

(1) 2
(0) 1

Saturday, 27th November 1993, Highbury　　　　　Att.: 36,091

ARSENAL

1	David	SEAMAN
2	Lee	DIXON
12	Steve	BOULD – *Booked*
14	Martin	KEOWN
3	Nigel	WINTERBURN
17	John	JENSEN
21	Steve	MORROW – *Booked*
11	Eddie	McGOLDRICK
8	Ian	WRIGHT – *Booked*
9	Alan	SMITH
10	Paul	MERSON

Subs

4	Paul	DAVIS
7	Kevin	CAMPBELL
13	Alan	MILLER

NEWCASTLE UNITED

30	Mike	HOOPER
19	Steve	WATSON
26	*Robbie*	*ELLIOTT (+59)*
4	Paul	BRACEWELL
5	Kevin	SCOTT
2	Barry	VENISON
7	Robert	LEE
8	Peter	BEARDSLEY
9	Andy	COLE
10	*Lee*	*CLARK (†59)*
11	Scott	SELLARS

1	Pavel	SRNICEK
6	*Steve*	*HOWEY (+59)*
14	*Alex*	*MATHIE (†59)*

Match Facts

• Arsenal 'keeper David Seaman had been sent of the previous Wednesday, for a professional foul in the Gunners' game at West Ham. Unfortunately for Newcastle, however, his suspension was not to begin until after this match.

Score Sheet

I. WRIGHT 16 min – 1-0
A. SMITH 60 min – 2-0
P. BEARDSLEY 62 min – 2-1

Referee:
Mr A. Gunn (Sussex)

FA Carling Premiership

		P	W	D	L	F	A	Pts
4	Blackburn Rovers	17	8	5	4	22	16	29
5	Aston Villa	16	8	5	3	18	13	29
6	**Newcastle United**	**17**	**8**	**4**	**5**	**32**	**17**	**28**
7	Norwich City	16	7	6	3	25	14	27
8	Queens Park Rangers	17	8	3	6	29	23	27

Result of this Season's Fixture

Newcastle Utd.
Arsenal

Down to earth

Whatever you say about them, Arsenal have the finest defence in the country and, although they were without captain Tony Adams, they were always going to be a stern test for Newcastle.

Despite the boring reputation of the opposition this was actually a very entertaining game, although the scoreline was disappointing from a Geordie viewpoint. Most of the real quality play came from United, but the shear professionalism of the opposition plus a few flashes from the likes of Wright and Merson was enough to win the points and highlight that there are a few things which Keegan's men still have yet to learn about the Premiership.

Andy Cole was returning to the club who let him go after just one appearance as substitute and he was desperate to have a good game, but he was given no rein and made little impact. The same could be said of Lee, Sellars and Clark and the lack of experience at full back eventually proved Newcastle's downfall.

Both Arsenal goals came from wide balls. The first was after just 16 minutes when a Merson corner was flicked on by Bould at the near post and Ian Wright was on hand to score. There was a lot of good entertaining football from now on, with Beardsley looking splendid and Merson and Morrow causing all sorts of problems down the flanks for the opposition, but it wasn't until a quarter of an hour into the second half before the second goal.

United should have learned. The second goal was identical to the first. Another Merson corner, another Bould flick-on and this time it was Alan Smith who was on hand to score. By this time, Keegan had put on both substitutes, including Steve Howey, returning from a lengthy injury, and he did cause some problems despite his lack of match practice. Inevitably though, if United were to score it would be Beardsley who would do it and he duly did just that two minutes later. Steve Watson ran with the ball, before feeding Cole, who quickly set up Beardsley to beat the keeper. Watson hit a post late on, but to be fair Hooper had to pull off good saves from Merson and Wright and, despite the quality of Newcastle's play, their at times naive defending and Arsenal's own strength meant that the Londoners just about deserved their win.

League Record

	Home					Away				
	P	W	D	L	F	A	W	D	L	F	A
FAPL 93/94	17	6	1	2	20	6	2	3	3	12	11
All Time FAPL	17	6	1	2	20	6	2	3	3	12	11
All Time FL/FAPL	3607	1032	385	387	3606	2046	448	443	912	2137	3159

	Home	Away	Total
Attendances	311,295	192,758	504,053

Tottenham Hotspur (0) 1
Newcastle United (0) 2

Saturday, 4th December 1993, White Hart Lane   Att.: 30,780

TOTTENHAM HOTSPUR

1	Erik	THORSTVEDT
22	*David*	*KERSLAKE (+74)*
5	Colin	CALDERWOOD
14	Steve	SEDGLEY
3	Justin	EDINBURGH
9	Darren	ANDERTON
4	Vinny	SAMWAYS
16	Micky	HAZARD
20	Darren	CASKEY
7	Nick	BARMBY
23	*Sol*	*CAMPBELL (†60)*

Subs

13	Ian	WALKER
2	*Dean*	*AUSTIN (+74)*
12	*Jason*	*DOZZELL (†60)*

NEWCASTLE UNITED

30	Mike	HOOPER
19	Steve	WATSON
2	Barry	VENISON
6	Steve	HOWEY
26	Robbie	ELLIOTT
7	Robert	LEE
4	Paul	BRACEWELL
10	Lee	CLARK
31	Mike	JEFFREY
9	Andy	COLE
8	Peter	BEARDSLEY

1	Pavel	SRNICEK
15	Brian	KILCLINE
16	Liam	O'BRIEN

Match Facts

• Newcastle's first win at White Hart Lane since 1976.

Score Sheet

P. BEARDSLEY 55 min – 0-1
N. BARMBY 61 min Pen – 1-1
P. BEARDSLEY 90 min – 1-2

Referee:
Mr M. Reed (Birmingham)

FA Carling Premiership

		P	W	D	L	F	A	Pts
1	Manchester United	18	14	3	1	36	15	45
2	Leeds United	18	9	6	3	32	21	33
3	**Newcastle United**	**18**	**9**	**4**	**5**	**34**	**18**	**31**
4	Arsenal	18	8	6	4	17	10	30
5	Aston Villa	18	8	6	4	21	17	30

Result of this Season's Fixture

Newcastle Utd.
Tottenham H.

Fame is the spur

Spurs had just started their downhill slide into a relegation battle when it was the Magpies' turn to visit White Hart Lane. After a good start to the season, the Londoners had gone seven games without a win and this was to be their eighth.

The home side had serious injury problems. Striker Teddy Sheringham was out with a long term injury and the team captain Gary Mabbutt had just had his face smashed by John Fashanu's elbow. Newcastle had their own injury problems with Scott Sellars missing, meaning that Mike Jeffrey was to make his debut. Steve Howey, however, was fit again and played.

Despite Spurs' problems they had not given up their belief in flowing football, so with United naturally playing an attractive game this turned out to be a hugely entertaining spectacle, one of the most enjoyable games of the season. The decisive factor that took the points north was to be Peter Beardsley.

Both sides created several chances, but it remained scoreless at half time. Lee Clark and Robert Lee were the main sources of inspiration for United with Beardsley on hand to try and make the most of the opportunities they created. Andy Cole had another rather ineffective game. For Spurs there was plenty of creative play in the midfield, with Anderton looking especially sharp, but they clearly missed a natural target man.

The deadlock was broken after ten minutes of the second half when Lee Clark's corner was nodded down by Robert Lee and Beardsley hammered the ball past Thorstvedt. Spurs equalised six minutes later when Steve Watson brought down Anderton in the area. Anderton went down rather too easily, but the penalty was given and Barmby made no mistake.

Beardsley had another chance to score soon after but he took too long with his shot and it was only in the dying seconds that he got the winner. Andy Cole took a quick free kick and Beardsley picked up the ball. Calderwood backed off him as more Spurs defenders turned up in support, but Beardsley had the control to beat three of them before smacking in the winner. It was a splendid goal to decide a splendid game.

League Record

| | Home | | | | | | Away | | | | |
	P	W	D	L	F	A	W	D	L	F	A
FAPL 93/94	18	6	1	2	20	6	3	3	3	14	12
All Time FAPL	18	6	1	2	20	6	3	3	3	14	12
All Time FL/FAPL	3608	1032	385	387	3606	2046	449	443	912	2139	3160

	Home	Away	Total
Attendances	311,295	223,538	534,833

Newcastle United (0) 1
Manchester United (0) 1

Saturday, 11th December 1993, St. James' Park   Att.: 36,388

NEWCASTLE UNITED

30	Mike	HOOPER
19	Steve	WATSON
2	Barry	VENISON
6	Steve	HOWEY
26	Robbie	ELLIOTT
7	Robert	LEE
4	Paul	BRACEWELL
10	Lee	CLARK
11	Scott	SELLARS
8	Peter	BEARDSLEY
9	Andy	COLE

Subs

1	Pavel	SRNICEK
16	Liam	O'BRIEN
21	Malcolm	ALLEN

MANCHESTER UNITED

1	Peter	SCHMEICHEL
2	Paul	PARKER
4	Steve	BRUCE
6	Gary	PALLISTER
3	Denis	IRWIN
5	Lee	SHARPE
7	Eric	CANTONA
8	Paul	INCE
9	*Brian*	*McCLAIR (+77)*
11	Ryan	GIGGS
10	*Mark*	*HUGHES (†56)*

13	Les	SEALEY
16	*Roy*	*KEANE (+77)*
14	*Andrei*	*KANCHELSKIS (†56)*

Match Facts

• Andy Cole's 17th Premiership goal of the season took him two clear of Alan Shearer in the leading goalscorer chart

Score Sheet

P. INCE 59 min – 0-1
A. COLE 71 min – 1-1

Referee:
Mr K. Hackett (Sheffield)

FA Carling Premiership

		P	W	D	L	F	A	Pts
1	Manchester United	20	15	4	1	40	16	49
2	Leeds United	19	10	6	3	33	21	36
3	Blackburn Rovers	19	10	5	4	26	17	35
4	**Newcastle United**	**19**	**9**	**5**	**5**	**35**	**19**	**32**
5	Arsenal	19	8	7	4	18	11	31

Result of this Season's Fixture

Newcastle Utd.
Manchester Utd.

Red hot

Just three days earlier, the home game against Coventry had been called off because of a waterlogged pitch and the St James' Park surface was heavy for the visit of the champions, but this didn't stop the Magpies from giving yet another display of pure, stylish football.

The unusual spectacle of a team wearing the numbers 1 to 11 on their shirts showed that Manchester were at full strength and as they were running away with the title at the time, they were favourites for the three points. However, if any side deserved to win this match it was Newcastle, whose performance, especially in the first half, gave Manchester United a real fright.

The visitors paid Keegan's men a massive compliment as they set out their stall to defend their goal to the hilt. They could only manage five shots all through the game and the likes of Cantona and Giggs hardly figured. Instead it was Robert Lee, Lee Clark, Sellars and Beardsley who showed the real flair.

Manchester managed to hang on to 0-0 right through to the break and then made a vital substitution which was to give them the lead. At this stage of the season, Andrei Kanchelskis was still not a regular in Man. Utd.'s starting line up but his speed on the right was enough for him to break down the right and get a cross in for Giggs. The Welshman made room for Ince who blasted the ball past Hooper. The visitors might have secured an undeserved victory had Hooper not been able to block Lee Sharpe after he had been given a good chance from a superb pass by Cantona, but the equaliser was not long in coming.

Clark and Watson played the ball out of defence and it was Peter Beardsley who beat Denis Irwin with a pinpoint pass for Robert Lee. Lee dashed to the by-line and put in the perfect cross for Andy Cole to nod in his 23rd goal of the season. It was a simple goal but perfectly executed and it won the point which was the least Newcastle deserved.

League Record

| | Home | | | | | | Away | | | | |
	P	W	D	L	F	A	W	D	L	F	A
FAPL 93/94	19	6	2	2	21	7	3	3	3	14	12
All Time FAPL	19	6	2	2	21	7	3	3	3	14	12
All Time FL/FAPL	3609	1032	386	387	3607	2047	449	443	912	2139	3160

	Home	Away	Total
Attendances	347,683	223,538	571,221

Everton (0) 0
Newcastle United (1) 2

Saturday, 18th December 1993, Goodison Park   Att.: 25,189

EVERTON			NEWCASTLE UNITED		
1	Neville	SOUTHALL	30	Mike	HOOPER
2	Matthew	JACKSON	19	Steve	WATSON
5	Dave	WATSON	2	Barry	VENISON
24	Ian	SNODIN	6	Steve	HOWEY
6	Gary	ABLETT	3	*John*	*BERESFORD (+77)*
8	Graham	STUART	7	Robert	LEE
7	Mark	WARD	4	Paul	BRACEWELL
14	John	EBRELL	10	Lee	CLARK
20	*Robert*	*WARZYCHA (+55)*	11	Scott	SELLARS
19	Stuart	BARLOW	9	Andy	COLE
9	Tony	COTTEE	8	Peter	BEARDSLEY

Subs

13	Jason	KEARTON	1	Pavel	SRNICEK
16	*Pedray*	*RADOSAVICEVIC (+55)*	14	Alex	MATHIE
10	Barry	HORNE	26	*Robbie*	*ELLIOTT (+77)*

Match Facts

• United had not won at Goodison Park since the 1959/60 season, losing 13 times and drawing 6 in the interim

Score Sheet

A. COLE 15 min – 0-1
P. BEARDSLEY 76 min – 0-2

Referee:
Mr M. Bodenham (Cornwall)

FA Carling Premiership

		P	W	D	L	F	A	Pts
1	Manchester United	20	15	4	1	40	16	49
2	Leeds United	21	11	6	4	37	24	39
3	Blackburn Rovers	20	11	5	4	28	17	38
4	**Newcastle United**	**20**	**10**	**5**	**5**	**37**	**21**	**35**
5	Arsenal	21	9	7	5	20	13	34

Result of this Season's Fixture

Newcastle Utd.

Everton

Stinging the blues

A lacklustre United performance, but perfectly adequate against a disappointing opposition. This was the stage of Everton's season in between Howard Kendall's surprise departure and Mike Walker's controversial arrival in the manager's position. It was also at the height of the boardroom battle for control of the club and with an unsettled side as well, there were always going to be rich pickings for the visitors.

Barry Venison was returning to his 'old enemy' and was determined to put in a good show, as was Paul Bracewell, returning to his old club. With their lightweight forward line and rather ineffectual midfield, the Merseysiders were never going to be able to impose themselves on such a resolute United. But of course it was Peter Beardsley, discarded by the home team, who had the most to prove and the loyal Toon Army had great fun taunting the opposition fans as Beardsley got the winning goal.

It was Andy Cole, though, who got the first. A long kick from Hooper found Beardsley, who put it into the path of the back-on-form striker and his right foot shot squeezed between Southall and the post. That was after just a quarter of an hour and although Everton tried hard, it had really decided the game. Barlow and Stuart were the opposition's best players and if Mike Hooper hadn't been on top form it might have been different. Everton managed six on-target shots as opposed to Newcastle's four, but a combination of good goalkeeping and weak finishing maintained the balance of form.

It was with great delight that Beardsley struck the winner. John Beresford played a good through ball, Beardsley exchanged passes with Cole and then slid the ball into the net. One of the duller games of the season maybe, but the three points were in the bag.

League Record

| | Home | | | | | | Away | | | | |
	P	W	D	L	F	A	W	D	L	F	A
FAPL 93/94	20	6	2	2	21	7	4	3	3	16	12
All Time FAPL	20	6	2	2	21	7	4	3	3	16	12
All Time FL/FAPL	3610	1032	386	387	3607	2047	450	443	912	2141	3160

	Home	Away	Total
Attendances	347,683	248,727	596,410

Newcastle United (0) 1
Leeds United (0) 1

Wednesday, 22nd December 1993, St James' Park   Att.: 36,388

NEWCASTLE UNITED

30	Mike	HOOPER
19	Steve	WATSON
2	Barry	VENISON
6	Steve	HOWEY
3	John	BERESFORD
7	Robert	LEE
4	Paul	BRACEWELL
10	*Lee*	*CLARK (+75)*
11	Scott	SELLARS
8	Peter	BEARDSLEY
9	Andy	COLE

Subs

1	Pavel	SRNICEK
14	*Alex*	*MATHIE (+75)*
26	Robbie	ELLIOTT

LEEDS UNITED

13	Mark	BEENEY
22	Gary	KELLY – *Booked*
12	John	PEMBERTON
16	John	NEWSOME – *Booked*
3	Tony	DORIGO
5	Chris	FAIRCLOUGH – *Bkd*
10	Gary	McALLISTER – *Bkd*
14	Steve	HODGE – *Booked*
25	*Noel*	*WHELAN (+87)*
9	Brian	DEANE
8	Rod	WALLACE

1	John	LUKIC
20	*Kevin*	*SHARP (+87)*
14	David	WETHERALL

Match Facts

- Leeds had five players booked in this 'rugged' game.

Score Sheet

C. FAIRCLOUGH 66 min – 0-1

A. COLE 85 min – 1-1

Referee:
Mr P. Don (Middlesex)

FA Carling Premiership

		P	W	D	L	F	A	Pts
1	Manchester United	21	16	4	1	43	17	52
2	Leeds United	22	11	7	4	38	25	40
3	Blackburn Rovers	20	11	5	4	28	17	38
4	**Newcastle United**	**21**	**10**	**6**	**5**	**38**	**22**	**36**
5	Arsenal	21	9	7	5	20	13	34

Result of this Season's Fixture

Newcastle Utd.

Leeds United

Tough at the top

A dour and hard top-of-the-table clash saw United snatch a well deserved point with a late equaliser from Andy Cole. High flyers Leeds came to St James' Park intent on stifling Newcastle's more fluid style and this they did, with Cole and Beardsley marked out of the game for much of the time.

At the start, however, the opposition struggled to contain Newcastle and on another night might have taken Leeds apart. Beardsley's one touch play was wonderful and he, along with Lee and Clark, created plenty of chances, but Cole unfortunately wasted a couple of good opportunities to give United the lead. Both Lee and Clark also shot over the bar and it remained scoreless at half time.

By the second half, the Leeds stranglehold had tightened and Newcastle were forced to resort to a more direct approach, just as Leeds' manager Howard Wilkinson had planned. As Gary McAllister and the rest of the Leeds midfield came more and more into the game, the balance swung.

Still it was Newcastle who had the first really good chance of a goal. Just past the hour, Robert Lee was brought down inside the area by Dorigo, but Beardsley's weak spot-kick was saved by Beeney. Just a few minutes later the visitors took the lead. Watson brought down Whelan and McAllister's floated free-kick was met by a crashing header from Fairclough.

But it's not like this Newcastle side to give up and the goal gave the home side the boost they needed. With just five minutes remaining and the anxious crowd in a frenzy, Paul Bracewell found Cole twenty yards from goal and the striker's shot took a deflection off Beardsley to wrong-foot Beeney.

After the game Keegan said "We saw two of the sides who are going to chase Manchester United but probably aren't going to catch them." As it turned out, Leeds' challenge was to fade more quickly than expected.

This was a real blood and guts encounter, with the visitors' physical approach sometimes getting out of hand – they received five yellow cards – but in the end a draw was probably a fair result.

League Record

	Home						Away				
	P	W	D	L	F	A	W	D	L	F	A
FAPL 93/94	21	6	3	2	22	8	4	3	3	16	12
All Time FAPL	21	6	3	2	22	8	4	3	3	16	12
All Time FL/FAPL	3611	1032	387	387	3608	2048	450	443	912	2141	3160

	Home	Away	Total
Attendances	384,071	248,727	632,798

Chelsea
Newcastle United

(1) 1
(0) 0

Tuesday, 28th December 1993, Stamford Bridge · Att.: 23,133

CHELSEA

1	Dimitri	KHARINE
12	Steve	CLARKE
6	Frank	SINCLAIR
5	Erland	JOHNSEN
26	Andy	DOW
24	Craig	BURLEY
18	Eddie	NEWTON
10	*Gavin*	*PEACOCK (+70)*
11	Dennis	WISE
21	Mark	STEIN
19	*Neil*	*SHIPPERLEY (†81)*

Subs

13	Kevin	HITCHCOCK
17	*Nigel*	*SPACKMAN (+70)*
7	*John*	*SPENCER (†81)*

NEWCASTLE UNITED

30	Mike	HOOPER
19	*Steve*	*WATSON (+63)*
2	Barry	VENISON
6	Steve	HOWEY
3	John	BERESFORD
7	Robert	LEE
10	*Lee*	*CLARK (†63)*
4	Paul	BRACEWELL
11	Scott	SELLARS
9	Andy	COLE
8	Peter	BEARDSLEY

1	Pavel	SRNICEK
12	*Mark*	*ROBINSON (+63)*
14	*Alex*	*MATHIE (†63)*

Match Facts

• United had gone 21 games since they last failed to score in a League game on the first day of the season against Spurs

Score Sheet

M. STEIN 11 min – 1-0

Referee:
Mr J. Worrall (Warrington)

FA Carling Premiership

		P	W	D	L	F	A	Pts
3	Blackburn Rovers	21	11	6	4	29	18	39
4	Arsenal	22	10	7	5	24	13	37
5	**Newcastle United**	**22**	**10**	**6**	**6**	**38**	**23**	**36**
6	Norwich City	20	9	7	4	32	22	34
7	Queens Park Rangers	21	10	4	7	36	28	34

Result of this Season's Fixture

Newcastle Utd
Chelsea

Christmas Turkey

The one bright spot of this post-Christmas fixture was the welcome return of Mark Robinson as substitute after injury. Apart from that, it was dreadful.

To start with, the travelling support was less than Newcastle are used to, not surprising as the minimum ticket price was a massive £25, apparently due to the construction work at Stamford Bridge. This, added to the long journey, the dismal weather and the even worse performance meant those of the Toon Army who did travel were in for the worst of Christmas presents.

With Gavin Peacock boasting in the press beforehand about how he would get one over on his old team, it would have been more than satisfying to beat the struggling Londoners, but it was not to be. The decisive goal was just eleven minutes in coming, one consolation being that it was Stein, not Peacock, who scored it.

With his own team-mate Sinclair lying injured, Chelsea captain Dennis Wise ignored him and sent a perfect forty yard ball over the head of Beresford to Stein. The little striker controlled it, turned the defence and shot through Howey's legs and past Hooper.

The Chelsea fans were now in full voice and for once United had no response. Dennis Wise controlled the midfield, Beardsley, Lee and co barely getting a look-in and the home side may have taken a bigger lead. Stein wasted a good chance after Shipperley had nodded down Kharin's punt and might have got on the end of Dow's cross as well.

It was a slightly better performance in the second half but Andy Cole was slow to react to the only two real chances he had all game.

Chelsea were fired up for this game and it proved to be the start of a revival in their fortunes. Glenn Hoddle's side desperately needed the points and they made sure they got them. All that Newcastle's men got from this game was a thoroughly deserved roasting from their manager.

League Record

| | Home | | | | | | Away | | | | |
	P	W	D	L	F	A	W	D	L	F	A
FAPL 93/94	22	6	3	2	22	8	4	3	4	16	13
All Time FAPL	22	6	3	2	22	8	4	3	4	16	13
All Time FL/FAPL	3612	1032	387	387	3608	2048	450	443	913	2141	23161

	Home	Away	Total
Attendances	384,071	271,860	655,931

Newcastle United (2) 2
Manchester City (0) 0

Saturday, 1st January 1994, St James' Park — Att.: 35,658

NEWCASTLE UNITED

30	Mike	HOOPER
12	*Mark*	*ROBINSON (+77)*
3	John	BERESFORD
15	Brian	KILCLINE
6	Steve	HOWEY
7	Robert	LEE
4	*Paul*	*BRACEWELL (†45)*
10	Lee	CLARK
11	Scott	SELLARS
8	Peter	BEARDSLEY
9	Andy	COLE

Subs

1	Pavel	SRNICEK
14	*Alex*	*MATHIE (+77)*
19	*Steve*	*WATSON (†45)*

MANCHESTER CITY

1	Tony	COTON
	John	FOSTER
15	Alan	KERNAGHAN
6	Michael	VONK
22	Richard	EDGHILL
7	David	ROCASTLE
21	Steve	LOMAS
19	Fitzroy	SIMPSON
12	Ian	BRIGHTWELL
8	*Mike*	*SHERON (+61)*
28	Carl	SHUTT

25	Andy	DIBBLE
26	*Kare*	*INGEBRIGTSEN (+61)*
		FINNEY

Match Facts

- Another double strike takes Andy Cole's goal tally to 27 for the season.

Score Sheet

A. COLE 28 min – 1-0

A. COLE 45 min – 2-0

Referee:

K. Morton (Bury St Edmunds)

FA Carling Premiership

		P	W	D	L	F	A	Pts
3	Arsenal	24	12	7	5	30	13	43
4	Leeds United	24	11	9	4	38	26	42
5	**Newcastle United**	**23**	**11**	**6**	**6**	**40**	**21**	**39**
6	Norwich City	22	10	7	5	35	24	37
7	Liverpool	23	10	6	7	36	28	36

Result of this Season's Fixture

Newcastle Utd

Manchester City

Happy New Year

This was just the sort of game that was needed after the dreadful performance at Chelsea and in the end United comfortably took the three points. You had to feel a bit sorry for City, however – with just one win fourteen games before this and with a team devastated by injuries they put up a good fight, although they were never likely to get anything out of the game.

City's team had a very unfamiliar look about it with youngsters such as Foster, Edghill and Lomas and the veteran Carl Shutt on loan from Birmingham City. For the Magpies, Mark Robinson was making his first start of the season.

It was an unspectacular, workmanlike win with the two goals coming in the first half. Just before the half hour, City's £1.6 million defender Alan Kernaghan made a hash of dealing with Hooper's long kick from goal and Sellars latched onto the loose ball. He put in a deep cross which Beardsley nodded down for Cole to strike past Coton. The second goal came on the stroke of half time as Lee Clark's pass found Cole alone, having beaten the off side trap, and he ran on to score.

United might have gone on to destroy the visitors, but the game fizzled out in the second half, with the result already decided. Coton pulled off a couple of good saves, but it was really a case of concluding the formalities.

A comfortable three points but United suffered an injury blow as Paul Bracewell sustained a groin injury which was to keep him out of the team for more than a fortnight.

League Record

	Home						Away				
	P	W	D	L	F	A	W	D	L	F	A
FAPL 93/94	23	7	3	2	24	8	4	3	4	16	13
All Time FAPL	23	7	3	2	24	8	4	3	4	16	13
All Time FL/FAPL	3613	1033	387	387	3610	2048	450	443	913	2141	3161

	Home	Away	Total
Attendances	419,729	271,860	691,589

Norwich City
Newcastle United

(1) 1
(1) 2

Tuesday, 4th January 1994, Carrow Road   Att.: 19,564

NORWICH CITY		
1	Bryan	GUNN
5	Ian	CULVERHOUSE
3	Rob	NEWMAN
17	Ian	BUTTERWORTH
8	Colin	WOODTHORPE
14	Ruel	FOX
9	Gary	MEGSON
4	Ian	CROOK
2	Mark	BOWEN
7	Efan	EKOKU
22	Chris	SUTTON

NEWCASTLE UNITED		
30	Mike	HOOPER
12	Mark	ROBINSON
3	John	BERESFORD
6	Steve	HOWEY
5	Kevin	SCOTT
7	Robert	LEE
10	Lee	CLARK
26	Robbie	ELLIOTT
9	Andy	COLE
11	Scott	SELLARS
8	Peter	BEARDSLEY

Subs

13	Scott	HOWIE
18	Robert	ULLATHORNE
21	David	SMITH

1	Pavel	SRNICEK
19	Steve	WATSON
15	Brian	KILCLINE

Match Facts

• Peter Beardsley's equaliser was the 200th goal of his career.

Score Sheet

M. BOWEN 4 min – 1-0
P. BEARDSLEY 20 min – 1-1
A. COLE 79 min – 1-2

Referee:
Mr T. Holbrook (Walsall)

FA Carling Premiership

		P	W	D	L	F	A	Pts
2	Blackburn Rovers	23	13	6	4	32	18	45
3	Arsenal	25	12	8	5	30	13	44
4	**Newcastle United**	**24**	**12**	**6**	**6**	**42**	**22**	**42**
5	Leeds United	24	11	9	4	38	26	42
6	Sheffield Wednesday	25	9	10	6	45	33	37

Result of this Season's Fixture

Norwich City
Newcastle Utd

Canaries off Song

With the absence of two senior players, Venison and Bracewell, United could have been forgiven for struggling against a Norwich side still in good form after their European exploits, but with Kevin Scott and young Robbie Elliott back in the side as replacements, the team turned in perhaps the most consistently excellent performance of the season, to move back to fourth place in the league.

This was, as it turned out, Mike Walker's last game in charge of the Canaries before his controversial move to Everton and with the passionate home crowd chanting for him to stay. Norwich made a good start to the game. We got a glimpse of the skill which Ruel Fox was to bring to Tyneside later in the season in just the fourth minute, as he moved down the right, exchanging passes with both Ekoku and Sutton to leave Elliott and Beresford floundering. Fox got to the byeline, dribbling to the box and crossing to the unmarked Bowen, who smacked a crisp volley past Hooper. It was a fine goal, but all it did was inspire Newcastle, who instantly turned on the pressure, never letting up until the final whistle.

On 20 minutes, Beardsley and Lee Clark exchanged passes, bisecting the home defence and Beardsley ran through to chip the ball over Gunn and into the net. Despite a wet pitch, the quality of passing from both sides was superb and although United were having the best of the game, their attack-minded play always left opportunities for Norwich to counter-attack and it was gripping stuff. In all there was a total of 28 attempts on goal, but only one more was to count. With ten minutes left, Clark dummied Megson in midfield and his pass set Elliott free. His pinpoint pass found Cole who knocked the ball wide of Gunn and then ran on to knock it home. The striker had already hit the woodwork and missed a good chance, but it was inevitable that Cole would get the winner.

At the post match press conference, Keegan described Newcastle's performance as "dream football" and, with Norwich also playing their part, this was a thrilling match.

League Record

	P	Home					Away				
		W	D	L	F	A	W	D	L	F	A
FAPL 93/94	24	7	3	2	24	8	5	3	4	18	14
All Time FAPL	24	7	3	2	24	8	5	3	4	18	14
All Time FL/FAPL	3614	1033	387	387	3610	2048	451	443	913	2143	3162

	Home	Away	Total
Attendances	419,729	291,424	711,153

Newcastle United
Coventry City

(1) 2
(0) 0

Saturday, 8th January 1994, St James' Park   Att.: 35,444

NEWCASTLE UNITED

30	Mike	HOOPER
12	Mark	ROBINSON
3	John	BERESFORD
6	Steve	HOWEY
5	Kevin	SCOTT
7	Robert	LEE
10	Lee	CLARK
26	Robbie	ELLIOTT
9	Andy	COLE
11	Scott	SELLARS (+80)
8	Peter	BEARDSLEY

Subs

1	Pavel	SRNICEK
19	Steve	WATSON (+80)
15	Brian	KILCLINE

COVENTRY CITY

1	Steve	OGRIZOVIC
2	Brian	BORROWS
20	Phil	BABB
4	Peter	ATHERTON
3	Steve	MORGAN
18	Sean	FLYNN
15	Paul	WILLIAMS (+60)
24	Julian	DARBY
12	Peter	NDLOVU
7	John	WILLIAMS
17	Roy	WEGERLE (†31)

Subs

23	Jon	GOULD
10	Mick	QUINN (†31)
6	David	RENNIE (+60)

Match Facts

• Andy Cole's first ever FA Cup goal, and Newcastle have not failed to reach the fourth round since 1989.

Score Sheet

A. COLE 21 min – 1-0
P. BEARDSLEY 76 min – 2-0

Referee:
Mr P. Foakes (Clacton)

Cup of Cheer

A straightforward and comfortable win saw United ease into the Fourth Round of the Cup. Coventry's new manager Phil Neal had left former Magpie Mick Quinn on the bench, but he came on after just half an hour. The nightmare scenario of Quinnie scoring the goal that knocked United out of the Cup never looked likely however, and it was the deadly duo of Beardsley and Cole who stole the show.

Beardsley was the man of the match, acting as captain in the continued absence of Venison and Bracewell, and he was involved in both goals. The first came on 21 minutes when a fierce Beardsley shot came back off the post. Cole's goal-scoring instinct inevitably meant that he was the first to the loose ball and he knocked in the rebound. Steve Howey especially, and the rest of the Magpies defence, comfortably controlled Coventry's attack and the visitors only managed one shot on target all game, winning just one corner. With City never likely to score, United could be patient in their build up and with Sellars in splendid form, the second goal was only a matter of time. It was Robert Lee who exchanged passes with Peter Beardsley as he sliced through the defence, running into the area and chipping the ball over the advancing Ogrizovic.

Coming on the back of the win at Carrow Road, this was a confident and clinical Newcastle performance and, although the FA Cup dream was soon to turn to a nightmare, Keegan's men could be well pleased with this third round victory.

League Record

	Home						Away				
	P	*W*	*D*	*L*	*F*	*A*	*W*	*D*	*L*	*F*	*A*
FA Cup	301	83	34	29	320	159	63	37	55	242	216

	Home	*Away*	*Total*
Cup Attendances	61,331	17,599	78,930

Queens Park Rangers (1) 1
Newcastle United (1) 2

Sunday, 16th January 1994, Loftus Road   Att.: 15,774

QUEENS PARK RANGERS

1	Tony	ROBERTS
2	David	BARDSLEY
5	Darren	PEACOCK
24	Steve	YATES
3	Clive	WILSON
7	Andy	IMPEY (+65)
14	Simon	BARKER
4	Ray	WILKINS
11	Trevor	SINCLAIR
12	Gary	PENRICE
9	Les	FERDINAND

Subs

13	Jan	STEJSKAL
22	Michael	MEAKER (+65)
18	Karl	READY

NEWCASTLE UNITED

30	Mike	HOOPER
12	Mark	ROBINSON
2	Barry	VENISON
6	Steve	HOWEY
3	John	BERESFORD
4	Paul	BRACEWELL
7	Robert	LEE
10	LEE	CLARK
11	Scott	SELLARS
9	Andy	COLE
10	LEE	CLARK

1	Pavel	SRNICEK
5	Kevin	SCOTT
26	Robbie	ELLIOTT

Match Facts

• Lee Clark became the first Newcastle player other than Beardsley and Cole to score since October.

Score Sheet

L. CLARK 5 min – 0-1
G. PENRICE 20 min – 1-1
P. BEARDSLEY 63 min – 1-2

Referee:
Mr D Gallagher (Banbury)

FA Carling Premiership

		P	W	D	L	F	A	Pts
1	Manchester United	26	18	7	1	53	23	61
2	Blackburn Rovers	24	14	6	4	34	19	48
3	Newcastle United	25	13	6	6	44	23	45
4	Arsenal	26	12	9	5	30	13	45
5	Leeds United	25	11	10	4	38	26	43

Result of this Season's Fixture

QPR
Newcastle Utd

On the Road Again

United gained revenge over Rangers for the defeat at St James' Park when Peter Beardsley scored a magnificent winner, just two days before his 33rd birthday. It was Beardsley who made the difference in a contest that had been just about equal until the winning goal.

Before the match, Keegan had announced that he was no longer interested in signing Ranger's England striker Les Ferdinand and at this time there was no hint that Darren Peacock would soon be a United player. With Bracewell and Venison fit again, Elliott and Scott were back on the bench, Elliott in particular being unlucky to lose his place after being a splendid stand-in.

Unusually, Newcastle took an early lead. Sellars hassled Rangers defender Wilson into playing a poor back pass and Roberts came out to try and win the ball. Cole, however, won it off him and it came to Clark on the edge of the area, who had only the right back Bardsley on the line to beat. Rangers' main ploy was to put high balls up to Ferdinand but Steve Howey did a splendid job of marking him and he rarely threatened. In fact, it was his little striking partner Penrice who got the home team's equaliser. A good sweeping cross from Bardsley found Penrice running on. He controlled the ball on his chest and beat Robinson and Hooper with a good shot.

It remained even up to half time as both sides, although playing some nice football, rather cancelled each other out. It took a stroke of real genius to break the deadlock. With less than half an hour to go, Beardsley passed to Clark on the halfway line. Clark's return pass was intercepted by Barker but Beardsley won it back, then set Cole free. As Beardsley ran into the area, it looked as though Cole's pass was too long for him, but he stretched to reach it and sent a flying volley past Roberts.

This one moment of brilliance decided the game and the three points were enough to put United up into third place for the first time.

League Record

| | Home | | | | | | Away | | | | |
	P	W	D	L	F	A	W	D	L	F	A
FAPL 93/94	25	7	3	2	24	8	6	3	4	20	15
All Time FAPL	25	7	3	2	24	8	6	3	4	20	15
All Time FL/FAPL	3615	1033	387	387	3610	2048	452	443	913	2145	3163

	Home	Away	Total
Attendances	419,729	307,168	726,897

Newcastle United
Southampton

(1) 1
(1) 2

Saturday, 22nd January 1994, St James' Park   Att.: 32,129

NEWCASTLE UNITED

30	Mike	HOOPER
12	Mark	ROBINSON
3	John	BERESFORD
2	Barry	VENISON
6	Steve	HOWEY
4	Paul	BRACEWELL
17	Robert	LEE
10	Lee	CLARK
11	Scott	SELLARS
8	Peter	BEARDSLEY
9	Andy	COLE

Subs

1	Pavel	SRNICEK
5	Kevin	SCOTT
14	Alex	MATHIE

SOUTHAMPTON

1	Dave	BEASANT
2	Jeff	KENNA
6	Ken	MONKOU
17	Kevin	MOORE
18	Steve	WOOD
4	Simon	CHARLTON
7	Matt	Le TISSIER
10	Neil	MADDISON
27	Paul	ALLEN
9	Iain	DOWIE
16	Nicky	BANGER

13	Ian	ANDREWS
25	Frankie	BENNETT
21	Tom	WIDDRINGTON

Match Facts

• Andy Cole's goal was his 30th of the
season and he became the fastest United
player to reach that mark in a season, but the
Saints became the first team to do the league
double over United since April 1992.

Score Sheet

N. MADDISON 5 min 0-1
A. COLE 38 min 1-1
M. Le TISSIER 83 min 1-2

Referee:
Mr A. Gunn, Sussex

FA Carling Premiership

		P	W	D	L	F	A	Pts
2	Blackburn Rovers	24	14	6	4	34	19	48
3	Arsenal	27	12	10	5	31	14	46
4	**Newcastle United**	**26**	**13**	**6**	**7**	**45**	**25**	**45**
5	Liverpool	26	12	7	7	44	32	43
6	Leeds United	25	11	10	4	38	26	43

**Result of this
Season's Fixture**

Newcastle Utd

Southampton

Matt Made Welcome

It's a good job United only have to face up to Matt Le Tissier twice a season, because the skilful striker certainly seems to have the Indian sign over Newcastle. This was Alan Ball's first game in charge of the south coast side and, with all the players eager to impress the new boss, Southampton's work rate and one player's magic touch was enough to give the strugglers the points.

It was a poor performance by United, with the normal commitment and effort sadly missing. Southampton's early goal might have spurred the home team into life but it didn't and despite dominating the second half, Keegan's men could have no complaint at the defeat.

After just five minutes Southampton won a corner and with Newcastle more concerned about the tall men, Dowie and Monkou, Maddison was left unmarked. Le Tissier's floating ball found him and he nodded comfortably past Hooper. Cole got the equaliser shortly before the break when Mark Robinson set him free. His shot was mis-hit, hammered into the ground, but the bounce fooled Beasant and it was in.

United had all the play after the break but Southampton defended solidly and with less than ten minutes left, a breathtaking run from Le Tissier led to the winning goal. He was well inside his own half when he got the ball but he ambled right through to the edge of United's area before Robinson brought him down. Le Tissier himself took the free kick and his deceptive curling shot left Mike Hooper leaden footed as he watched it hit the net.

Some late urgency came into Newcastle's play but there was no way back and Southampton could enjoy their long trip home. Newcastle could not afford more performances like this if they were to get anything from the season.

League Record

		Home					Away				
	P	W	D	L	F	A	W	D	L	F	A
FAPL 93/94	26	7	3	3	25	10	6	3	4	20	15
All Time FAPL	26	7	3	3	25	10	6	3	4	20	15
All Time FL/FAPL	3616	1033	387	388	3611	2050	452	443	913	2145	3163

	Home	Away	Total
Attendances	451,858	307,168	759,897

Newcastle United
Luton Town

(0) 1
(1) 1

Saturday, 29th January 1994, St. James' Park   Att.: 32,216

NEWCASTLE UNITED

30	Mike	HOOPER
19	Steve	WATSON
3	John	BERESFORD
2	Barry	VENISON
6	Steve	HOWEY
7	Robert	LEE
4	Paul	BRACEWELL
10	Lee	CLARK
11	Scott	SELLARS
8	Peter	BEARDSLEY
9	Andy	COLE

Subs

1	Pavel	SRNICEK
5	Kevin	SCOTT
14	Alex	MATHIE

LUTON TOWN

1	Jurgen	SOMMER
2	Des	LINTON
3	Trevor	PEAKE
4	John	DREYER
5	Julian	JAMES
6	David	PREECE
7	Tony	*THORPE (+80)*
8	Scott	OAKES
9	Paul	TELFER
10	Alan	HARPER
11	Kerry	DIXON

12	Andy	PETTERSON
13	John	HARTSON
14	Jamie	*CAMPBELL (+80)*

Match Facts

• The sixth consecutive season in which at least one of United's FA Cup ties has gone to a replay.

Score Sheet

T. THORPE 35 min – 0-1
P. BEARDSLEY 65 min Pen – 1-1

Referee:
Mr J. Parker (Preston)

Luton Pay the Penalty

On the face of it this was an easy draw, a leading Premiership side at home to a struggling First Division outfit. But it was to prove a disaster for United.

David Pleat, the Luton manager, is renowned for his tactical sense and he prepared his young team perfectly to deal with United's stars. Everything the Magpies did was countered by Luton who, although they had few attacks, thoroughly deserved at least the draw.

Steve Watson was starting a game for the first time since Christmas and he gave a good account of himself, but many of the team were well below par and the first goal can really be put down to a Paul Bracewell error. His mistake gave the ball to Luton's Alan Harper whose pass to Thorpe brought a cracking 25 yard shot that whistled past Hooper.

Luton were well and truly fired up for this match and although Newcastle had plenty of the ball and amassed seven shots on target, it was a lacklustre display. The only way United were going to equalise was through a penalty, which duly arrived in the 65th minute. Peter Beardsley was brought down by Harper inside the box and despite the visitors' protestations, the spot kick was awarded. Beardsley comfortably converted.

Given what was to follow in the replay, it might have been as well for United to lose this game, but there was a general sense of relief at the final whistle. Everybody believed that the First Division side had missed their opportunity and that United would win comfortably at Kenilworth Road.

Cup Record

| | Home | | | | | | Away | | | | |
	P	W	D	L	F	A	W	D	L	F	A
FA Cup	303	83	35	29	321	160	63	37	56	242	218

	Home	Away	Total
Cup Attendances	93,547	17,599	111,146

Luton Town
Newcastle United

(1) 2
(0) 0

Wednesday, 9th February 1994, Kenilworth Road   Att.: 12,503

LUTON TOWN			**NEWCASTLE UNITED**		
1	Jurgen	SOMMER	30	Mike	HOOPER
2	Des	LINTON	19	Steve	WATSON
3	Trevor	PEAKE	2	Barry	VENISON
4	John	DREYER	6	Steve	HOWEY
5	Julian	JAMES	3	John	BERESFORD
6	Paul	TELFER	7	Robert	LEE
7	Alan	HARPER	10	Lee	CLARK
8	David	PREECE	26	Robbie	ELLIOTT
9	*Jamie*	*CAMPBELL (+80)*	11	Scott	SELLARS
10	John	HARTSON	8	Peter	BEARDSLEY
11	*Scott*	*OAKES (†85)*	9	Andy	COLE

Subs

13	Andy	PETTERSEN	1	Pavel	SRNICEK
12	*Tony*	*THORPE (+80)*	12	Mark	ROBINSON
14	*Scott*	*HOUGHTON (†85)*	20	Alan	NEILSON

Match Facts

• Another early Cup exit. United haven't reached the sixth round since 1976.

Score Sheet

J. HARTSON 16 min – 1-0
S. OAKES 77 min – 2-0

Referee:
Mr J. Parker (Preston)

Down and Out

This was depressing stuff. Luton had done their homework on United, knew exactly what to expect and played with more passion, more commitment and more skill than their supposed superiors. United were never in this match and failed dismally to live up to their billing as second favourites in the competition.

Bracewell was out of the side and Robbie Elliott back in, but it was the general team performance, rather than individual mistakes, that was the reason for this loss. A major blow came early on when Andy Cole suffered a shoulder injury. Although he played out the full ninety minutes, he was always struggling and was to miss the next two games. With Lee Clark and Scott Sellars off form and Robert Lee never really getting into the game, it was only Peter Beardsley who posed any threat at all, but a goal never looked likely – United only managed two shots on target all evening.

Luton were without striker Kerry Dixon and their team of veterans and youngsters shouldn't have posed a threat, but their captain Trevor Peake was to get a wonderful 37th birthday present.

The first goal came after little more than a quarter of an hour and could be put down to Hooper's error. The 18-year-old Hartson was left free on the right and Peake's through ball found him in space. He ran onto the ball as Hooper came charging off his line but Hartson was there first and only had to tap the ball on to have an open goal at his mercy, with the keeper stranded. He duly slotted the ball home.

You would think Newcastle would have fought back, but they were lucky not to go two down before the break when Oakes beat Hooper, only for Venison to clear off the line.

In the second half, Beardsley struck a post and Sommer had to make a good save from Cole, but Oakes got a deserved second goal for the First Division team with thirteen minutes left. He beat Beresford and shot. Hooper could only palm it away and it fell to Linton who quickly played the ball back in. Oakes couldn't miss.

After the second goal, Newcastle became a shambles and the result was never in doubt. The fact that Luton went on to reach the semi-finals may make this defeat more excusable, but at the time it was hard to bear.

Cup Record

			Home					Away			
	P	W	D	L	F	A	W	D	L	F	A
FA Cup	303	83	35	29	321	160	63	37	56	242	218

	Home	Away	Total
Cup Attendances	93,547	30,102	123,649

Wimbledon
Newcastle United

(2) 4
(0) 2

Saturday, 12th February 1994, Selhurst Park   Att. 13,358

WIMBLEDON		
1	Hans	SEGERS
2	Warren	BARTON
4	Vinny	JONES
6	Scott	FITZGERALD
8	Robbie	EARLE
9	*John*	*FASHANU (+75)*
10	Dean	HOLDSWORTH
15	John	SCALES
24	Peter	FEAR
33	Gary	ELKINS
36	Gary	BLISSETT

Subs

23	Neil	SULLIVAN
5	Dean	BLACKWELL
7	Andy	CLARKE

NEWCASTLE UNITED		
30	Mike	HOOPER
19	Steve	WATSON
2	Barry	VENISON
6	Steve	HOWEY
3	John	BERESFORD
5	Ruel	FOX
26	Robbie	ELLIOTT
10	Lee	CLARK
11	Scott	SELLARS
7	*Robert*	*LEE (+69)*
8	Peter	BEARDSLEY

1	Pavel	SRNICEK
14	*Alex*	*MATHIE (+69)*
12	Mark	ROBINSON

Match Facts

• Of the last 32 goals that Newcastle had scored, including these two, only one had not been scored by either Cole or Beardsley.

Score Sheet

R. EARLE 9 min – 1-0
G. BLISSETT 26 min – 2-0
BEARDSLEY 50 min Pen – 2-1
J. FASHANU 55 min – 3-1
HOLDSWORTH 63 min – 4-1
BEARDSLEY 90 min Pen – 4-2

Referee:
Mr. D. Elleray (Harrow)

FA Carling Premiership

		P	W	D	L	F	A	Pts
1	Manchester United	28	20	7	1	57	25	67
2	Blackburn Rovers	27	17	6	4	41	20	57
3	Arsenal	27	12	10	5	31	14	46
4	**Newcastle United**	**27**	**13**	**6**	**8**	**47**	**29**	**45**
5	Liverpool	27	12	8	7	46	34	44

Result of this Season's Fixture

Wimbledon
Newcastle Utd

Done by the Dons

To round off a dreadful week, United were completely outplayed by Wimbledon and were lucky to only lose by two goals. The £2.25 million signing Ruel Fox made his debut on a day when his new team-mates were disheartened and disjointed and Newcastle's lightweight players were hustled out of this game by the muscular crazy gang. That's not to knock Wimbledon in anyway, they played some good football, but if United have a weakness, it's when faced with the direct style of play at which Wimbledon are past masters.

Wimbledon's first goal came after just nine minutes, when Hooper got his fist to Elkins' corner but the clearance only went as far as Earle, who blasted it back past the keeper. Then came United's best spell of the game as Fox showed pace and skill down the right hand side, but without Cole, United's attacks were impotent. Blissett got Wimbledon's second as he beat Howey and Venison to Barton's cross and put a powerful header past Hooper.

By now Fox was fading from the game and not even Beardsley could find any way to liven up Newcastle's performance. Soon after the break, Beresford was bundled over by Jones in the Wimbledon area and Beardsley converted the penalty, but the home side quickly struck back. Their third goal came when Barton and Fear worked the ball to Holdsworth. The striker set up Fear for a run down the right and when the cross came in, Hooper hesitated, leaving Fashanu to head home. Another defensive error put Wimbledon three up when Howey, under pressure from Fashanu, gifted the ball to Holdsworth, who couldn't miss.

Newcastle were lucky to get another goal, although by the time it came it was far too late. The referee decided that Fitzgerald had handled, although it looked as if the ball struck his hip, and Beardsley got his second spot kick of the match.

Wimbledon were on a roll and their final league placing shows that they are not a team to be scoffed at, but Newcastle had some work to do if they were to realistically think of a European place.

League Record

			Home				Away				
	P	W	D	L	F	A	W	D	L	F	A
FAPL 93/94	27	7	3	3	25	10	6	3	5	22	19
All Time FAPL	27	7	3	3	25	10	6	3	5	22	19
All Time FL/FAPL	3617	1033	387	388	3611	2050	452	443	914	2147	3167

	Home	Away	Total
Attendances	451,858	320,526	772,384

Blackburn Rovers (0) 1
Newcastle United (0) 0

Saturday 19th February 1994, Ewood Park   Att.: 21,269

BLACKBURN ROVERS

26	Tim	FLOWERS
2	David	MAY
6	Graeme	Le SAUX
7	Stuart	RIPLEY
8	Kevin	GALLACHER
9	Alan	SHEARER
11	*Jason*	*WILCOX (+72)*
22	Mark	ATKINS
20	Henning	BERG
21	Kevin	MORAN
23	David	BATTY

Subs

1	Bobby	MIMMS
3	*Alan*	*WRIGHT (+72)*
12	Nicky	MARKER

NEWCASTLE UNITED

1	Pavel	SRNICEK
2	Barry	VENISON
3	John	BERESFORD
5	Ruel	FOX
6	Steve	HOWEY
7	Robert	LEE
8	Peter	BEARDSLEY
10	Lee	CLARK
11	Scott	SELLARS
19	Steve	WATSON
26	Robbie	ELLIOTT

30	Mike	HOOPER
20	Alan	NEILSON
14	Alex	MATHIE

Match Facts

• The third of just five Premiership games in which United failed to score.

Score Sheet

D. MAY 76 min – 1-0

Referee:
Mr K. Burge (Tonypandy)

FA Carling Premiership

		P	W	D	L	F	A	Pts
3	Arsenal	29	12	12	5	31	16	48
4	Leeds United	28	12	10	6	41	29	46
5	**Newcastle United**	28	13	6	9	47	30	45
6	Aston Villa	27	12	8	7	36	27	44
7	Liverpool	29	12	8	9	48	40	44

Result of this Season's Fixture

Blackburn Rovers
Newcastle Utd

Playing the Wild Rovers

If there was one team to avoid, after a run of three defeats in a row, it was Blackburn Rovers. With nine wins in their last ten Premiership matches, the Lancashire club had pegged back Manchester United's lead at the top of the table to ten points – it was to be just seven after today and before the season was out they were to close right up on the eventual champions.

Still this was a much better performance, at least defensively, from Newcastle. To the great relief of a large section of the Toon Army fans, Pavel Srnicek was back in goal and he had a fine game, ensuring that he was to retain the number one spot for the rest of the season. Steve Howey did a wonderful marking job on the prolific Alan Shearer and Blackburn's star striker could only manage one shot all game.

With Cole still out of the team, Newcastle again didn't have any real firepower to threaten the home team. Robert Lee worked hard to no avail, as did Sellars and Clark, while Beardsley showed a few nice touches but was not at his best. New signing Fox got little change from Le Saux and Batty.

It was much the same story for Blackburn, with their best play coming from defence. Le Saux forced Srnicek to make a good save from a free kick in the first half and Kevin Moran also brought the best from the keeper in the second, but until Blackburn scored, the game had nil-nil written all over it.

In the 76th minute, a Blackburn corner was cleared but the defence was slow to break out and when Batty head the ball back into the area, it fell to David May, who hit his first Premiership goal of the season.

It was another three points dropped but there were definite signs that things were on the mend. If only Cole was fit...

League Record

	Home						Away				
	P	W	D	L	F	A	W	D	L	F	A
FAPL 93/94	28	7	3	3	25	10	6	3	6	22	20
All Time FAPL	28	7	3	3	25	10	6	3	6	22	20
All Time FL/FAPL	3618	1033	387	388	3611	2050	452	443	915	2147	3168

	Home	Away	Total
Attendances	451,858	341,795	793,653

Newcastle United (0) 4
Coventry City (0) 0

Wednesday 23rd February 1994, St James Park   Att.: 32,216

NEWCASTLE UNITED

1	Pavel	SRNICEK
24	Matty	APPLEBY
19	Steve	WATSON
20	Alan	NEILSON
26	Robbie	ELLIOTT
5	Ruel	FOX
10	Lee	CLARK
7	*Robert*	*LEE (+45)*
11	*Scott*	*SELLARS (†84)*
8	Peter	BEARDSLEY
9	Andy	COLE

Subs

30	Mike	HOOPER
12	*Mark*	*ROBINSON (+45)*
14	*Alex*	*MATHIE (†84)*

COVENTRY CITY

1	Steve	OGRIZOVIC
2	Brian	BORROWS
4	Peter	ATHERTON
20	*Phil*	*BABB (+45)*
3	Steve	MORGAN
18	*Sean*	*FLYNN (†69)*
6	David	RENNIE
25	Julian	DARBY
22	Leigh	JENKINSON
12	Peter	NDLOVU
15	Paul	WILLIAMS

23	Jon	GOULD
14	*David*	*BUSST (+45)*
26	*Sandy*	*ROBERTSON (†69)*

Match Facts

• Andy Cole's sixth hat-trick of his Newcastle career put him back at the top of the list of scorers in the Premiership. His total of 26 was one more than Blackburn's Alan Shearer.

• Referee Bob Hart was a last minute replacement for Roger Dilkes, who was snowed in at his Mossley home!

Score Sheet

A. COLE 49 min – 1-0

A. COLE 70 min – 2-0

A. COLE 77 min – 3-0

A. MATHIE 86 min – 4-0

Referee:
Mr R. Hart (Darlington)

FA Carling Premiership

		P	W	D	L	F	A	Pts
1	Manchester United	28	20	7	1	57	25	67
2	Blackburn Rovers	29	18	7	4	44	23	61
3	**Newcastle United**	**29**	**14**	**6**	**9**	**51**	**30**	**48**
4	Arsenal	29	12	12	5	31	16	48
5	Leeds United	28	12	10	6	41	29	46

Result of this Season's Fixture

Newcastle Utd

Coventry City

Back on Track

The bad run came to end, thanks to a brilliant second half performance from the returning Andy Cole. Back in the team after injury, Cole was not fully fit and Keegan admitted after the game that he had nearly been replaced at half-time!

With the game having been rearranged after postponement in December, the visitors, having a solid season, were in 11th place in the Premiership when they arrived at St James' Park. They must have been confident, given United's form and indeed only Srnicek's fine save from Ndlovu's volley kept the scores level at half-time, but the second forty five was to be a very different story.

For the first goal, Srnicek's long ball up field should have been comfortably cleared, but the lightning quick Cole pressurised Atherton, whose back pass was too short for Ogrizovic and the striker pounced, leaving the dumbstruck defender in his wake. Cole's threat was obvious and Flynn was soon booked for a rough tackle on the striker, but when Fox's run and shot brought a parry from the Coventry keeper, it was Cole again who was on hand to knock in the rebound.

The hat trick came after a goalmouth scramble, with Cole blasting home from 10 yards and Mathie completed the scoring with virtually his first touch of the game.

Cole's performance drew praise from his manager, but Keegan had as much to say about the performance of the young back four. With Venison suspended, Scott gone south to Spurs and both Howey and Beresford out through injury, it had a very inexperienced look about it, but was rarely stretched and Srnicek had little to do. "They must be the youngest ever to play for Newcastle", said Keegan, "and they came up trumps."

But the night belonged to Cole and his importance to the side could be seen from the fact that, until Mathie's strike, only he, Beardsley and Clark (once) had scored for United since mid November. But he was fit again, the team regained third place in the table and the season was back on track.

League Record

	Home						Away				
	P	W	D	L	F	A	W	D	L	F	A
FAPL 93/94	29	8	3	3	29	10	6	3	6	22	20
All Time FAPL	29	8	3	3	29	10	6	3	6	22	20
All Time FL/FAPL	3619	1034	387	388	3615	2050	452	443	915	2147	3168

	Home	Away	Total
Attendances	484,074	341,795	825,869

Sheffield Wednesday (0) 0
Newcastle United (0) 1

Match 36

Saturday, 5th March 1994, Hillsborough   Att.: 33,224

SHEFFIELD WEDNESDAY

13	Kevin	PRESSMAN
2	Roland	NILSSON
12	Andy	PEARCE
17	Des	WALKER
28	Simon	COLEMAN
16	*Graham*	*HYDE (+23)*
4	Carlton	PALMER
14	Chris	BART-WILLIAMS
15	Andy	SINTON
10	*Mark*	*BRIGHT (†80)*
20	Gordon	WATSON

Subs

23	Paul	KEY
18	*Phil*	*KING (+23)*
19	*Nigel*	*JEMSON (†80)*

NEWCASTLE UNITED

1	Pavel	SRNICEK
12	Mark	ROBINSON
3	John	BERESFORD
6	*Steve*	*HOWEY (+48)*
20	Alan	NEILSON
5	Ruel	FOX
7	Robert	LEE
11	Scott	SELLARS
19	Steve	WATSON
8	Peter	BEARDSLEY
9	Andy	COLE

30	Mike	HOOPER
26	*Robbie*	*ELLIOTT (+48)*
14	Alex	MATHIE

Match Facts

• Peter Beardsley celebrated his return to the England team by creating the winning goal.

Score Sheet

A. COLE 88 min – 1-0

Referee:
Mr P. Durkin (Portland)

FA Carling Premiership

		P	W	D	L	F	A	Pts
2	Blackburn Rovers	31	19	7	5	46	23	64
3	Arsenal	31	14	12	5	39	17	54
4	**Newcastle United**	**30**	**15**	**6**	**9**	**52**	**30**	**51**
5	Leeds United	30	12	12	6	42	30	48
6	Liverpool	31	13	8	10	49	42	47

Result of this Season's Fixture

Sheffield Wed
Newcastle Utd

89

Riding our Luck

The look on Wednesday manager Trevor Francis' face at the end of the game said it all about this disappointing clash, but his team had only themselves to blame for gifting the three points to United.

After being humiliated by Manchester United in their League Cup semi-final during the week, Wednesday were in need of a boost and a lacklustre United gave them every chance, but in the end it was a typically opportunist late strike from Cole that decided the game.

Wednesday, lacking the injured Hirst up front, created the best chances in the first half, and Carlton Palmer should have given them the lead in the 23rd minute when he was left unmarked at the far post, only to put his free header against the outside of the post. Palmer was also the culprit later on as he placed a soft header straight into Srnicek's hands, when a nod down to either Bright or Watson could have lead to a goal.

United were without Lee Clark through illness and his influence was sorely missed. With Walker in the Wednesday defence dominating proceedings, Beardsley was stifled out of the game, only occasionally linking up with Fox to any effect, and Cole had little service. Fox looked lively at times but his occasional runs brought nothing in the way of end product.

The ineffectual jousting continued through the second half, the best chance coming when Bright beat Alan Neilson on the right. With Sinton running into the area unmarked, United were only spared when Bright's cross took a deflection.

The decisive moment came with just two minutes to go. Beardsley played a ball through to Cole from midfield, leaving the striker a clear run on goal. Andy Pearce, who up to that point had had a fine game, was caught out for pace and ten yards from the area lunged out to concede the free-kick. With Cole through, the referee had no option but to dismiss the defender, but the punishment for Wednesday was to be even more severe.

Sellars touched the free-kick to Beardsley, whose low shot was going nowhere until it deflected off the wall. It then hit Fox in the back and bounced invitingly to the incoming Cole, who wasted no time in slotting the ball past Pressman.

Not the best performance of the season, not the best match, but another three points was enough to keep UEFA cup hopes alive.

League Record

	Home						Away				
	P	W	D	L	F	A	W	D	L	F	A
FAPL 93/94	30	8	3	3	29	10	7	3	6	23	20
All Time FAPL	30	8	3	3	29	10	7	3	6	23	20
All Time FL/FAPL	3620	1034	387	388	3615	2050	453	443	915	2148	3168

	Home	Away	Total
Attendances	484,074	375,019	859,093

Newcastle United (2) 7
Swindon Town (0) 1

Saturday, 12th March 1994, St James' Park   Att.: 32,216

NEWCASTLE UNITED

1	Pavel	SRNICEK
19	Steve	WATSON
3	John	BERESFORD
12	Mark	ROBINSON
2	Barry	VENISON
26	Robbie	ELLIOTT
7	Robert	LEE
8	Peter	BEARDSLEY
9	Andy	COLE
11	Scott	SELLARS
5	Ruel	FOX

SWINDON TOWN

1	Fraser	DIGBY
3	Paul	BODIN (+45)
5	Luc	NIJHOLT
6	Shaun	TAYLOR
7	John	MONCUR
26	Terry	FENWICK
10	Martin	LING
9	Jan-Aage	FJORTOFT
27	Keith	SCOTT (†77)
16	Kevin	HORLOCK
32	Frank	McAVENNIE

Subs

30	Mike	HOOPER (gk)
14	Alex	MATHIE
20	Alan	NEILSON

23	Nicky	HAMMOND (gk)
	Ty	GOODEN (+45)
17	Chris	HAMON (†77)

Match Facts

- 7-1 became the biggest Premiership victory, by any side, this season.

- Robert Lee's first goal was his first in the Premiership, while Ruel Fox's strike was his first since his arrival from Norwich.

Score Sheet

BEARDSLEY 12 min Pen – 1-0
R. LEE 17 min – 2-0
R. LEE 67 min – 3-0
P. BEARDSLEY 70 min – 4-0
S. WATSON 76 min – 5-0
J. MONCUR 77 min – 5-1
S. WATSON 79 min – 6-1
R. FOX 84 min – 7-1

Referee:
Mr M. Reed (Birmingham)

FA Carling Premiership

		P	W	D	L	F	A	Pts
1	Manchester United	30	20	8	2	59	28	68
2	Blackburn Rovers	31	19	7	5	46	23	64
3	**Newcastle United**	**31**	**16**	**6**	**9**	**59**	**31**	**54**
4	Arsenal	31	14	12	5	39	17	54

Result of this Season's Fixture

No Fixture

Seven Up – Again!

Just a year ago, both these teams were on the up and up, heading for promotion to the Premiership. Now, fortunes had changed with Swindon doomed to relegation and United eyeing a place in Europe, and this result clearly reflected the difference in class between the two sides.

Much admired for their passing, entertaining brand of football, poor Swindon just didn't have the defensive nous to contain a rampant United and it took just twelve minutes for the home team to open their account. Beardsley, sprinting for a return pass inside the opposition area, was tripped by Taylor and Beardsley himself made light of the resultant penalty. Just five minutes later, the game was as good as over when Sellars sent Lee through and, with two defenders closing in, he shot high into the roof of the net for his first Premiership goal.

Things settled down for the rest of the half, although Swindon's much-travelled striker, McAvennie, drew a good save from Srnicek.

This was the only real moment of worry for United and Sellars twice came close after the interval before Lee made it three in the 67th minute, tapping in after Cole's shot had been blocked by Digby. Beardsley glided past the keeper to slot in his second and Newcastle's fourth, after a poor back pass from Fenwick, and Watson put a nice drive wide of the keeper for the fifth.

Swindon's heads had dropped by this stage, but Moncur got a consolation goal, his free-kick from just outside the area taking an odd bounce that caught Srnicek unawares.

It wasn't long before Watson got his second, this time again after a Cole shot could only be parried and Fox rounded things off by guiding Sellars' cross in from 6 yards.

This was a comprehensive victory, with United looking a complete team. Beardsley, fresh from his return to international duties and his fiftieth cap the previous Wednesday, was hugely influential, but Fox, Watson and Sellars all showed that, on their day, they can be as good as anybody in the league. Admittedly, Swindon didn't provide the sternest of tests but United's confident second half performance would have stretched anybody.

Something else. Seven goals and not one of them scored by Cole? Would the striker be able to keep his place in the side for the next match?

League Record

| | Home | | | | | | Away | | | | |
	P	W	D	L	F	A	W	D	L	F	A
FAPL 93/94	31	9	3	3	36	11	7	3	6	23	20
All Time FAPL	31	9	3	3	36	11	7	3	6	23	20
All Time FL/FAPL	3621	1035	387	388	3622	2051	453	443	915	2148	3168

	Home	Away	Total
Attendances	516,290	375,019	891,309

West Ham United   (0) 2
Newcastle United   (1) 4

Saturday, 19th March 1994, Upton Park   Att.: 23,132

WEST HAM UNITED

1	Ludek	MIKLOSKO
2	Tim	BREACKER
4	Steve	POTTS
8	Peter	BUTLER
9	*Trevor*	*MORLEY (+80)*
14	Ian	BISHOP
16	Matt	HOLMES
18	Alvin	MARTIN
23	Keith	ROWLAND
25	Lee	CHAPMAN
34	Mike	MARSH

Subs

13	Gary	KELLY
	Jeroen	BOERE
15	Kenny	BROWN

NEWCASTLE UNITED

1	Pavel	SRNICEK
12	Mark	ROBINSON
2	Barry	VENISON
26	Robbie	ELLIOTT
3	John	BERESFORD
5	*Ruel*	*FOX (+79)*
7	Robert	LEE
19	*Steve*	*WATSON (†19)*
11	Scott	SELLARS
9	Andy	COLE
8	Peter	BEARDSLEY

30	Mike	HOOPER
14	*Alex*	*MATHIE (+79)*
20	*Alan*	*NEILSON (†19)*

Match Facts

• Robert Lee scored twice against the team he supported as a boy. He stayed behind in London after the game to act as best man at a friend's wedding.

Score Sheet

R. LEE 34 min – 0-1
T. BREACKER 57 min – 1-1
A. COLE 69 min – 1-2
R. LEE 73 min – 1-3
A. MARTIN 81 min – 2-3
A. MATHIE 90 min – 2-4

Referee:
K. Morton (Bury St. Edmunds)

FA Carling Premiership

		P	W	D	L	F	A	Pts
1	Manchester United	32	21	9	2	66	30	72
2	Blackburn Rovers	31	19	7	5	46	23	64
3	**Newcastle United**	**32**	**17**	**6**	**9**	**63**	**33**	**57**
4	Arsenal	32	15	12	5	43	17	57
5	Leeds United	33	14	13	6	47	32	55

Result of this Season's Fixture

West Ham Utd
Newcastle Utd

Lee on Home Soil

This game came just four days before the Hammers were to be beaten in their quarter final Cup replay against Luton, Newcastle's conquerors in the fourth round, and you could certainly see the weaknesses in both teams that allowed the First Division team their wins. Neither side's defence had any coherence in this game but it did make for a highly entertaining game. The Magpies deserved their victory because they had that little bit more solidity at the back and the devastating form of the front men meant that goals were inevitable.

Robert Lee was brilliant against his boyhood heroes, playing in central midfield in the absence of Clark, and he brought an extra dimension to United, the focus no longer being simply on Cole and Beardsley.

Fox and Robinson were involved in the build-up which led to Cole laying the ball to Lee for the first goal. His right foot shot took a deflection off Steve Potts, which put it out of the reach of Miklosko and it was 1-0 at half time.

As so often with Newcastle this season, most of the goals came late in the game and there was little more than half an hour to go when West Ham equalised. Holmes played the ball to Bishop who found Mike Marsh. Marsh put a fine ball into the path of Breacker, who fired past Srnicek. There was still no hint of the drama to come when with just twenty minutes to go, Andy Cole stretched to turn in Fox's cross and restore United's lead. Just four minutes later and it looked all over, as Beardsley played the ball to Cole, who quickly found Lee. His shot gave Miklosko no chance.

West Ham continued to come forward and Alvin Martin gave them hope as his strength in the air outdid the Newcastle defence and he headed in, but substitute Alex Mathie had the last word with an injury-time winner. Beardsley worked the ball to Cole who turned in the area to set up the Scot for a low shot.

League Record

	Home					Away				
	P	W	D	L	F	A	W	D	L	F	A
FAPL 93/94	32	9	3	3	36	11	8	3	6	27	22
All Time FAPL	32	9	3	3	36	11	8	3	6	27	22
All Time FL/FAPL	3622	1035	387	388	3622	2051	454	443	915	2152	3170

	Home	Away	Total
Attendances	516,290	398,151	914,441

Newcastle United
Ipswich Town

(1) 2
(0) 0

Wednesday, 23rd March 1994, St James' Park   Att.: 32,216

NEWCASTLE UNITED

1	Pavel	SRNICEK
12	Mark	ROBINSON
2	Barry	VENISON
26	*Robbie*	*ELLIOTT (+79)*
3	John	BERESFORD
19	*Steve*	*WATSON (†45)*
23	Chris	HOLLAND
11	Scott	SELLARS
7	Robert	LEE
9	Andy	COLE
8	Peter	BEARDSLEY

IPSWICH TOWN

13	Clive	BAKER
2	Mick	STOCKWELL
5	John	WARK
15	Phil	WHELAN
8	Gavin	JOHNSON
4	Paul	MASON
7	Geraint	WILLIAMS
18	*Steve*	*PALMER (+74)*
21	Stuart	SLATER
10	Ian	MARSHALL
11	Chris	KIWOMYA

Subs

30	Mike	HOOPER			
14	*Alex*	*MATHIE (†45)*	22	*Lee*	*DURRANT (+74)*
20	*Alan*	*NEILSON (+79)*			

Match Facts

• Scott Sellars scored his first Premiership goal of the season, in his 21st appearance.

Score Sheet

S. SELLARS 37 min – 1-0

A. COLE 73 min – 2-0

Referee:
Mr K. Cooper (Pontypridd)

FA Carling Premiership

		P	W	D	L	F	A	Pts
2	Blackburn Rovers	33	21	7	5	51	25	70
3	Arsenal	34	16	13	5	46	19	61
4	**Newcastle United**	33	18	6	9	65	33	60
5	Leeds United	34	14	13	7	47	33	55
6	Liverpool	34	15	8	11	53	45	53

Result of this Season's Fixture

Newcastle Utd
Ipswich Town

Easy Does It

This was a comfortable win for United and the 2-0 scoreline does not reflect the gulf between the two sides. Ipswich arrived with an ultra-defensive formation but with Robert Lee still in sparkling form and Cole working incredibly hard, there was only ever going to be one result.

Off the field, negotiations were being finalised in the deal that was to bring Darren Peacock to Tyneside, but the big bonus of the night, however, was the debut of young Chris Holland. The £100,000 signing from Preston had never before started a league game but, playing wide on the right in place of Fox, he was crucial to both goals.

In the opening minutes, Lee headed just wide and then saw a good shot pushed onto the bar. Despite having all the play it looked as though Newcastle might be held right through to half-time, but with just eight minutes to go before the break, Sellars broke the deadlock. He played the ball to Holland who put in a long cross, setting Sellars up for a right foot shot.

Immediately after the break, Ipswich might have got an equaliser when they had a confident penalty appeal turned down. Marshall fell under a challenge from Srnicek but it would have been unjust for the Suffolk team to get anything from this match. They had just three shots all game, only one on target. Instead, the Magpies were to score again. Holland showed just how much potential he has with another pinpoint cross, this time for Cole to head in at the far post.

It was a comfortable victory, but with uncomfortable results for two players. Barry Venison fractured a cheek bone, and more seriously Robbie Elliott tore knee ligaments, an injury that was to keep him out for the rest of the season.

League Record

	P	W	D	L	F	A	W	D	L	F	A
			Home						**Away**		
FAPL 93/94	33	10	3	3	38	11	8	3	6	27	22
All Time FAPL	33	10	3	3	38	11	8	3	6	27	22
All Time FL/FAPL	3623	1036	387	388	3624	2051	454	443	915	2152	3170

	Home	Away	Total
Attendances	48,506	398,151	946,657

Newcastle United (1) 3
Norwich City (0) 0

Tuesday, 29th March 1994, St James' Park   Att.: 32,216

NEWCASTLE UNITED

1	Pavel	SRNICEK
12	Mark	ROBINSON
3	John	BERESFORD
15	Darren	PEACOCK
20	Alan	NEILSON
5	Ruel	FOX (+80)
4	Paul	BRACEWELL (†74)
11	Scott	SELLARS
7	Robert	LEE
9	Andy	COLE
8	Peter	BEARDSLEY

Subs

30	Mike	HOOPER
14	Alex	MATHIE (+80)
23	Chris	HOLLAND (†74)

NORWICH CITY

1	Bryan	GUNN
2	Mark	BOWEN
8	Colin	WOODTHORPE
27	Spencer	PRIOR
5	Ian	CULVERHOUSE
6	Neil	ADAMS (+67)
4	Ian	CROOK
9	Gary	MEGSON
11	Jeremy	GOSS
18	Robert	ULLATHORNE
20	Darren	EADIE

Subs

13	Scot	HOWIE
26	Ade	AKINBIWI (+67)
21	David	SMITH

Match Facts

• To show just how one-sided this match was, Norwich City did not manage one shot on target in the game.

• Andy Cole's 30th Premiership goal made him the first player to reach that mark in the top flight since Clive Allen in 1987.

Score Sheet

A. COLE 45 min – 1-0

R. LEE 50 min – 2-0

P. BEARDSLEY 70 min – 3-0

Referee:
Mr T. Holbrook (Walsall)

FA Carling Premiership

		P	W	D	L	F	A	Pts
1	Manchester United	33	21	10	2	58	32	73
2	Blackburn Rovers	34	21	7	6	52	29	70
3	**Newcastle United**	**34**	**19**	**6**	**9**	**68**	**33**	**63**
4	Arsenal	34	16	13	5	46	19	61
5	Leeds United	34	14	13	7	47	33	55

Result of this Season's Fixture

Newcastle Utd
Norwich City

The Goals Keep Coming

The double over Norwich brought the points which took United back to third place in the league and Andy Cole's opening strike took his Premiership tally to 30. With Darren Peacock making his debut and Alan Neilson starting the game, Newcastle's defence was more impressive and with the usual attacking excellence still in force, this was a fine win.

Norwich were without young striker Chris Sutton for the first time this season, which didn't help them, but although they didn't create much they made life difficult for United and played some nice football. Their season had died with their exit from Europe and there was already nothing for them to play for, but the visitors played their part in an entertaining game.

It took a long while for United to break down the opposition defence and it was only in injury time before the break that the first goal came. Darren Peacock repaid some of the £2.7 million fee when he went up for a Scott Sellars corner. His aerial power won the ball and after a scramble it fell to Cole to volley past Gunn.

Despite the enterprise of Goss, Norwich had no reply and just five minutes after half time, Robert Lee made it two with a cracking goal. A lovely back heel from Beardsley gave the ball to Cole who swept the ball into the area. Lee shook off Culverhouse and hammered the ball into the back of the net.

The third goal was another piece of Beardsley magic. Fox's through ball should have been cleared, but Prior hesitated and Beardsley rushed onto the ball. Gunn forced him wide but with consummate control, Pedro slotted the ball in from the tightest of angles.

Another thrilling performance gained a sixth successive victory and kept alive United's slim chance of claiming the runners-up spot in their first Premiership season.

League Record

			Home					Away				
	P	W	D	L	F	A	W	D	L	F	A
FAPL 93/94	34	11	3	3	41	11	8	3	6	27	22
All Time FAPL	34	11	3	3	41	11	8	3	6	27	22
All Time FL/FAPL	3624	1037	387	388	3627	2051	454	443	915	2152	3170

	Home	Away	Total
Attendances	580,722	398,151	978,873

Leeds United
Newcastle United

(0) 1
(1) 1

Friday, 1st April 1994, Elland Road   Att.: 40,005

LEEDS UNITED

1	John	LUKIC
22	Gary	KELLY
18	*David*	*WETHERALL (+72)*
16	Jon	NEWSOME
3	Tony	DORIGO
5	Chris	FAIRCLOUGH
7	Gordon	STRACHAN
11	Gary	SPEED
10	Gary	McALLISTER
8	Rod	WALLACE
9	Brian	DEANE

Subs

13	Mark	BEENEY
4	*David*	*WHITE (+72)*
23	Mark	TINKLER

NEWCASTLE UNITED

1	Pavel	SRNICEK
12	Mark	ROBINSON
3	John	BERESFORD
15	Darren	PEACOCK
20	Alan	NEILSON
4	Paul	BRACEWELL
5	Ruel	FOX
7	*Robert*	*LEE (+57)*
11	Scott	SELLARS
9	Andy	COLE
8	Peter	BEARDSLEY

30	Mike	HOOPER
2	*Barry*	*VENISON (+57)*
14	Alex	MATHIE

Match Facts

- Cole's strike was the 50th goal of his brief Newcastle career.

Score Sheet

A. COLE 3 min – 0-1

FAIRCLOUGH – 89 min – 1-1

Referee:
Mr K. Cooper (Pontypridd)

FA Carling Premiership

		P	W	D	L	F	A	Pts
1	Manchester United	34	22	10	2	59	32	76
2	Blackburn Rovers	34	21	7	6	52	29	70
3	**Newcastle United**	**35**	**19**	**7**	**9**	**69**	**34**	**64**
4	Arsenal	34	16	13	5	46	19	61
5	Leeds United	35	14	14	7	48	34	56

Result of this Season's Fixture

Leeds United

Newcastle Utd

Rock Solid

An unusual game for Newcastle. Against fellow high-flyers Leeds, the Magpies got an early goal and then hung on desperately, the opposition having most of the possession before getting a late equaliser.

In the third minute, Robert Lee played a cross into the middle and Sellars hit it first time. Lukic made a good save, but Andy Cole pounced on the rebound. His fiftieth Newcastle goal led to wild celebrations and stunned the home fans, but there were to be few chances after this.

Leeds put on a great deal of pressure. Srnicek made a good save at the near post and Deane very nearly scored after a Ruel Fox error gave him a run on goal. The big striker beat two defenders and fired past Srnicek, but the lightning reactions of Neilson allowed him to make a desperate goal line clearance. Newcastle's defenders continued to harry the home side and everything they tried was rushed. Newsome might have scored from a Strachan cross, and both Strachan and McAllister tried long range shots but to no avail.

An indication of the way things were going came when Robert Lee went off through injury. His replacement was not Mathie, but the defender Venison, making a comeback just nine days after fracturing a cheek bone. No matter what the home team tried, they couldn't get the breakthrough, and Cole always looked dangerous whenever Newcastle broke. Then, with just a minute on the clock, a Gordon Strachan corner finally unlocked the Magpies defence. Newsome nodded it on at the near post leaving Srnicek stranded and Fairclough had the easiest of tasks to head home.

So the two games against Leeds this season both ended in 1-1 draws and there was clearly little to separate the two teams. The winning streak had come to an end, but seven games without defeat meant that United were well placed to earn the third place finish that could secure a place in Europe.

League Record

	Home					Away				
	P	W	D	L	F	A	W	D	L	F	A
FAPL 93/94	35	11	3	3	41	11	8	4	6	28	23
All Time FAPL	35	11	3	3	41	11	8	4	6	28	23
All Time FL/FAPL	3625	1037	387	388	3627	2051	454	444	915	2153	3171

	Home	Away	Total
Attendances	580,722	438,156	1,018,878

Newcastle United (0) 0
Chelsea (0) 0

Monday, 4th April 1994, St James' Park   Att.: 32,216

NEWCASTLE UNITED

1	Pavel	SRNICEK
12	Mark	ROBINSON
3	*John*	*BERESFORD (+73)*
2	Barry	VENISON
15	Darren	PEACOCK
7	Robert	LEE
23	*Chris*	*HOLLAND (†63)*
4	Paul	BRACEWELL
11	Scott	SELLARS
8	Peter	BEARDSLEY
9	Andy	COLE

CHELSEA

1	Dimitri	KHARIN
12	Steve	CLARKE
15	Mal	DONAGHY
35	Jakob	KJELDBJERG
6	Frank	SINCLAIR
5	Erland	JOHNSEN
11	Dennis	WISE
17	Nigel	SPACKMAN
9	Tony	CASCARINO
7	John	SPENCER
24	*Craig*	*BURLEY (+90)*

Subs

30	Mike	HOOPER
20	*Alan*	*NEILSON (+73)*
14	*Alex*	*MATHIE (†63)*

13	Kevin	HITCHCOCK
2	Darren	BARNARD
	David	LEE

Match Facts

• Chelsea became the only side this season to prevent Newcastle scoring in both their Premiership games.

Score Sheet

Referee:
Mr S. Lodge (Barnsley)

FA Carling Premiership

		P	W	D	L	F	A	Pts
1	Manchester United	36	23	10	3	72	36	79
2	Blackburn Rovers	36	23	7	6	57	29	76
3	**Newcastle United**	**36**	**19**	**8**	**9**	**69**	**34**	**65**
4	Arsenal	36	16	15	5	48	21	63
5	Leeds United	36	15	14	7	52	34	59

Result of this Season's Fixture

Newcastle Utd
Chelsea

Stalemate

The only 0-0 of the season as the visitors set out their stall right from the start to play for a draw. Glenn Hoddle's tactics made this a very disappointing spectacle for the bank holiday crowd as their time-wasting and off side ploys killed the game stone dead.

In Chelsea's favour, it should be said that they were preparing for the vital FA Cup semi-final against Luton and had a long injury list. Star striker Mark Stein and the influential Eddie Newton were both sidelined, as was ex-Magpie Gavin Peacock and Chelsea were more concerned about not picking up more injuries than picking up points.

Newcastle were caught offside 10 times in the first half alone and whenever they did beat the trap, the Chelsea defence, especially Kharin in goal, were up to the challenge. The Russian keeper saved well from Sellars and both Beardsley and Lee missed chances.

With Cole and Beardsley marked out of the game, and Lee and the young Chris Holland never really getting going, it was left to Beresford and Bracewell to try and create the openings. Beresford was going forward more often than usual but it was on one of these forays into the opposition half that he tangled with Dennis Wise and damaged an ankle. He had to be substituted and would be out of the next game at Maine Road.

After the match, Keegan singled out Kharin in particular for his time-wasting, but in reality it was a professional, if dull, performance by the Londoners and United didn't have any answers.

League Record

| | Home | | | | | | Away | | | | |
	P	W	D	L	F	A	W	D	L	F	A
FAPL 93/94	36	11	4	3	41	11	8	4	6	28	23
All Time FAPL	36	11	4	3	41	11	8	4	6	28	23
All Time FL/FAPL	3626	1037	388	388	3627	2051	454	444	915	2153	3171

	Home	Away	Total
Attendances	612,938	438,156	1,051,094

Manchester City
Newcastle United

(2) 2
(1) 1

Saturday, 9th April 1994, Maine Road   Att.: 33,774

MANCHESTER CITY			NEWCASTLE UNITED		
25	Andy	DIBBLE	1	Pavel	SRNICEK
2	Andy	HILL	2	Mark	ROBINSON
18	David	BRIGHTWELL	20	Alan	NEILSON
5	Keith	CURLE	2	Barry	VENISON
6	Michael	VONK	15	Darren	PEACOCK
7	David	ROCASTLE	5	Ruel	FOX
4	Steve	McMAHON	7	Robert	LEE
31	*Stefan*	*KARL (+80)*	31	*Mike*	*JEFFREY (+81)*
32	Peter	BEAGRIE	11	Scott	SELLARS
30	Paul	WALSH	9	Andy	COLE
28	Uwe	ROSLER	8	Peter	BEARDSLEY

Subs

13	Martyn	MARGETSON	30	Mike	HOOPER
21	*Steven*	*LOMAS (+80)*	14	*Alex*	*MATHIE (+81)*
3	Terry	PHELAN	34	Brian	REID

Match Facts

- This defeat marked the end of United's eight game unbeaten run.

Score Sheet

S. SELLARS 19 min – 0-1
P. WALSH 33 min – 1-1
D. BRIGHTWELL 48 min 2-1

Referee:
J. Borrett (Great Yarmouth)

FA Carling Premiership

		P	W	D	L	F	A	Pts
1	Manchester United	36	23	10	3	72	36	79
2	Blackburn Rovers	36	23	7	6	57	29	76
3	**Newcastle United**	**37**	**19**	**8**	**10**	**70**	**36**	**65**
4	Arsenal	36	16	15	5	48	21	63
5	Leeds United	36	15	14	7	52	34	59

Result of this Season's Fixture

Manchester City
Newcastle Utd

City Serve up a Case of the Blues

With all the other top teams not playing, this was a chance for United to close the gap on Blackburn and make third place their own, but with City fighting for their lives, the home side's desire was that much stronger.

Since the arrival of Francis Lee as chairman, the Manchester team had picked up their form and there had been a big reshuffle in the team. Paul Walsh had arrived from Portsmouth along with the German pair Karl and Rosler. Peter Beagrie, the ex-Everton player, was also at Maine Road and he was perhaps the star of this game. Newcastle gave a second start of the season to Mike Jeffrey, amid a deepening midfield injury crisis.

United made a bright start and it was Jeffrey's cross, after he had been set free by Fox, that led to the opening goal. His cross was turned in from close range by Sellars. There was a feeling about Newcastle that the job had been done already, but City were fighting for their lives and believed that they were still in the game. After half an hour Peter Beagrie beat Robinson down the left and the nippy Walsh crept in to head home off the underside of the bar. Soon afterwards, Cole hit a cracking shot which beat Dibble but it bounced back off the woodwork.

Four minutes after the break, City got the winning goal. David Brightwell had got his place in the team through an injury to Terry Phelan after being out of favour. He had an excellent game, stifling Fox and crowned the performance with a goal. Stefan Karl's cross was met by Peacock in the middle, but his headed clearance fell to the City defender, whose left foot shot beat Srnicek.

After that, the game was decided and City might have won by more. Steve McMahon was switched to marking Beardsley in the second half and United's attacking options dried up. Both Karl and Beagrie went close, but in the end a 2-1 win for City was a fair result.

League Record

	P	W	D	L	F	A	W	D	L	F	A
			Home						**Away**		
FAPL 93/94	37	11	4	3	41	11	8	4	7	29	25
All Time FAPL	37	11	4	3	41	11	8	4	7	29	25
All Time FL/FAPL	3627	1037	388	388	3627	2051	454	444	916	2154	3173

	Home	Away	Total
Attendances	612,938	471,930	1,084,868

Liverpool
Newcastle United

(0) 0
(1) 2

Saturday, 16th April 1994, Anfield | Att.: 44,601

LIVERPOOL

13	David	JAMES
2	Rob	JONES
4	Steve	NICOL
25	Neil	RUDDOCK
3	Julian	DICKS
17	Steve	McMANAMAN (+71)
15	Jamie	REDKNAPP
12	Ronnie	WHELAN
10	John	BARNES
9	Ian	RUSH
23	Robbie	FOWLER (†60)

Subs

1	Bruce	GROBBELAAR
16	Michael	THOMAS (+71)
16	Don	HUTCHISON (†60)

NEWCASTLE UNITED

1	Pavel	SRNICEK
2	Barry	VENISON (+88)
3	John	BERESFORD
15	Darren	PEACOCK
20	Alan	NEILSON
5	Ruel	FOX
7	Robert	LEE
4	Paul	BRACEWELL
11	Scott	SELLARS
9	Andy	COLE
8	Peter	BEARDSLEY (†90)

30	Mike	HOOPER
2	Mark	ROBINSON (+88)
14	Alex	MATHIE (†90)

Match Facts

• Andy Cole's winner equalled Hughie Gallacher and George Robledo's record of 39 goals in a season.

Score Sheet

R. LEE 4 min – 0-1
A. COLE 56 min – 0-2

Referee:
Mr P. Don (Middlesex)

FA Carling Premiership

		P	W	D	L	F	A	Pts
1	Manchester United	37	23	10	4	72	37	79
2	Blackburn Rovers	38	24	7	7	59	32	79
3	**Newcastle United**	**38**	**20**	**8**	**10**	**72**	**36**	**68**
4	Arsenal	37	17	15	5	49	21	66
5	Leeds United	36	15	14	7	52	34	59

Result of this Season's Fixture

Liverpool
Newcastle Utd

Red Letter Day

This was an emotionally charged day. The fifth anniversary of the Hillsborough tragedy and before the game two of United's ex-Anfield contingent, Peter Beardsley and assistant manager Terry McDermott, both laid wreaths to mark the event. It was also the penultimate game for the famous Kop terrace, but for Newcastle it was another League game, and they didn't let the occasion change the way they played.

Liverpool had improved under new boss Roy Evans but they were still not a match for a rampant United, for whom Lee, Fox and Beardsley were in top form.

After the emotional preamble to the game it was perhaps essential that Newcastle made a good start and it took just four minutes for Robert Lee to give the Magpies the lead. Scott Sellars laid the ball to Cole and he threaded a pass through the defence. Lee was sharply onto it, chipping past James and into the net.

Liverpool had plenty of pressure but Newcastle's industry limited their opportunities. Only John Barnes posed any real problems as the home team, despite plenty of possession, struggled for ideas and could only try a series of hopeful long shots. The occasion inspired the former Anfield favourite Beardsley to great heights and he showed his skill, but a lot of the credit for the win has to go to the defence. Young Alan Neilson might have been intimidated by the atmosphere, but he coped admirably.

Fox was sharp and pacey, Lee was everywhere and Scott Sellars showed exceptional skills. Ten minutes after the break, as Liverpool were threatening to come into the game, it was Fox who created the winner. He took the ball on the right and slid a perfect pass just where Cole wanted it. The striker gave James no chance.

Just before the end, Keegan substituted the two ex-Liverpool players, Venison and Beardsley, and they left the pitch to a rousing reception. United had now completed the double over both Merseyside teams without conceding a single goal, totally dominating a game against one of the biggest teams in the land.

League Record

	Home						Away				
	P	W	D	L	F	A	W	D	L	F	A
FAPL 93/94	38	11	4	3	41	11	9	4	7	31	25
All Time FAPL	38	11	4	3	41	11	9	4	7	31	25
All Time FL/FAPL	3628	1037	388	388	3627	2051	455	444	916	2156	3173

	Home	Away	Total
Attendances	612,938	516,531	1,129,469

Newcastle United
Oldham Athletic

(1) 3
(1) 2

Saturday, 23rd April 1994, St James' Park

Att.: 32,216

NEWCASTLE UNITED

1	Pavel	SRNICEK
2	Barry	VENISON
3	John	BERESFORD
15	Darren	PEACOCK
20	Alan	NEILSON
4	Paul	BRACEWELL
5	Ruel	FOX
7	Robert	LEE
11	Scott	SELLARS
8	Peter	BEARDSLEY
9	Andy	COLE

Subs

30	Mike	HOOPER
12	Mark	ROBINSON
14	Alex	MATHIE

OLDHAM ATHLETIC

13	Jon	HALLWORTH
2	Craig	FLEMING
22	Chris	MAKIN
5	Richard	JOBSON
6	Steve	REDMOND
4	Nick	HENRY
10	Mike	MILLIGAN
11	*Paul*	*BERNARD (+45)*
20	Mark	BRENNAN
14	Graeme	SHARP
21	Sean	McCARTHY

1	Paul	GERRARD
25	*Rick*	*HOLDEN (+45)*
15	Andy	BARLOW

Match Facts

● Peter Beardsley's 21st Premiership goal of the season took him to sixth place in the scoring table.

Score Sheet

R. FOX 19 min – 1-0

R. JOBSON 42 min – 1-1

BEARDSLEY 56 min – 2-1

G. SHARP 57 min – 2-2

R. LEE 63 min – 3-2

Referee:
Mr D. Allison (Lancaster)

FA Carling Premiership

		P	W	D	L	F	A	Pts
1	Manchester United	38	24	10	4	74	35	85
2	Blackburn Rovers	38	24	7	7	59	32	79
3	**Newcastle United**	**39**	**21**	**8**	**10**	**75**	**38**	**71**
4	Arsenal	39	18	16	5	52	23	70
5	Leeds United	38	16	15	7	55	35	63

Result of this Season's Fixture

No Fixture

When Luck's on your Side

You had to feel sorry for Oldham. They missed a Wembley appearance by a matter of seconds when Mark Hughes got the equaliser that took their semi-final against Manchester United to a replay and, with a string of games to cram into the last few days of the season, relegation beckoned. They arrived on Tyneside desperately in need of points and against a United side playing well below their best, they came very close. The fact that they left empty handed was largely due to a magnificent performance from Robert Fox, who seemed to be the only United player firing on all cylinders. In defence, United were shaky, Venison and Peacock in particular, and the visitors were given every chance, but Newcastle's scoring power was enough to win the day.

United went in front after 19 minutes when Andy Cole's shot was going off target but found Fox running in to knock it home. It was a very open game with both sides showing indecision in defence and Oldham were right back in it by half-time. A Brennan corner was won by Jobson, beating Peacock to the ball and although Srnicek batted out his first attempt, the Oldham captain didn't waste his second chance.

Early in the second half a decisive ball set Cole free on the right and Peter Beardsley converted his cross, but Oldham had levelled again within a minute. A terrible defensive mix up led to Graeme Sharp blasting past Srnicek. The goal flurry continued just four minutes later as Robert Lee got the winner. Cole and Beardsley combined to produce the centre which Lee converted.

A desperate fight back from the visitors made United cling on to their lead and Oldham might have won a late penalty, but it was not to be. In front of the Match of the Day cameras, Andy Cole had failed to set a new scoring record, but Newcastle had another three points in their European quest. For Oldham, it was one defeat too many.

League Record

		Home					Away				
	P	W	D	L	F	A	W	D	L	F	A
FAPL 93/94	39	12	4	3	44	13	9	4	7	31	25
All Time FAPL	39	12	4	3	44	13	9	4	7	31	25
All Time FL/FAPL	3629	1038	388	388	3630	2053	455	444	916	2156	3173

	Home	Away	Total
Attendances	645,154	516,531	1,161,685

Newcastle United   (3) 5
Aston Villa   (1) 1

Wednesday, 27th April 1994, St James' Park   Att.: 32,216

NEWCASTLE UNITED

1	Pavel	SRNICEK
2	Barry	VENISON
15	Darren	PEACOCK
20	Alan	NEILSON
3	John	BERESFORD
4	Paul	BRACEWELL *(+69)*
5	Ruel	FOX
7	Robert	LEE
11	Scott	SELLARS
8	Peter	BEARDSLEY
9	*Andy*	*COLE (†87)*

Subs

30	Mike	HOOPER
19	*Steve*	*WATSON (+69)*
14	*Alex*	*MATHIE (†87)*

ASTON VILLA

1	Nigel	SPINK
2	Earl	BARRETT
3	Steve	STAUNTON
4	*Shaun*	*TEALE (+50)*
16	Ugo	EHIOGU
6	Kevin	RICHARDSON
7	Ray	HOUGHTON
14	Andy	TOWNSEND
19	Stefan	BEINLICH
25	Graham	FENTON
21	*Dave*	*FARRELL (†69)*

30	Michael	OAKES
11	Tony	DALEY
20	Matthias	BREITKREUTZ

Match Facts

• Andy Cole's strike gave him a new season's scoring record for United – 40 and counting.

Score Sheet

S. BEINLICH 10 min – 0-1
P. BRACEWELL 15 min – 1-1
BEARDSLEY 23 min Pen – 2-1
A. COLE 41 min – 3-1
P. BEARDSLEY 66 min 4-1
S. SELLARS 79 min – 5-1

Referee:
Mr J. Lloyd (Wrexham)

FA Carling Premiership

		P	W	D	L	F	A	Pts
1	Manchester United	39	25	10	4	76	35	85
2	Blackburn Rovers	40	25	8	7	62	34	83
3	**Newcastle United**	40	22	8	10	80	39	74
4	Arsenal	40	18	17	5	53	24	71
5	Leeds United	39	16	15	8	55	37	63

Result of this Season's Fixture

Newcastle Utd

Aston Villa

Record Breaker

A night of celebration at St James' Park as Andy Cole set a new scoring record as part of a thrilling display. It was a weakened Villa team but this should take nothing away from yet another terrific Magpies performance.

The evening, however, got off to a bad start. The signs weren't good when, following on from the shaky performance against Oldham, Villa took an early lead. After ten minutes, the German Stefan Beinlich picked up a weak Neilson clearance, and ran on to round Srnicek and score. This did nothing but stir United to action and amid a flurry of attacking football, Newcastle took over the game.

Five minutes later, Villa only partially cleared a Scott Sellars cross and the ball came to Bracewell on the edge of the box. The unlikely scorer crashed in a magnificent shot for his only Premiership strike of the season. Bracewell was carrying a groin strain and very nearly didn't make the team, but Keegan was pleased he had taken the risk. Still United came forward and in the 23rd minute, Sellars played the ball through to Beardsley in the box. Pedro was brought down, made no mistake with the spot kick and it was 2-1.

Just before the break, however, came the big moment of the night. Another Sellars assist found Cole running through the middle. He rounded the keeper and slotted it home – the crowd went wild as Cole's achievement registered.

The second half was all Newcastle and in the 66th minute Beardsley capped a fine display with a superb 25 yard shot to beat Spink. With 11 minutes left, Scott Sellars made it five, latching on to the end of a Beardsley cross.

Just before the end, Cole was brought off and left the field to an incredible ovation. His 40 goals would now live in Magpies history forever.

League Record

		Home					Away				
	P	W	D	L	F	A	W	D	L	F	A
FAPL 93/94	40	13	4	3	49	14	9	4	7	31	25
All Time FAPL	40	13	4	3	49	14	9	4	7	31	25
All Time FL/FAPL	3630	1039	388	388	3635	2054	455	444	916	2156	3173

	Home	Away	Total
Attendances	677,370	516,531	1,193,901

Sheffield United (0) 2
Newcastle United (0) 0

Saturday, April 30th 1994, Bramall Lane   Att.: 29,013

SHEFFIELD UNITED

13	Simon	TRACEY
17	Carl	BRADSHAW
14	*David*	*TUTTLE (+16)*
16	Paul	BEESLEY
33	Rodger	NILSEN
4	John	GANNON
8	Paul	ROGERS
11	Mitch	WARD
30	Nathan	BLAKE
12	Jostein	FLO
18	Dane	WHITEHOUSE

Subs

1	Alan	KELLY
27	Ross	DAVISON
10	*Glynn*	*HODGES (+16)*

NEWCASTLE UNITED

1	Pavel	SRNICEK
2	Barry	VENISON
15	Darren	PEACOCK
20	Alan	NEILSON
3	John	BERESFORD
4	Paul	BRACEWELL
5	Ruel	FOX
7	Robert	LEE
11	Scott	SELLARS
8	Peter	BEARDSLEY
9	Andy	COLE

30	Mike	HOOPER
19	Steve	WATSON
14	Alex	MATHIE

Match Facts

- The sixth and final game of the season in which Newcastle failed to score – out of a total of 48.

Score Sheet

N. BLAKE 63 min – 1-0

N. BLAKE 90 min – 2-0

Referee:
Mr I Worrall (Warrington)

FA Carling Premiership

		P	W	D	L	F	A	Pts
1	Manchester United	39	25	10	4	76	37	85
2	Blackburn Rovers	40	25	8	7	62	34	83
3	**Newcastle United**	**41**	**22**	**8**	**11**	**80**	**41**	**74**
4	Arsenal	41	18	17	6	53	26	71
5	Leeds United	40	17	15	8	58	37	66

Result of this Season's Fixture

No Fixture

Bassett's Battlers Win the Day

Yet again, Newcastle went down to one of the division's more direct, physical sides. It was a definite factor this season, with Wimbledon and Sheffield United providing big problems for Keegan's men. The Magpies defence just don't seem to be able to handle bustling and battling big men and it is something which has to be looked at for the coming season.

However, today it was perhaps a case of who wanted it more. Newcastle had nothing definite to play for, but Sheffield were desperately fighting to avoid the drop. As it turned out they failed, conceding a last minute goal on the last day of the season to drop out of the Premiership, but Dave Bassett's men fought like tigers every inch of the way.

Sheffield were hampered by injuries. Big Brian Gayle was out and after just a quarter of an hour, defender David Tuttle had to be replaced after twisting his knee. His substitute was the winger Hodges and as the Yorkshiremen reorganised it was to be the Welshman who would cause Newcastle the biggest problems.

For United, none of the front men showed their true form. With Fox and Lee having off days, there was no service for Cole and Beardsley and the Magpies managed just one shot on target. Immediately after the break, Newcastle had their best spell of the game, Lee just missing after a good run, but a quarter of an hour into the second half, the home team struck. John Gannon's corner was met by Blake, Sheffield's promising new signing from Cardiff, and his header was ruled to have crossed the line before Srnicek could paw it away.

Newcastle didn't have the spirit to fight back and Blake got his second in injury time. He chased a long ball, held off Neilson and pushed the ball in at the second attempt. It was not a good Newcastle performance, but with Arsenal losing as well, United were certain of finishing third and quite possibly earning a place in the UEFA Cup.

League Record

		Home					Away			
	P	*W*	*D*	*L*	*F*	*A*	*W*	*D*	*L*	*F*	*A*
FAPL 93/94	41	13	4	3	49	14	9	4	8	31	27
All Time FAPL	41	13	4	3	49	14	9	4	8	31	27
All Time FL/FAPL	3631	1039	388	388	3635	2054	455	444	917	2156	3175

	Home	Away	Total
Attendances	677,370	545,544	1,222,914

Newcastle United (0) 2
Arsenal (0) 0

Saturday, 7th May 1994, St James' Park   Att.: 32,216

NEWCASTLE UNITED

1	Pavel	SRNICEK
2	Barry	VENISON
3	John	BERESFORD
15	Darren	PEACOCK
20	Alan	NEILSON
19	Steve	WATSON (+58)
5	Ruel	FOX
7	Robert	LEE
11	Scott	SELLARS
9	Andy	COLE
8	Peter	BEARDSLEY

Subs

30	Mike	HOOPER
12	Mark	ROBINSON (+58)
31	Mike	JEFFREY

ARSENAL

13	Alan	MILLER
2	Lee	DIXON (+81)
3	Nigel	WINTERBURN
4	Paul	DAVIS (†55)
6	Tony	ADAMS
12	Steve	BOULD
21	Steve	MORROW
22	Ian	SELLEY
11	Eddie	McGOLDRICK
8	Ian	WRIGHT
9	Alan	SMITH

26	Jim	WILL
5	Andy	LINIGHAN (+81)
23	Ray	PARLOUR (†55)

Match Facts

• Newcastle's 14th home win of the season, a record equalled only by Manchester United and Blackburn Rovers. The two goals made United the Premiership's highest scorers.

Score Sheet

A. COLE 46 min – 1-0

BEARDSLEY 66 min Pen – 2-0

Referee:
Mr R. Dilkes (Mossley)

FA Carling Premiership

		P	W	D	L	F	A	Pts
1	Manchester United	41	27	10	4	80	38	91
2	Blackburn Rovers	42	25	9	8	63	36	84
3	**Newcastle United**	**42**	**23**	**8**	**11**	**82**	**41**	**77**
4	Arsenal	42	18	17	7	53	28	71
5	Leeds United	42	18	16	8	65	39	70

Result of this Season's Fixture

Newcastle Utd

Arsenal

End of Term

It was a real day of celebration at St. James' Park. It was a lovely sunny day, Newcastle were certain of being England's third candidate for the UEFA Cup should another place become available and the visitors were still on a high after their magnificent Cup-Winners' Cup triumph. It was a real carnival in the crowd, fancy dress and good cheer abounding and the team gave us the result the occasion deserved.

Arsenal had a few fringe players in the first team, some regulars recovering after their midweek excursions, but Newcastle's players and fans gave them a good welcome. However, once the game was under way, Newcastle instantly gained the upper hand. Fittingly it was Beardsley and Cole who dominated the game and secured the goals which won it.

In the first half, the formidable Arsenal centre back pair of Adams and Bould kept Newcastle in check, but just a minute after the break, Cole got his 41st and final goal of the season. Fox brought the ball in from the right, Beardsley carried the move on and blasted a shot. Alan Miller, the Gunners' stand-in keeper, parried well but it fell to Cole who struck. "Thank you very much for Andy Cole" sang the fans, taunting the striker's former club. Beardsley nearly made it two soon after with a good chip that was just over the bar.

Beresford was having a splendid game and looking for his first goal in open play for the Magpies, but he was brought down by Dixon when free in the area. Peter Beardsley stepped up to hammer in the penalty. Lee and Cole had chances late on but the score was to remain 2-0.

As the fans departed, celebrating a probable return to Europe, the sun set on St James' Park for the last time in a memorable season.

League Record

	Home						Away				
	P	W	D	L	F	A	W	D	L	F	A
FAPL 93/94	42	14	4	3	51	14	9	4	8	31	27
All Time FAPL	42	14	4	3	51	14	9	4	8	31	27
All Time FL/FAPL	3632	1040	388	388	3637	2054	455	444	917	2156	3175

	Home	Away	Total
Attendances	709,586	545,544	1,255,130

Newcastle United
Player by Player

Darren Peacock

Pavel Srnicek

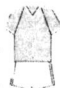

Date of Birth: 10th March 1968, Ostrava, Czechoslovakia

Debut: 17th April, 1991 *v* Sheffield Wednesday
First Goal: None

Since the Czech born keeper joined the club more than three years ago, he has had several long spells in the first team, but never quite made the goalkeeper's jersey his own. First Tommy Wright and then this season Mike Hooper have muscled in on his place in the team, but Pavel reclaimed the spot to round off the season. Popular with the crowd, Pavel's keeping is often spectacular though sometimes erratic.

International Details – Czech Republic

Previous Clubs and Appearance record

Clubs	Signed	Fee	Appearances Lge	FLC	FAC	Goals Lge	FLC	FAC
Banik Ostrava								
Newcastle United	1/91	£350,000	74	3	5			
FA Premier League Record								
	92/93							
	93/94		23			0		

Honours

Estimated value: £1,000,000

Barry Venison

Date of Birth: 16th August 1964, Consett

Debut: 15th August, 1992 *v* Southend United
First Goal: None

The hugely experienced defender was a vital part in Newcastle's First Division winning squad of 1993, bringing a solidity that was previously lacking. Born in County Durham, Barry is a huge influence on the team, despite having played for the Wearside rivals! He will turn 30 at the start of next season, but still has plenty of games left in him.

International Details – none

Previous Clubs and Appearance record

| Clubs | Signed | Fee | *Appearances* | | | *Goals* | | |
			Lge	FLC	FAC	Lge	FLC	FAC
Sunderland	1/82		169/4	21	7/1	2	0	0
Liverpool	17/86	£200,000	103/7	14/3	16/5	1	0	0
Newcastle United	7/92	£250,000	81/1	7	6	0	0	0
FA Premier League Record								
	92/93							
	93/94		38/1			0		

Honours
Football League Championship Winner: 1988, 1990
FA Cup Winner: 1989

Estimated value: £650,000

John Beresford

Date of Birth: 4th September 1966, Sheffield

Debut: 15th August, 1992 v Southend United
First Goal: 7th April, 1993 v Barnsley

John was another experienced player to come into the team for the promotion winning season and has continued to be a big influence despite the arrival of so many young Magpie defenders. Born in Sheffield, John was always a Sheffield United supporter and turned down a move to Wednesday, coming to St James' Park instead!

International Details – none

Previous Clubs and Appearance record

Clubs	Signed	Fee	Appearances			Goals		
			Lge	FLC	FAC	Lge	FLC	FAC
Manchester City	9/83							
Barnsley	8/86		79/9	5/2	5	5	2	1
Portsmouth	3/89	£300,000	102/5	12	11	8	2	0
Newcastle United	6/92	£650,000	73	7	7	0	0	0
FA Premier League Record								
	92/93							
	93/94		32			0		

Honours

Estimated value: £500,000

Paul Bracewell

Date of Birth: 19th July 1962, Heswall, Cheshire

Debut: 15th August, 1992 *v* Southend United
First Goal: 15th August, 1992 *v* Southend United

Paul was another of the defenders brought in for the Promotion year. Again despite his red and white connections, the two times League Championship winner has become a linchpin of the Newcastle defence.

International Details – none

Previous Clubs and Appearance record

Clubs	Signed	Fee	Appearances			Goals		
			Lge	FLC	FAC	Lge	FLC	FAC
Stoke City	2/80		123/6	6	6	5	1	0
Sunderland	7/83	£250,000	38	4	2	4	0	0
Everton	5/84	£425,000	95	11	19/2	7	2	0
Sunderland	9/89	£250,000	112/1	9	10	2	0	0
Newcastle United	6/92	£250,000	51/12	3	3/2	3	0	0
FA Premier League Record								
	92/93							
	93/94		32			1		

Honours

League Championship Winner: 1985,1987
FA Cup Finalist: 1985, 1986, 1989, 1992
                               (four losers medals)

Estimated value: £300,000

Kevin Scott

Date of Birth: 17th December 1966, Easington

Signed: December, 1984   **Fee:** From Juniors
Debut: 6th September, 1986 *v* Sheffield Wednesday
First Goal: 6th September, 1986 *v* Sheffield Wednesday

Kevin rose up from the junior ranks to pro status in December 1984 and since joining Newcastle had become an essential member of Newcastle's team for many years, this year losing his place in the centre of defence with the graduation of players such as Steve Watson. He now plays at White Hart Lane, helping to secure their Premiership future this season

International Details – none

Previous Clubs and Appearance record

Clubs	Signed	Fee	Appearances			Goals		
			Lge	FLC	FAC	Lge	FLC	FAC
Newcastle United	12/84	–	227	8/1	18	8	0	0
Tottenham Hotspur	2/94	£850,000	12	0	0	1	0	0
FA Premier League Record								
Newcastle United	93/94		18			0		
Tottenham Hotspur	93/94		12			1		

Honours

Estimated value: £350,000

Ruel Fox

Date of Birth: 14th January 1968, Ipswich

Signed:	February, 1994	**Fee:** £2,250,000	
Debut:	12th February, 1994 *v* Wimbledon		
First Goal:	12th March, 1994, Swindon Town		

When the lightning winger arrived on Tyneside he became United's most expensive signing, although this record was to be topped by Darren Peacock later in the season. The 26 year old was born and bred in Ipswich, but played his football for East Anglian rivals Norwich, with whom he appeared in Europe last season. Ruel has two children, James and Tasharna.

International Details – none

Previous Clubs and Appearance record

			Appearances			Goals		
Clubs	Signed	Fee	Lge	FLC	FAC	Lge	FLC	FAC
Norwich City	1/86		123/2 4	9/3	9/2	15	1	0
Newcastle United	2/94	£2.25m	14			2		
FA Premier League Record								
Norwich City	92/93-93/94		57/2			11		
Newcastle United	93/94		14			2		

Honours

Estimated value: £2,500,000

Steve Howey

Date of Birth: 26th October 1971, Sunderland

Signed:	December, 1989	**Fee:** From Juniors
Debut:	13th May, 1989 v Manchester United	
First Goal:	9th October, 1991 v Crewe Alexandra	

Steve rose up from the juniors, making his debut at the age of just eighteen in the final game of the 1988/89 season and is now an established first team regular – when he's fit that is. Steve's season was dogged with a persistent knee injury and there were fears that it could finish his career, but things are now looking up for next season.

International Details – none

Previous Clubs and Appearance record

			Appearances			Goals		
Clubs	Signed	Fee	Lge	FLC	FAC	Lge	FLC	FAC
Newcastle United	12/89	–	70/18	6/2	6	3	1	
FA Premier League Record								
	92/93							
	93/94		13/1			0		

Honours

Estimated value: £1,500,000

Robert Lee

Date of Birth: 1st February 1966, Plaistow

Debut: 26th September, 1992 *v* Peterborough United
First Goal: 21st November, 1992 *v* Watford

The London born Lee came into the Newcastle team near the beginning of the First Division Championship campaign and his class was a vital factor in that success. This season, usually playing just behind Cole and Beardsley, sometimes deeper, he has really flourished and is on the verge of England recognition. Just before he signed for the Magpies, he had turned down a move to Middlesbrough and his old Charlton boss Lennie Lawrence. The reason he gave? Middlesbrough was too far north.

International Details – none

Previous Clubs and Appearance record

Clubs	Signed	Fee	Appearances			Goals		
			Lge	FLC	FAC	Lge	FLC	FAC
Charlton Athletic	7/83	–	274/24	16/3	14	58	1	2
Newcastle United	9/92	£700,000	76	6	7	17	2	2
FA Premier League Record								
92/93								
93/94			41			7		

Honours

Estimated value: £1,750,000

Peter Beardsley

Date of Birth: 18th January 1961, Newcastle

Debut: 24th September, 1983 v Barnsley
First Goal: 19th October, 1983 v Cardiff City

What can you say about Pedro? A footballing enigma as despite his obvious talent he was released by both the Merseyside giants and ignored by England. Now rightfully back in the International scene, Peter has found a truly appreciative audience in his home town and despite his 33 years, there is a lot of life in the old dog yet.

International Details – England
Debut: 1986 v Egypt
First Goal:
Played: 53
Goals: 9

Previous Clubs and Appearance record

| | | | Appearances | | | Goals | | |
Clubs	Signed	Fee	Lge	FLC	FAC	Lge	FLC	FAC
Carlisle United	8/79		93/11	6/1	15	2	0	7
Vancouver Whitecaps	4/81	£275,000						
Manchester United	9/82	£300,000	0	1	0	0	0	0
Vancouver Whitecaps	9/83							
Newcastle United	9/83	£150,000	146/1	10	6	61	0	0
Liverpool	7/87	£1,900,000	120/11	13/1	22/3	46	1	11
Everton	8/91	£1,000,000	81	8	4	25	5	1
Newcastle United	6/93	£1,400,000	34	3	3	20	1	1

FA Premier League Record

92/93								
93/94			35			21		

Honours
League Championship Winner: 1988, 1990
FA Cup Winner: 1989
FA Cup Finalist: 1988
World Cup Semi-Finalist: 1990

Estimated value: £1,200,000

Andy Cole

Date of Birth: 19th October 1971, Nottingham

Debut: 13th March, 1993 *v* Swindon Town
First Goal: 20th March, 1993 *v* Notts. County

Newcastle's goal machine has had an incredible year. He scored 53 goals in just 56 appearances for the Magpies, smashing the record for one season, a record previously held by Hughie Gallacher and George Robledo. Ditched by George Graham early in his career, Andy is still only 22 years old and has the whole world at his feet.

International Details – England

Previous Clubs and Appearance record

Clubs	Signed	Fee	Appearances			Goals		
			Lge	FLC	FAC	Lge	FLC	FAC
Arsenal	10/89		0/1	0	0	0	0	0
Fulham	5/91	Loan						
Bristol City	3/92	£500,000	41			20		
Newcastle United	3/93	£1,750,000	50/1	2	3	45	6	1
FA Premier League Record								
	92/93							
	93/94		40			34		

Honours

Estimated value: £5,000,000

Lee Clark

Date of Birth: 27th October 1972, Wallsend

Debut: 29th September, 1990 *v* Bristol City
First Goal: 10th November, 1990 *v* Wolverhampton Wanderers

Lee came up from the juniors, making his debut for the Magpies while he was still just 17 years of age. He played in every game during the Promotion in 1992/93 and his infectious enthusiasm and devastating runs from deep played a big part in United's success. This season, however, has been less happy with injury ruling him out of many games, but off the field his sense of humour is as lively as ever.

International Details – none

Previous Clubs and Appearance record

Clubs	Signed	Fee	Appearances			Goals		
			Lge	FLC	FAC	Lge	FLC	FAC
Newcastle United	11/89	–	103/10	10	9	19		
FA Premier League Record								
92/93								
93/94			29			2		

Honours

Estimated value: £1,000,000

Scott Sellars

Date of Birth: 27th November 1965, Sheffield

Debut: 10th March, 1993 *v* Charlton Athletic
First Goal: 7th April, 1993 *v* Barnsley

Scott was a hugely popular player during his spell at Blackburn, but his second spell with Leeds was an unhappy one. Since joining Newcastle however, especially towards the end of this season, his midfield class has been hugely impressive, picking up a few goals along the way.

International Details – none

Previous Clubs and Appearance record

Clubs	Signed	Fee	Appearances			Goals		
			Lge	FLC	FAC	Lge	FLC	FAC
Leeds United	7/83		72/2	4	4	12	1	0
Blackburn Rovers	7/86	£20,000	194/8	12	11	35	3	1
Leeds United	7/92	£800,000	6/1	1/1	0	0	0	0
Newcastle United	3/93	£700,000	41/1	1/1	3	5	1	0
FA Premier League Record								
Leeds United	92/93		6/1			0		
Newcastle United	93/94		29/1			3		

Honours

Estimated value: £500,000

Mark Robinson

Date of Birth: 21st November 1968, Manchester

Debut: 10th March, 1993 *v* Charlton Athletic
First Goal: –

Mark was another player with injury worries, being out of contention until Christmas. Since then, however, he has played a part in most games, vying for places with Newcastle's crop of young defenders.

International Details – none

Previous Clubs and Appearance record

Clubs	Signed	Fee	Appearances			Goals		
			Lge	FLC	FAC	Lge	FLC	FAC
West Bromwich Alb	1/87		2	0/1	0	0	0	0
Barnsley			118/19	5/2	4/1	5	0	0
Newcastle United	3/93	£450,000	13/11	0	1	0	0	0
FA Premier League Record								
92/93								
93/94			11/4			0		

Honours

Estimated value: £750,000

Tommy Wright

Date of Birth: 29th August 1963, Belfast

Signed: March, 1988   **Fee:** £30,000
Debut: 14th January, 1989 *v* Aston Villa
First Goal:

The Northern Irish 'keeper gave admirable service to the Magpies in more than five years at the club, but with the arrival of Mike Hooper became third choice between the posts, so he moved on. He has been the Northern Ireland number one for several years and will be returning to the Premiership next season with his new club.

International Details – Northern Ireland
Debut: 1989 *v* Malta
Appearances:

Previous Clubs and Appearance record

Clubs	Signed	Fee	Appearances			Goals		
			Lge	FLC	FAC	Lge	FLC	FAC
Linfield								
Newcastle United	3/88	£30,000	70/1	6	4			
Hull City	2/91	Loan	6					
Nottingham Forest	9/93	£450,000	10	2				

FA Premier League Record

	92/93							
Newcastle United	93/94		0/1			1		

Honours

Estimated value: £250,000

Alex Mathie

Date of Birth: 20th December 1968, Bathgate

Signed: 1993   **Fee:** £285,000
Debut: 13th September, 1993 *v* Sheffield Wednesday
First Goal: 13th September, 1993 *v* Sheffield Wednesday

Alex moved to United from Morton in the summer and scored a cracking winner on his debut as substitute against Wednesday. He has rarely started a game but often appeared as substitute, adding fresh legs to United's attack. Alex scored his second goal of the season against Coventry in February, but immediately after the game was rushing back to Scotland, where his wife Elaine was giving birth to their first child, Craig!

International Details – none

Previous Clubs and Appearance record

Clubs	Signed	Fee	Appearances			Goals		
			Lge	FLC	FAC	Lge	FLC	FAC
Morton **								
Port Vale	3/93	Loan	0/3					
Newcastle United	7/93	£285,000	0/15	1		3		
FA Premier League Record								
	92/93							
	93/94		0/15			3		

Honours

<table>
<tr><td>Estimated value: £300,000</td></tr>
</table>

Brian Kilcline

Date of Birth: 7th May 1962, Nottingham

Signed:	February, 1992	**Fee:** £250,000	
Debut:	22nd February, 1992 *v* Barnsley		
First Goal:			

Killer's greatest moment came at Wembley in 1987, when he lifted the Cup for Coventry City. In his brief Newcastle career he added character to the defence, but his strength was not enough to prevent relegation for his new club Swindon.

International Details – none

Previous Clubs and Appearance record

			Appearances			Goals		
Clubs	Signed	Fee	Lge	FLC	FAC	Lge	FLC	FAC
Notts. County	5/80		156/2	16	10	9	1	2
Coventry City	6/84	£60,000	173	16/1	15	28	4	3
Oldham Athletic	8/91	£400,000	8	2	0	0	0	0
Newcastle United								
Swindon Town	1/94							

FA Premier League Record

Newcastle United	93/94	1	0	
Swindon Town	93/94	10	0	

Honours
FA Cup Winner: 1987

Estimated value: £150,000

Liam O'Brien

Date of Birth: 5th September 1964, Dublin

Signed: November, 1988   **Fee:** £300,000
Debut: 19th November, 1988 v Millwall
First Goal: 26th February, 1989 v Middlesborough

Liam had an illustrious Newcastle career, but when he became surplus to requirements he took his talents to Tranmere, with whom he reached the First Division play-offs. A big disappointment was being left out of the Republic of Ireland squad for the 1994 World Cup Finals.

International Details – Republic of Ireland
Debut: 1986 v Uruguay
First Goal:
Played: 9
Goals:

Previous Clubs and Appearance record

Clubs	Signed	Fee	Appearances Lge	FLC	FAC	Goals Lge	FLC	FAC
Shamrock Rovers								
Manchester United	10/86	£60,000	16/15	0/2	1/2	2	0	0
Tranmere Rovers	1/94							
Newcastle United								
FA Premier League Record								
	92/93							
Newcastle United	93/94		4/2			0		

Honours

Estimated value: £200,000

Niki Papavasiliou

Date of Birth: 30st August 1970, Limassol

Signed:	29th July, 1993	**Fee:** £120,000	
Debut:	14th August, 1993 *v* Tottenham Hotspur		
First Goal:			

The young Cypriot striker had an impressive few games at the start of the season, after his arrival during the summer. Sadly for him, he has been unable to regain his first team place after a promising start.

International Details – Cyprus

Debut:
First Goal:
Played:
Goals:

Previous Clubs and Appearance record

			Appearances			Goals		
Clubs	Signed	Fee	Lge	FLC	FAC	Lge	FLC	FAC
OFI Crete								
Newcastle United	7/93	£120,000	7					
FA Premier League Record								
	92/93							
	93/94		7					

Honours

Estimated value: £250,000

Steve Watson

Date of Birth: 1st April 1974, North Shields

Signed:	July, 1990	**Fee:**	From Juniors
Debut:	10th November 1990 *v* Wolverhampton Wanderers		
First Goal:	29th February 1992 *v* Port Vale		

The find of the season. Only just 20, Steve has become a regular first team choice. When he made his debut as a sub in 1990 he became the youngest ever United player. An England Youth and Under 21 International, we could well have seen the beginnings of a great career.

International Details – none

Previous Clubs and Appearance record

			Appearances			Goals		
Clubs	Signed	Fee	Lge	FLC	FAC	Lge	FLC	FAC
Newcastle United	7/90	–	75/11	3	7/1	3		
FA Premier League Record								
92/93								
93/94			30/3			2		

Honours

Estimated value: £750,000

Alan Neilson

Date of Birth: 26th September 1972, Weyburg, Germany

Signed: February, 1991   **Fee:** From Juniors
Debut: 27th August, 1991 *v* Middlesborough
First Goal: 21st September, 1991 *v* Millwall

Alan became a frequent first team choice towards the end of the season and his impressive form has now won him International recognition with Wales.

International Details – Wales
Debut: 1994 *v* Sweden
Played: 2

Previous Clubs and Appearance record

Clubs	Signed	Fee	Appearances			Goals		
			Lge	FLC	FAC	Lge	FLC	FAC
Newcastle United	2/91		29/9	3		1		
FA Premier League Record								
	92/93							
	93/94		10/4			0		

Honours

Estimated value: £1,000,000

Malcolm Allen

Date of Birth: 21st March 1967, Deiniolen

Signed:	August, 1993	**Fee:**
Debut:	14th August, 1993 *v* Tottenham Hotspur	
First Goal:	25th August, 1993 *v* Everton	

The much travelled striker was bought at the last minute to deputise for the injured Peter Beardsley at the start of the season. Expecting to struggle for a place at First Division Millwall he suddenly found himself in the Premiership limelight and had an impressive scoring record before losing his place. Malcolm is married with two children.

International Details – Wales

Debut:	1986 *v* Saudi Arabia
First Goal:	
Played:	12
Goals:	3

Previous Clubs and Appearance record

Clubs	Signed	Fee	Appearances			Goals		
			Lge	FLC	FAC	Lge	FLC	FAC
Watford	3/85	–	39	5	14	5	2	6
Aston Villa	9/87	Loan	4			0		
Norwich City	8/88	£175,000	35			8		
Millwall	3/90	£400,000	81	7	1	24	2	
Newcastle United	8/93	£300,000	9	3		5	2	
FA Premier League Record								
	92/93							
	93/94		9			5		

Honours

Estimated value: £500,000

Mattie Appleby

Date of Birth: 16th April 1972, Middlesborough

Signed: 2nd April, 1990   **Fee:** From Juniors
Debut: 5th October, 1991 *v* Portsmouth
First Goal:

Young Matty has been on the Newcastle scene for some time now, but made only one appearance this season, giving an impressive display as part of the back four babes in the 4-0 win at home to Coventry.

International Details – none

Previous Clubs and Appearance record

Clubs	Signed	Fee	Appearances			Goals		
			Lge	FLC	FAC	Lge	FLC	FAC
Newcastle United	5/90	–	15/1	1				
FA Premier League Record								
	92/93		1			0		
	93/94							

Honours

Estimated value: £

Robbie Elliott

Date of Birth: 25th December 1973, Newcastle

Signed: 4th June, 1990   **Fee:** From Juniors
Debut: 12th March, 1991 *v* Middlesborough
First Goal:

Robbie made his debut more than three years but had a long spell in the wilderness, partly through injury. However, when John Beresford was injured he was given a chance and seized it with both hands. Essentially a left back, Robbie has filled in both central defence and midfield, making himself and essential member of the squad.

International Details – none

Previous Clubs and Appearance record

			Appearances			Goals		
Clubs	Signed	Fee	Lge	FLC	FAC	Lge	FLC	FAC
Newcastle United	4/91	–	27/3	1	2			
FA Premier League Record								
	92/93							
	93/94		13/2			0		

Honours

Mike Hooper

Date of Birth: 10th February 1962, Bristol

Signed: September, 1993 **Fee:** £550,000
Debut: 25th September, 1993 *v* West Ham United
First Goal:

After years of limited opportunities as Liverpool reserve. Mike moved to United for more than half a million in mid-season, when it became clear he was only third choice at Anfield. He was given his chance almost immediately at the expense of Pavel Srnicek. But, despite goalkeeping coach John Burridge suggesting he should be considered for the England team, he was to lose his place back to the Czech after a poor run in February.

International Details – none

Previous Clubs and Appearance record

Clubs	Signed	Fee	Appearances			Goals		
			Lge	FLC	FAC	Lge	FLC	FAC
Bristol City	1/84		1	1	0	0	0	0
Wrexham	2/85		34	0	4	0	0	0
Liverpool	10/85		50/1	5	10	0	0	0
Leicester City	9/90	Loan	14	0	0	0	0	0
Newcastle United	9/93	£550,000	19	2	3	0	0	0
FA Premier League Record								
Liverpool	92/93		8/1			0		
Newcastle United	93/94		19			0		

Honours
League Championship Winner: 1986, 1988, 1990

Estimated value: £300,000

Mike Jeffrey

Date of Birth: 11th August 1971, Liverpool

Signed: 1st October, 1993   **Fee:** Exchange deal + £60,000
Debut: 4th December, 1993 v Tottenham Hotspur
First Goal:

Afforded only rare opportunities in the first team, young Mike gave an impressive display on his debut against Spurs, but had to wait more than four months for his next first team appearance.

International Details – none

Previous Clubs and Appearance record

Clubs	Signed	Fee	Appearances			Goals		
			Lge	FLC	FAC	Lge	FLC	FAC
Bolton Wanderers	2/89	–	9/6	1/2	1			
Doncaster Rovers	3/92	£20,000	48/1	4		19		
Newcastle United	10/93	£60,000	2					
FA Premier League Record								
	92/93							
	93/94		2			0		

Honours

Estimated value: £500,000

Chris Holland

Date of Birth: 11th September 1975, Whalley

Signed: January, 1994   **Fee:** £100,000
Debut: 23rd March, 1994 *v* Ipswich Town
First Goal:

Perhaps Keegan took a gamble in spending so much on a player who had never started a league game, but Chris Holland is one of the most promising youngsters in the country. Although he only got a handful of run-outs at the end of the season, Chris made a huge impact on his debut. Playing wide on the right, which is not his preferred position, he provided the two crosses which led to the goals in a 2-0 victory. Definitely one for the future.

International Details – none

Previous Clubs and Appearance record

Clubs	Signed	Fee	Appearances			Goals		
			Lge	FLC	FAC	Lge	FLC	FAC
Preston North End		–	0/2					
Newcastle United	1/94	£100,000	2/1					
FA Premier League Record								
92/93								
93/94			2/1			0		

Honours

Estimated value: £750,000

Darren Peacock

Date of Birth: 3rd February 1968, Bristol

Signed: March, 1994   **Fee:** £2,700,000
Debut: 29th March, 1993 v Norwich City
First Goal:

United's most recent and most expensive acquisition. Keegan splashed out a fortune on the established 26 year old defender, brought in to shore up the defence after the sale of Kevin Scott. He certainly looked the part at the end of the season despite a couple of shaky performance when he first joined. With his long main of blond hair, you certainly can't miss him on the field.

International Details – none

Previous Clubs and Appearance record

Clubs	Signed	Fee	Appearances			Goals		
			Lge	FLC	FAC	Lge	FLC	FAC
Newport County	2/86	–	22/4	2	1	0	0	0
Hereford United	3/89	–	56/7	6	6	5	1	0
Queens Park Rangers	12/90	£200,000	123/3	8	2	6	0	0
Newcastle United	3/94	£2.7m	8	0	0	0	0	0
FA Premier League Record								
Queens Park Rangers	92/93-93/4		65/3			5		
Newcastle United	93/94		9			0		

Honours

Estimated value: £2,500,000

Season's Records 1993-94

Attendance by Number – *F A Premier League*

	Home			Away	
11/12/93	Manchester United	36,388	16/04/94	Liverpool	44,601
22/12/93	Leeds United	36,388	21/08/93	Manchester United	41,829
21/11/93	Liverpool	36,374	01/04/94	Leeds United	40,005
01/01/94	Manchester City	35,658	02/10/93	Aston Villa	37,336
14/08/93	Tottenham Hotspur	35,216	27/11/93	Arsenal	36,091
24/11/93	Sheffield United	35,101	09/04/94	Manchester City	33,774
25/08/93	Everton	34,833	05/03/94	Sheffield Wednesday	33,224
25/09/93	West Ham United	34,336	04/12/93	Tottenham Hotspur	30,780
29/08/93	Blackburn Rovers	34,272	30/04/94	Sheffield United	29,013
13/09/93	Sheffield Wednesday	33,890	18/12/93	Everton	25,189
16/10/93	Queens Park Rangers	33,926	28/12/93	Chelsea	23,133
30/10/93	Wimbledon	33,392	19/03/94	West Ham United	23,132
23/02/94	Coventry City	32,216	19/02/94	Blackburn Rovers	21,269
12/03/94	Swindon Town	32,216	04/01/94	Norwich City	19,564
23/03/94	Ipswich Town	32,216	31/08/93	Ipswich Town	19,102
29/03/94	Norwich City	32,216	16/01/94	Queens Park Rangers	15,774
04/04/94	Chelsea	32,216	18/08/93	Coventry City	15,760
23/04/94	Oldham Athletic	32,216	18/09/93	Swindon Town	15,015
27/04/94	Aston Villa	32,216	08/11/93	Oldham Athletic	13,821
07/05/94	Arsenal	32,216	24/10/93	Southampton	13,804
22/01/94	Southampton	32,129	12/02/94	Wimbledon	13,358

Sending Off

Pavel	SRNICEK	18/8/93	v	Coventry City	(a)

Bookings

Peter	BEARDSLEY	12/2/94	v	Wimbledon	(a)
		30/4/94	v	Sheffield United	(a)
John	BERESFORD	25/9/93	v	West Ham United	(h)
Paul	BRACEWELL	25/8/93	v	Everton	(h)
		24/10/93	v	Southampton	(a)
		1/4/94	v	Leeds United	(a)
Lee	CLARK	25/8/93	v	Everton	(h)
		22/12/93	v	Leeds United	(h)
Andy	COLE	18/8/93	v	Coventry City	(a)
		18/12/93	v	Everton	(a)
Robbie	ELLIOTT	19/2/94	v	Blackburn Rovers	(a)
Mike	JEFFREY	4/12/93	v	Tottenham Hotspur	(a)
Alan	NEILSON	5/3/94	v	Sheffield Wednesday	(a)
Mark	ROBINSON	4/4/94	v	Chelsea	(h)
		19/3/94	v	West Ham United	(a)
Kevin	SCOTT	21/8/93	v	Manchester United	(a)
		13/9/93	v	Sheffield Wednesday	(h)
Scott	SELLARS	4/4/94	v	Chelsea	(h)
Barry	VENISON	14/8/93	v	Tottenham Hotspur	(h)
		18/8/93	v	Coventry City	(a)
		25/8/93	v	Everton	(h)
Barry	VENISON	27/10/93	v	Wimbledon	(a)
		16/1/94	v	Queens Park Rangers	(a)
		9/2/94	v	Luton Town	(a)
Steve	WATSON	22/12/93	v	Leeds United	(h)

Goals Scored by Five Minute Period

5	10	15	20	25	30	35	40	45	50	55	60	65	70	75	80	85	90
4	1	5	5	5	4	2	5	4	7	4	5	7	9	8	9	7	6

Goals Conceded by Five Minute Period

5	10	15	20	25	30	35	40	45	50	55	60	65	70	75	80	85	90
2	3	1	4	1	2	3	2	1	3	2	6	5	2	1	4	3	3

Score by Number

Score	Frequency	Score	Frequency	Score	Frequency
2-0	8	0-1	3	3-1	1
1-1	7	7-1	2	3-2	1
1-2	7	3-0	2	2-2	1
4-0	3	1-0	2	0-0	1
4-2	3	0-2	2	2-4	1
2-1	3	5-1	1		

Transfers to Newcastle United

Player		Date Signed	From	Fee
Peter	BEARDSLEY	Summer 1993	Everton	£1,400,000
Alex	MATHIE	Summer 1993	Morton	£285,000
Niki	PAPAVASILIOU	Summer 1993	OFI Crete	£120,000
Mike	JEFFREY	1/10/93	Doncaster Rovers	Exchange
Chris	HOLLAND	20/1/94	Preston North End	£100,000
Ruel	FOX	2/2/94	Norwich City	£2,250,000
Brian	REID	23/3/94	Rangers	Loan
Darren	PEACOCK	24/3/94	Queens Park Rangers	£2,700,000

Transfers from Newcastle United

Player		Date Sold	To	Fee
Gavin	Peacock	Summer 1993	Chelsea	£1,250,000
David	Kelly	Summer 1993	Wolves	£750,000
Andy	Hunt	Summer 1993	West Bromwich Albion	£100,000
Mark	Stimson	Summer 1993	Portsmouth	£100,000
Alan	Thompson	Summer 1993	Bolton Wanderers	Tribunal
Kevin	Sheedy	Summer 1993	Blackpool	Free
John	Watson	Summer 1993	Scunthorpe United	Free
David	Roche	1/10/93	Doncaster Rovers	Exchange
Liam	O'Brien	**	Tranmere Rovers	**
Tommy	Wright	**	Nottingham Forest	**
Brian	Kilcline	**	Swindon Town	**
Kevin	Scott	1/2/94	Tottenham Hotspur	**

1993-94 Appearances

Match no.	1	2	3	4	5	6	7	8	9	10	11	12
1 Pavel Srnicek	*	*+	*	*	*	*	–	S	*	S	S	S
2 Barry Venison	*	*	*	*	*	*	*	*	*	*	*	*69
3 John Beresford	*	*	*	*	*	*	*	*	*	*	*	*
4 Paul Bracewell	*	*	*	*	*	*	*	*	*	*	*	*69
5 Kevin Scott	*	*	*	*	*	*	*	*	–	*	*	*
5 Ruel Fox												
6 Steve Howey	*	–	–	–	–	–	–	–	–	–	–	–
7 Robert Lee	*	*	*	–	*	*	*	*	*	*	*	*
8 Peter Beardsley	–	–	–	–	–	–	–	*	*	*	*	*
9 Andy Cole	*	*	*	*	*	*	*	*	*	*	*	*
10 Lee Clark	*	*	*	*	*	*59	*	*	*	*	*	*
11 Scott Sellars	–	–	–	–	–	–	–	–	–	–	S	69
12 Mark Robinson	–											
13 Tommy Wrigh	–	†	S	S	S	S	*	*	–			
14 Alex Mathie	–	–	–	–	–	–	62	S	S	S	–	–
15 Brian Kilcline	–	–	–	–	–	–	–	S	*	S	S	69
16 Liam O'Brien	75	*	*	*	*	59	S	–	–	–	–	–
17 Niki Papavas	*75	*†	*	*	*	*86	*62	–	S	–	–	–
18 Kevin Brock												
19 Steve Watson	61	*	*	*	*	*	*	*	*	*	*	*
20 Alan Neilson	–	–	–	–	S	S	86	–	–	–	–	–
21 Malcolm Allen	*61	S	S	*	S	*	*	*	*	*	*	*
22 Richie Appleby												
23 Matty Appleby	–	S	S	S	–	–	–	–				
25 Nathan Murray												
26 Robbie Elliott	–	–	–	–	–	–						
27 Peter Cormack												
29 John Burridge	S	–	–	–	–	–	S	–	S	–	–	–
30 Mike Hooper	–	–	–	–	–	–	–	–	–	*	*	*
31 Mike Jeffrey											–	–
32 Chris Holland												
33 Darren Peacock												
34 Brian Reid												

Match no.	13	14	15	16	17	18	19	20	21	22	23	24
1 Pavel Srnicek	S	S	S	S	S	S	S	S	S	S	S	S
2 Barry Venison	*	*	*	*	*	*	*	*	*	*	*	*
3 John Beresford	*	*	*	*	–	–	–	–	–	–	*77	*
4 Paul Bracewell	*	*	*	*	*	*	*75	*	*	*	*	*
5 Kevin Scott	*	*	*	*	*	*	*	*	–	–	–	–
5 Ruel Fox												
6 Steve Howey	–	–	–	–	–	–	–	59	*	*	*	*
7 Robert Lee	*	*	*	*	*	*	*	*	*	*	*	*
8 Peter Beardsley	*	*	*	*	*	*	*	*	*	*	*	*
9 Andy Cole	*	*	*	*	*	*	*	*	*	*	*	*
10 Lee Clark	*	*70	–	*	*	*	*	*59	*	*	*	*75
11 Scott Sellars	S	70	*	*	*	*	*	*	–	*	*	*
12 Mark Robinson	–	–										
13 Tommy Wrigh			Transferred to Nottingham Forest									
14 Alex Mathie	–	70	*	S	S	S	75	59	–	–	S	75
15 Brian Kilcline	S	–	77	S	–	–	S	–	S	–	–	–
16 Liam O'Brien	–	–	–	–	–	–	–	–	–	S	S	
17 Niki Papavas	–	–	–	–	–	–	–					
18 Kevin Brock												
19 Steve Watson	*	*	*	*	*	*	*	*	*	*	*	*
20 Alan Neilson	–	–	S	–	S	–	–	–	–	–	–	–
21 Malcolm Allen	*	*70	*77	–	–	S	–	–	–	S	–	–
22 Richie Appleby												
23 Matty Appleby	–	–	–	–								
25 Nathan Murray												
26 Robbie Elliott	–	–	–	–	*	*	*	*59	*	*	77	S
27 Peter Cormack												
29 John Burridge	–	–	–	–	–	–	–	–	–	–	–	–
30 Mike Hooper	*	*	*	*	*	*	*	*	*	*	*	*
31 Mike Jeffrey	–	–	–	–	–	–	–	–	*	–	–	
32 Chris Holland												
33 Darren Peacock												
34 Brian Reid												

Match no.	25	26	27	28	29	30	31	32	33	34	35	36
1 Pavel Srnicek	S	S	S	S	S	S	S	S	S	*	*	*
2 Barry Venison	*	–	–	–	*	*	*	*	*	*	–	–
3 John Beresford	*	*	*	*	*	*	*	*	*	*	–	*
4 Paul Bracewell	*	*45	–	–	*	*	*	–	–	–	–	–
5 Kevin Scott	–	–	*	*	S	S	S	Transferred to Spurs				
5 Ruel Fox	Transpered from Norwich City								*	*	*	*
6 Steve Howey	*	*	*	*	*	*	*	*	*	*	–	*47
7 Robert Lee	*	*	*	*	*	*	*	*	*69	*	*45	*
8 Peter Beardsley	*	*	*	*	*	*	*	*	*	*	*	*
9 Andy Cole	*	*	*	*	*	*	*	*	*	*	*	*
10 Lee Clark	*63	*	*	*	*	*	*	*	*	*	*	–
11 Scott Sellars	*	*	*	*80	*	*	*	*	*	*	*85	*
12 Mark Robinson	63	*77	*	*	*	*	–	S	S	–	45	*
13 Tommy Wrigh												
14 Alex Mathie	63	77	–	–	–	S	S	–	69	S	85	S
15 Brian Kilcline	–	*	S	S	Transferred to Swindon Town							
16 Liam O'Brien			Transfered to Tranmere Rovers									
17 Niki Papavas	–	–	–	–	–	–	–	–	–	–	–	–
18 Kevin Brock												
19 Steve Watson	*63	45	S	80	–	–	*	*	*	*	*	*
20 Alan Neilson	–	–	–	–	–	–	–	S	–	S	*	*
21 Malcolm Allen	–											
22 Richie Appleby												
24 Matty Appleby	–	–	–	–	–	–	–	–	–	–	*	–
25 Nathan Murray												
26 Robbie Elliott	–	–	*	*	S	–	–	*	*	*	*	47
27 Peter Cormack												
29 John Burridge	–	–	–	–	–	–	–	–	–	–	–	–
30 Mike Hooper	*	*	*	*	*	*	*	*	*	S	S	S
31 Mike Jeffrey	–	–	–	–	–	–	–	–	–	–	–	–
32 Chris Holland								–	–	–	–	–
33 Darren Peacock												
34 Brian Reid												

Match no.	37	38	39	40	41	42	43	44	45	46	47	48
1 Pavel Srnicek	*	*	*	*	*	*	*	*	*	*	*	*
2 Barry Venison	*	*	*	–	57	*	*	*88	*	*	*	*
3 John Beresford	*	*	*	*	*	*73	–	*	*	*	*	*
4 Paul Bracewell	–	–	–	*74	*	*	–	*	*	*69	*	–
5 Kevin Scott												
5 Ruel Fox	*	*79	–	*80	*	–	*	*	*	*	*	*
6 Steve Howey	–	–	–	–	–	–	–	–	–	–	–	–
7 Robert Lee	*	*	*	*	*57	*	*	*	*	*	*	*
8 Peter Beardsley	*	*	*	*	*	*	*	*90	*	*	*	*
9 Andy Cole	*	*	*	*	*	*	*	*	*	*87	*	*
10 Lee Clark	–	–	–	–	–	–	–	–	–	–	–	–
11 Scott Sellars	*	·	*	*	*	*	*	*	*	*	*	*
12 Mark Robinson	*	*	*	*	*	*	*	88	S	–	–	58
13 Tommy Wrigh												
14 Alex Mathie	S	79	45	80	S	63	81	90	S	87	S	–
15 Brian Kilcline												
16 Liam O'Brien												
17 Niki Papavas	–	–	–	–	–	–	–	–	–	–	–	–
18 Kevin Brock												
19 Steve Watson	*	*19	*45	–	–	–	–	–	–	69	S	*58
20 Alan Neilson	S	19	79	*	*	73	*	*	*	*	*	*
21 Malcolm Allen	–	–	–	–	–	–	–	–	–	–	–	–
22 Richie Appleby												
24 Matty Appleby	–	–	–	–	–	–	–	–	–	–	–	–
25 Nathan Murray												
26 Robbie Elliott	*	*	*79	–								
27 Peter Cormack												
29 John Burridge	–	–	–	–	–	–	–	–	–	–	–	–
30 Mike Hooper	S	S	S	S	S	S	S	S	S	S	S	S
31 Mike Jeffrey	–	–	–	–	–	–	*81	–	–	–	–	S
32 Chris Holland	–	–	*	74	–	*63	–	–	–	–	–	–
33 Darren Peacock				*	*	*	*	*	*	*	*	*
34 Brian Reid	–	–	–	–	–	S	–	–				

149

Barry Venison tussles with Manchester United's Mark Hughes.

General Records

Football League

Biggest Home Win:	13-0 v Newport County	05/10/46
Biggest Away Win:	6-0 v Everton	26/10/12
	6-0 v Walsall	29/09/62
	7-1 v Manchester United	10/09/27
Biggest Home Defeat:	1-9 v Sunderland	05/12/08
Biggest Away Defeat:	0-9 v Burton Wanderers	15/04/1895
Highest Home Attendance:	68,386 v Chelsea (Won 1-0)	03/09/30
Most Appearances:	432 Jimmy Lawrence	
Leading Goalscorer:	177 Jackie Milburn	
Most Goals in a Season:	36 Hughie Gallacher	
Most Goals in a Game:	6 Len Shackleton	05/10/46
	v Newport County (h)	
Most Consecutive Wins:	11 15/8/92 to 24/12/92	

This sequence of wins began with the first game of the 1992/93 season.

Most Consecutive Defeats:	10 23/8/77 to 22/12/77	

Beginning with the second game of the season, after winning the opener against Leeds United

Longest Unbeaten Run:	14 22/4/50 to 7/10/50	
Longest Run Without a Win:	21 14/1/78 to 26/8/78	

FA Premiership

Biggest Home Win:	7-1 v Swindon Town	12/3/94
Biggest Away Win:	4-2 v West Ham United	19/3/94
	3-1 v Oldham Athletic	8/11/93
	2-0 v Aston Villa	2/10/93
	2-0 v Everton	18/12/93
	2-0 v Liverpool	16/4/94
Biggest Home Defeat:	1-2 v Queens Park Rangers	16/10/93
	1-2 v Southampton	22/1/94
	0-1 v Tottenham Hotspur	14/8/93
Biggest Away Defeat:	2-4 v Wimbledon	12/2/94
	0-2 v Sheffield United	30/4/94
Highest Home Attendance:	36,388 v Manchester United	11/12/93
	36,388 v Leeds United	22/12/93

Lowest Home Attendance:	32,129 v Southampton	22/01/94
Most Appearances:	Robert Lee	41
Leading Goalscorer:	Andy Cole	34
Most Goals in a Season:	Andy Cole	34
Most Consecutive Wins:	6 23/2/94 to 1/4/94	
Games Without Defeat:	6 23/2/94 to 1/4/94	

FA Cup

Biggest Home Win:	8-1 v Notts. County – 3rd Round	03/01/27
Biggest Away Win	9-0 v Southport, at Hillsborough – 4th Round, 2nd Replay	01/02/32
Biggest Home Defeat	0-5 v Sheffield United – 1st Round	10/01/14
Biggest Away Defeat	1-7 v Aston Villa – 2nd Round	16/02/1895
Highest Home Attendance	67,596 v Bolton Wanderers – 4th R	27/01/51
Most Appearances	64 Jimmy Lawrence	
Leading Goalscorer	23 Jackie Milburn	
Most Goals in a Game	4 Andy Aitken v Willington A – Qualifying Round	30/10/1897
Longest Unbeaten Run	16 06/01/51 to 31/01/53	
Longest Run Without a Win	6 29/01/69 to 13/01/73	

Football League Cup

Biggest Home Win	6-0 v Doncaster Rovers – 2nd Round	08/10/73
	6-0 v Southport – 2nd Round	10/09/75
Biggest Away Win	7-1 v Notts. County – 2nd Round	05/10/93
Biggest Home Defeat	1-4 v Leeds United – 2nd Round	27/10/82
	0-3 v Blackpool – 3rd Round	04/10/72
Biggest Away Defeat	2-7 v Manchester United – 4th Round	27/10/76
Highest Home Attendance	49,902 v Tottenham Hotspur – Semi-Final	21/01/76
Most Appearances:	22 Irving Nattrass	
Leading Goalscorer	12 Malcolm MacDonald	
Most Goals in a Game	4 Alan Gowling v Southport – 2nd Round	10/09/75
Longest Unbeaten Run	8 10/9/75 to 27/10/76	
Longest Run Without a Win	5 6/1163 to 2/9/68	

Biggest Home Win	5-1 v Vitoria Setubal – 4th Round	12/03/69	
	4-0 v Feyenoord – 4th Round	11/09/68	
	4-0 v Bohemians – 1st Round	28/09/77	
Biggest Away Win	3-2 v Ujpesti Dozsa – Final	11/06/69	
	2-1 v Dundee United – 1st Round	15/09/70	
Biggest Home Defeat	1-3 v Bastia – 2nd Round	02/11/77	
Biggest Away Defeat	1-3 v Vitoria Setubal – 4th Round	26/03/69	
	0-2 v Pecsi Dozsa – 2nd Round	04/11/70	
Highest Home Attendance	59,309 v Anderlecht – 4th Round	18/03/70	
Most Appearances	24	Willie McFaul	
Leading Goalscorer	10	Wyn Davies	
Most Goals in a Game	2	on six separate occasions	
Most Consecutive Wins	5	21/05/69 to 18/11/69	
Most Consecutive Defeats	2	19/10/77 to 02/11/77	
Longest Unbeaten Run	10	14/05/69 to 11/03/70	
Longest Run Without A Win	3	17/12/69 to 18/03/70	

If football were a Pantomime, would Scott Sellars and Leeds' Gary Speed hear the chant *"it's behind you!"*

Newcastle United

St James' Park, Newcastle, NE1 4ST

Nickname: The Magpies
Colours: Black and White Stripes, Black Shorts   **Change:** All Blue
Capacity: 36,401   **Pitch:** 110yds x 73 yds

Officials

President:	T.L Bennett
Honorary President:	Bob Young
Chairman:	Sir John Hall
Chief Executive:	A.O. Fletcher
Directors:	W.F. Shepherd, D.S. Hall, R. Jones
Manager:	Kevin Keegan
Vice Presidents:	T. Brown, E. Boynton, B. Phillips, D.W. Henderson
Assistant Manager:	Terry McDermott
Physio:	Derek Wright
General Manager & Secretary:	R. Cushing

Honours

League Champions:	1905, 1907,1909,1927
1st Division Champions:	1993 *(since restructuring of league)*
2nd Division Champions:	1965
2nd Division Promotion:	1898, 1948, 1984
FA Cup Winners:	1910, 1924, 1932, 1951, 1952, 1955
FA Cup Runners-Up:	1905, 1906, 1908, 1911, 1974
Football League Cup Runners-Up:	1976
FA Charity Shield Winners:	1909

European Honours

Inter Cities Fairs Cup Winners:	1969

Other Honours

Texaco Cup Winners:	1974, 1975
Anglo-Italian Cup Winners:	1973

Miscellaneous Records

Record Attendance:	68,368 *v* Chelsea, Division 1, 03/09/30

League History

1893	Elected to Division 2	1978-1984	Division 2
1898-1934	Division 1	1984-1989	Division 1
1934-1948	Division 2	1989-1992	Division 2
1948-1961	Division 1	1992-1993	Division 1
1961-1965	Division 2	1993-	FA Premier League
1965-1978	Division 1		

Managers and Secretary Managers

1893-1929	Frank G Watt	1962-1975	Joe Harvey
1930-1935	Andy Cunnigham	1975-1977	Gordon Lee
1935-1939	Tom Mather	1977	Richard Dinnis
1939-1947	Stan Seymour	1977-1980	Bill McGarry
1947-1950	George Martin	1980-1984	Arthur Cox
1950-1954	Stan Seymour	1984-1985	Jackie Charlton
1954-1956	Duggie Livingstone	1985-1988	Willie McFaul
1956-1958	Position Vacant	1988-1991	Jim Smith
1958-1961	Charlie Mitten	1991-1992	Ossie Ardiles
1961-1962	Norman Smith	1992-	Kevin Keegan

Telephone Numbers

Main Switchboard:	091-232 8361
Promotions:	091-230 2861
Commercial Dept:	091-232 0406
Ticket Office Hotline:	091-261 1571
Club Shop:	091-261 6357
Club Shop Answerphone:	091-232 4080
Football in the Community Scheme:	091-261 9715
Conference and Banqueting Suite:	091-222 1860
Club Fax:	091-232 9875
Clubcall:	(0898) 121590
Clubcall Ticket Line:	(0898) 121190

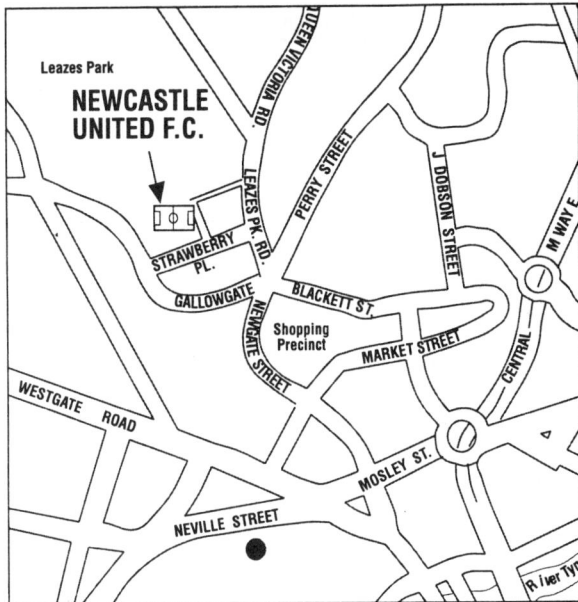

Directions

From South:
Follow A1, A68 then A6127 to cross the Tyne. At the next roundabout, take the first exit into Moseley Street. Turn left into Neville Street, then right at the end for Clayton Street and then Newgate Street. Then turn left for Leaze Park Road.

From West:
Take the A69 towards the city centre. Turn left into Clayton Street for Newgate Street, then left again for Leaze Park Road.

From North:
Take the A1, then follow signs for Hexham until Percy Street and then turn right into Leaze Park Road.

Rail:
Newcastle Central (¹/₂ mile).

Arsenal

Arsenal Stadium, Avenell Road, Highbury, London N5 1BU

Nickname:	The Gunners
Colours:	Red and White shirts, White shorts, Red &White socks
Change:	Blue with Turquoise shirts,Blue shorts, Blue & Turquoise socks
Capacity:	39,497 **Pitch:** 110yds x 71yds

Directions:

From North: M1 Junction 2 follow signs for City. After Holloway Road station take third left into Drayton Park. Then right into Aubert Street and 2nd left into Avenell Road. *From South:* Signs for Bank of England then Angel from London Bridge. Right at traffic lights towards Highbury roundabout. Follow Holloway Road then,third right into Drayton Park. Thereafter as above. *From West:* A40(M) to A501 ring road. Left at Angel to Highbury roundabout then as above. *Rail:* Drayton Park/Finsbury Park *Tube:* (Piccadilly Line) Arsenal

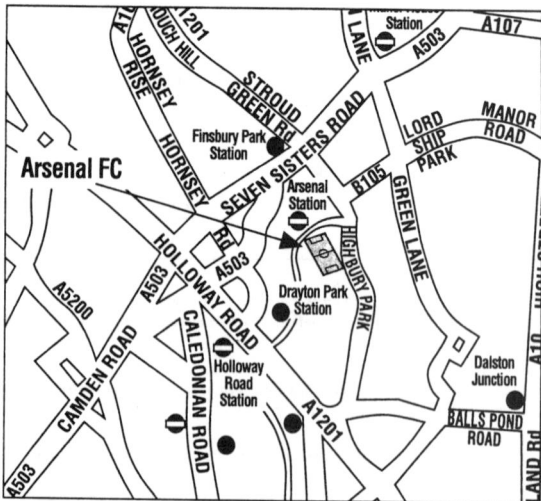

Telephone: 071-226 0304

Aston Villa

Villa Park, Trinity Rd, Birmingham, B6 6HE

Nickname: The Villains

Colours: Claret/Blue, White, Blue/Claret   **Change:** White, Black, White

All-seater Capacity: 40,530   **Pitch:** 115 yds x 75 yds

Directions:

M6 J6, follow signs for Birmingham NE. 3rd exit at roundabout then right into Ashton Hall Rd after $^1/_2$ mile.

Rail: Witton

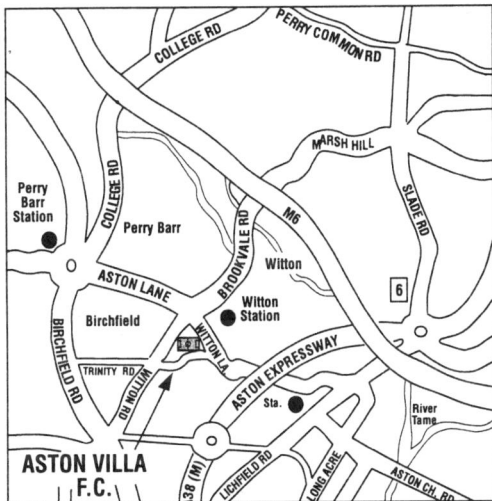

Telephone: 021-327 2299

Blackburn Rovers

Ewood Park, Blackburn, BB2 4JF

Nickname: Blue and Whites
Colours: Blue/White, White, Blue   **Change:** Black/Red, Black, Black/Red
All-seater Capacity: 30,591   **Pitch:** 115yds x 76yds

Directions:

From North, South & West: M6 J31 follow signs for Blackburn then Bolton Road.
Turn left after 1½ miles into Kidder Street.
From East: A677 or A679 following signs for Bolton Road, then as above.
Rail: Blackburn Central

Telephone: (0254) 55432

Chelsea

Stamford Bridge, London SW6

Nickname: The Blues
Colours: Royal Blue, Royal Blue, White   **Change:** White/Red, Black, Black
All-seater Capacity: 41,050   **Pitch:** 110 yds x 72 yds

Directions:

From North & East: A1 or M1 to central London and Hyde Park corner. Follow signs for Guildford (A3) and then Knightsbridge (A4). After a mile turn left into Fulham Road. *From South:* A219 Putney Bridge then follow signs for West End joining A308 and then into Fulham Road. *From West:* M4 then A4 to central London. Follow A3220 to Westminster, after ¼ mile right at crossroads into Fulham Road.

Rail/Tube: Fulham Broadway (District line).

Telephone: 071-385 5545

Coventry City

Highfield Road Stadium, King Richard Street, Coventry, CV2 4FW

Nickname: Sky Blues
Colours: All Sky Blue   **Change:** Yellow, Blue, Yellow
All-seater Capacity: 24,021   **Pitch:** 110 yds x 75 yds

Directions:

From North & West: M6 J3, after 3½ miles turn left into Eagle Street and straight on to Swan Lane. *From South & East:* M1 to M45 then A45 to Ryton-on-Dunsmore where 3rd exit at roundabout is A423. After 1 mile turn right into B4110. Left at T-junction then right into Swan Lane.
Rail: Coventry

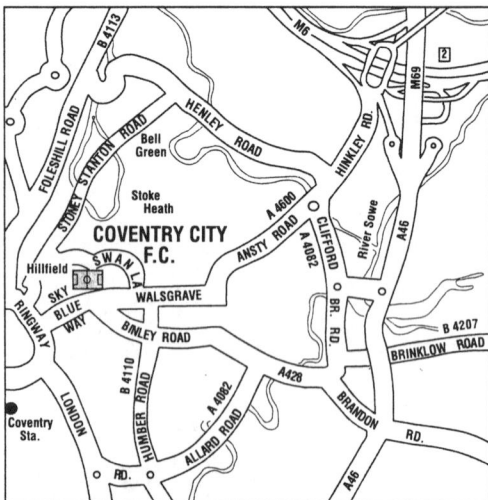

Telephone: (0203) 223535

162

Crystal Palace

Selhurst Park, London, SE25 6PU

Nickname: Eagles

Colours: Red/Blue, Red, Red

Change: Yellow, Light Blue, White

All-seater Capacity: 26,995

Pitch: 110 yds x 74 yds

Directions:

From North: M1 or A1 to A406 for Chiswick, then A205 to Wandsworth. A3 and then A214 for Streatham and then A23 to B273 for Whitehorse Lane.

From South: A23 and then B266. Turn right into High Street and then as above.

From East: A232 and then A215 to B266 for High Street and then as above.

From West: M4 to Chiswick and then as for the North.

Rail: Norwood Junction, Thornton Heath or Selhurst.

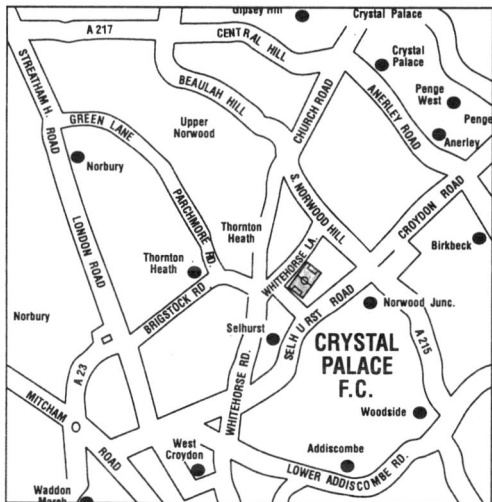

Telephone: 081-653 4462

Everton

Goodison Park, Liverpool, L4 4EL

Nickname: The Toffees
Colours: Royal Blue, White, Blue   **Change:** Salmon/Dark Blue, Salmon, Salmon
All-seater Capacity: 40,160   **Pitch:** 112 yds x 78 yds

Directions:

From North: M6 J8 take A58 to A580 and follow into Walton Hall Avenue.
From South & East: M6 J21A to M62, turn right into Queen's Drive then, after 4 miles, left into Walton Hall Avenue.
From West: M53 through Wallasey Tunnel, follow signs for Preston on A580. Walton Hall Avenue is signposted.
Rail: Liverpool Lime Street

Telephone: 051-521 2020

Ipswich Town

Portman Road, Ipswich, Suffolk, IP1 2DA

Nickname: Blues or Town
Colours: Blue/White, White, Blue **Change:** Red/Black, Black, Red/Black
All-seater Capacity: 22,823 **Pitch:** 112 yds x 70 yds

Directions:

Follow A45 and signs for Ipswich West. Through Post House traffic lights and turn right at second roundabout into West End Road. Ground is situated on the left.
Rail: Ipswich

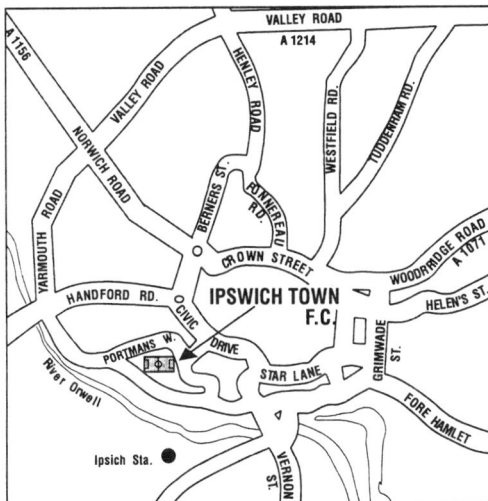

Telephone: (0473) 219211

Leeds United

Elland Road, Leeds, LS11 0ES

Nickname: United

Colours: All White

All-seater Capacity: 39,704

Change: All Yellow

Pitch: 117 yds x 76 yds

Directions:

From North & East: A58, A61, A63 or A64 into city centre and then onto M621.
Leave Motorway after 1½ miles onto A643 and Elland Road.
From West: take M62 to M621 then as above.
From South: M1 then M621 then as above
Rail: Leeds City

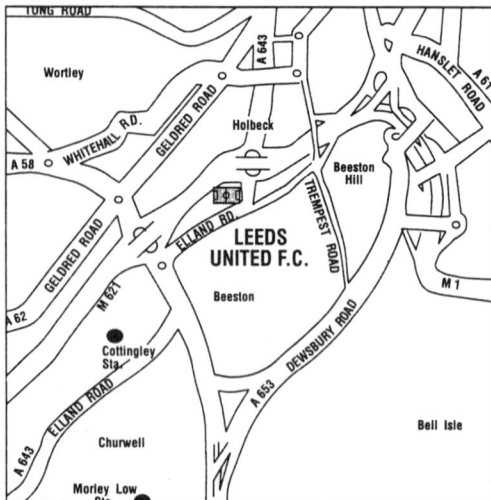

Telephone: (0532) 716037

Leicester City

City Stadium, Filbert Street, Leicester, LE2 7FL

Nickname: The Filberts or Foxes
Colours: Blue, White, Blue
All-seater Capacity: 27,722
Change: Red, Black, Black
Pitch: 112 yds x 75 yds

Directions:

From North: Leave M1 at J22 or take A46, A607 to town centre. Towards Rugby via Almond Road, Aylestone Road and left into Walnut Street and Filbert Street.
From South: M1 or M69 and then A46 to Upperton Road and Filbert Street.
From East: A47 into town centre, right along Oxford Street to Aylestone Road and then as North. *From West:* M69 and A50 to Aylestone Road and then as North.
Rail: Leicester

Telephone: (0533) 555000

Liverpool

Nickname: Reds or Pool
Colours: All Red/White Trim   **Change:** Racing Green/White Trim
All-seater Capacity: 44,243   **Pitch:** 110 yds x 75 yds

Directions:

From North: M6 J8, follow A58 to Walton Hall Avenue and pass Stanley Park turning left into Anfield Road. *From South/East:* To end of M62 and right into Queens Drive (A5058). After 3 miles turn left into Utting Avenue and right after 1 mile into Anfield Road. *From West:* M53 through Wallasey Tunnel, follow signs for Preston then turn into Walton Hall Avenue and right into Anfield Road before Stanley Park. *Rail:* Liverpool Lime Street

Manchester City

Maine Road, Moss Side, Manchester, M14 7WN

Nickname: Blues or City
Colours: Sky Blue, White, Sky Blue **Change:** Purple/Candystripe, Purple, Purple
All-seater Capacity: 45,053 **Pitch:** 117 yds x 77 yds

Directions:

From North & West: M61 to M63 J9. Follow signs into Manchester (A5103). Right after 3 miles into Claremont Road. Right after 400 yards into Maine Road.
From South: M6 J19 to A556 joining M56. Leave at J3 following A5103 as above.
From East: M62 J17 following signs for Manchester Airport (A56 and A57(M)). Then follow Birmingham signs to A5103. Left into Claremont Road after 1 mile then right into Maine Road. *Rail:* Manchester Piccadilly

Telephone: 061-226 1191/2

Manchester United

Old Trafford, Manchester, M16 0RA

Nickname: Red Devils
Colours: Red Shirts, White Shorts   **Change:** All Black or Yellow/Green Halves
All-seater Capacity: 44,622   **Pitch:** 116 yds x 76 yds

Directions:

From North: M63 J4 follow signs for Manchester (A5081). Right after 2½ miles into Warwick Rd.

From South: M6 J19 follow A556 then A56 (Altrincham). From Altrincham follow signs for Manchester turning left into Warwick Rd after 6 miles.

From East: M62 J17 then A56 to Manchester. Follow signs South and then Chester. Turn right into Warwick Rd after 2 miles.

Rail: Manchester Victoria, Piccadilly, Old Trafford.

Telephone: 061-872 1661

Norwich City

Carrow Road, Norwich, NR1 1JE

Nickname: The Canaries
Colours: Yellow, Green, Yellow   **Change:** All White
All-seater Capacity: 25,000   **Pitch:** 114yds x 74 yds

Directions:

From North: A140 to ring road and follow signs for Yarmouth A47. Turn right at T junction after 3$\frac{1}{2}$ miles then left after $\frac{1}{2}$ mile into Carrow Road.
From South & West: A11/A140 onto ring road. Follow signs for Yarmouth A47 etc as for North above.
From East: A47 into Norwich then left onto ring road.

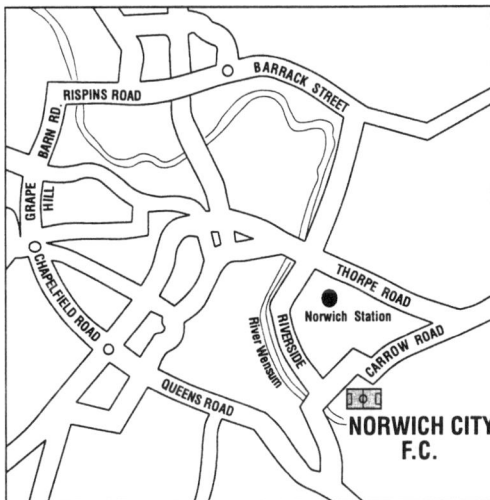

Telephone: (0603) 612131

Nottingham Forest

City Ground, Nottingham, NG2 5FJ

Nickname: The Reds or Forest
Colours: Red, White, Red
All-seater Capacity: 26,500

Change: Blue, Green, Blue
Pitch: 115 yds x 78 yds

Directions:

From North: Leave the M1 J26 for the A610 and the A606. Left into Radcliffe Road for the ground. *From South:* Leave the M1 J24 to Trent Bridge, turning right into Radcliffe Road. *From East:* A52 to West Bridgford and right for the ground. *From West:* A52 to A606 and then as for the North.
Rail: Nottingham.

Telephone: (0602) 526000

Queens Park Rangers

South Africa Road, W12 7PA

Nickname: Rangers or R's
Colours: Blue/White, White, White
All-seater Capacity: 19,300

Change: Red/Black, Black, Black
Pitch: 112 yds x 72 yds

Directions:

From North: M1 to north circular A406 towards Neasden. Left onto A404 for Hammersmith, past White City Stadium then right into South Africa Road. *From South:* A3 across Putney Bridge and signs for Hammersmith. A219 to Shepherds Bush and join A4020 towards Acton. Turn right after ¼ mile into Loftus Road. *From East:* From A40(M) towards M41 roundabout. Take 3rd exit at roundabout to A4020 then as above. *From West:* M4 to Chiswick then A315 and A402 to Shepherd's Bush joining A4020 then as for South. *Rail:* Shepherds Bush *Tube:* White City (Central Line)

Telephone: 081-743 0262

Sheffield Wednesday

Hillsborough, Sheffield, S6 1SW

Nickname: The Owls

Colours: Blue/White, Blue, Blue   **Change:** All Black with Yellow/Grey trim

All-seater Capacity: 40,000   **Pitch:** 115 yds x 75 yds

Directions:

From North: M1 J34 then A6109 to Sheffield. At roundabout after 1½ miles take 3rd exit then turn left after 3 miles into Herries Road.

From South & East: M1 J31 or 33 to A57. At roundabout take Prince of Wales Road exit. A further 6 miles then turn left into Herries Road South.

From West: A57 to A6101 then turn left after 4 miles at T junction into Penistone Road.

Rail: Sheffield Midland

Telephone: (0742) 343122

Southampton

The Dell, Milton Road, Southampton, SO9 4XX

Nickname: The Saints
Colours: Red/White, Black, Black **Change:** Turquoise/Blue, Turquoise, Blue
All-seater Capacity: 15,288 **Pitch:** 110 yds x 72 yds

Directions:

From North: A33 into The Avenue then right into Northlands Road. Right at the end into Archer's Road. *From East:* M27 then A334 and signs for Southampton along A3024. Follow signs for the West into Commercial Road, right into Hill Lane then first right into Milton Road.
From West: Take A35 then A3024 towards city centre. Left into Hill Lane and first right into Milton Road.
Rail: Southampton Central

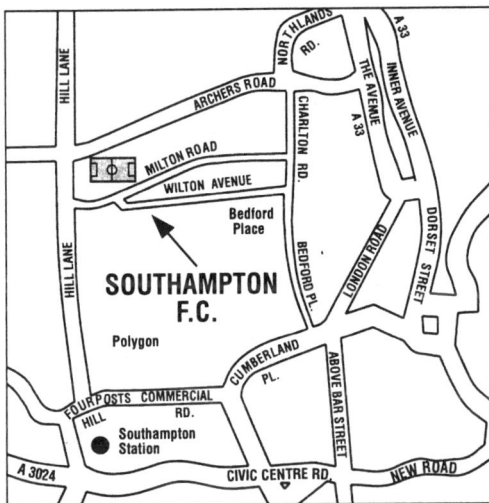

Telephone: (0703) 220505

175

Tottenham Hotspur

Nickname: Spurs
Colours: White, Navy Blue, White
All-seater Capacity: 30,246

Change: All Yellow or all Sky Blue
Pitch: 110 yds x 73 yds

Directions:

A406 North Circular to Edmonton. At traffic lights follow signs for Tottenham along A1010 then Fore Street for ground.
Rail: White Hart Lane (adjacent)
Tube: Seven Sisters (Victoria Line) or Manor House (Piccadilly Line).

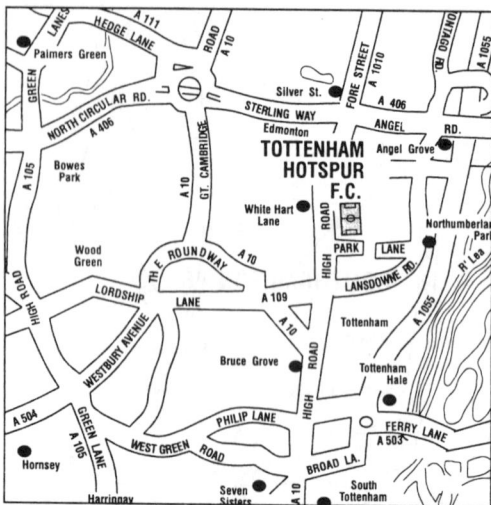

Telephone: 081-808 6666

West Ham United

Nickname: The Hammers
Colours: Claret, White, White
All-seater Capacity: 24,500

Change: All Blue
Pitch: 112 yds x 72 yds

Directions:

From North & West: North Circular to East Ham then Barking Rd for 1½ miles until traffic lights. Turn right into Green Street.

From South: Blackwall Tunnel then A13 to Canning Town. Then A124 to East Ham, Green Street on left after 2 miles.

From East: A13 then A117 and A124. Green Street on right after ¾ miles.

Rail/Tube: Upton Park (¼ mile)

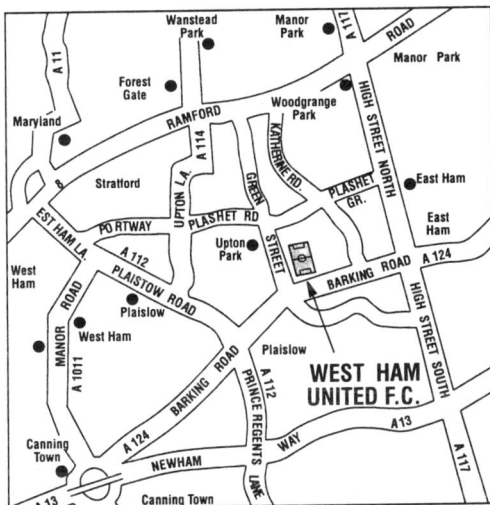

Telephone: 081-472 2740

177

Wimbledon

Selhurst Park, London, SE25 6PU

Nickname: The Dons
Colours: All Blue with Yellow trim
All-seater Capacity: 26,995

Change: All Red
Pitch: 110 yds x 74 yds

Directions:

From North: M1/A1 to North Circular A406 and Chiswick. Follow South Circular A205 to Wandsworth then A3 and A214 towards Streatham and A23. Then left onto B273 for 1 mile and turn left at end into High Street and Whitehorse Lane. *From South:* On A23 follow signs for Crystal Palace along B266 going through Thornton Heath into Whitehorse Lane. *From East:* A232 Croydon Road to Shirley joining A215, Norwood Road. Turn left after 2½ miles into Whitehorse Lane. *From West:* M4 to Chiswick then as above.

Rail: Selhurst, Norwood Junction or Thornton Heath.

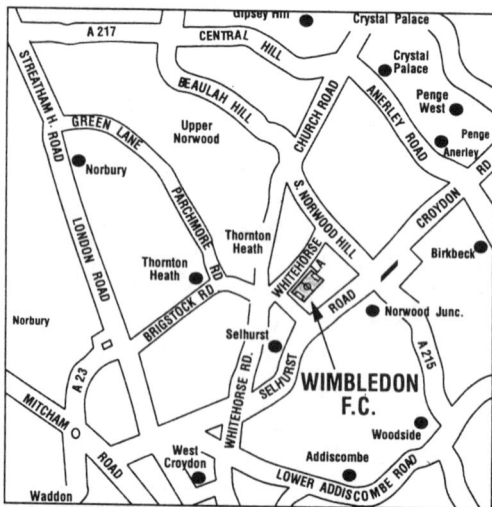

Telephone: 081-771 2233

All-time Records and Statistics

United against other clubs – *All Comps and Leagues*

The following list gives the Magpies' records against each other club they have played since joining the Football League in 1892. The figures include all Premiership, Football League, FA Cup, League Cup and European matches. Where clubs have changed names, the latest name only is used so games against Small Heath, for example, are listed under Birmingham City.

** Excludes 1990/91 and 1991/92

Club

	P	W	D	L	F	A
Aberdare Athletic	1	1	0	0	4	1
AFC Bournemouth	6	2	2	2	9	6
Anderlecht	2	1	0	1	3	3
Arsenal	129	58	27	44	204	177
Aston Villa	117	50	21	46	192	204
Barnsley	32	11	10	11	47	34
Bastia	2	0	0	2	2	5
Bedford Town	1	0	0	1	1	2
Birmingham City	86	34	23	29	140	122
Blackburn Rovers	103	45	19	39	164	161
Blackpool	57	25	8	24	91	99
Bohemians	2	1	1	0	4	0
Bolton Wanderers	94	43	18	33	170	124
Bradford Park Avenue	21	12	3	6	38	18
Bradford City	36	16	8	12	55	42
Brentford	8	5	0	3	15	13
Brighton and Hove Albion	16	7	3	6	27	17
Bristol City	22	8	8	6	32	20
Bristol Rovers	19	8	7	4	27	18
Burnley	98	40	17	41	149	139
Burton Swifts	10	5	0	5	26	23
Burton Wanderers	6	5	0	1	14	10
Bury	68	36	14	18	143	95
Cambridge United	16	9	3	4	21	9
Cardiff City	49	21	13	15	84	59
Carlisle United	7	3	1	3	11	10
Charlton Athletic	52	25	11	16	96	79
Chelsea	107	39	27	41	149	161
Chester City	4	1	1	2	3	4
Chesterfield	11	4	0	7	13	17

	P	W	D	L	F	A
Colchester United	3	1	1	1	6	8
Corinthians	1	1	0	0	3	1
Coventry City	50	21	13	16	89	66
Crewe Alexandra	8	5	1	2	21	10
Crystal Palace	22	12	3	7	31	17
Darwen	8	5	1	2	24	17
Derby County	104	41	29	34	161	137
Doncaster Rovers	7	6	1	0	24	4
Dundee United	2	2	0	0	3	1
Everton	122	48	25	49	182	185
Exeter City	2	0	1	1	1	5
FC Porto	2	1	1	0	1	0
Feyenoord	2	1	0	1	4	2
Fulham	45	18	10	17	91	75
Gainsborough Trinity	4	2	0	2	9	7
Gillingham	1	1	0	0	2	1
Glasgow Rangers	2	1	1	0	2	0
Glossop	3	2	1	0	2	0
Grimsby Town	40	15	9	16	65	51
Halifax Town	1	1	0	0	2	1
Hartlepool United	1	1	0	0	4	1
Hendon	2	1	1	0	5	1
Hereford United	2	0	1	1	3	4
Huddersfield Town	59	24	15	20	94	81
Hull City	15	9	3	3	34	16
Inter Milan	2	1	1	0	3	1
Ipswich Town	38	11	12	15	56	50
Leeds United	71	26	13	32	94	118
Leicester City	96	40	21	35	161	159
Leyton Orient	19	8	4	7	31	19
Lincoln City	11	7	0	4	27	18
Liverpool	126	39	32	55	162	205
Loughborough Town	6	4	0	2	11	6
Luton Town	50	22	11	17	89	78
Manchester City	137	62	31	44	217	191
Manchester United	115	35	27	53	184	216
Mansfield Town	2	1	1	0	2	1
Middlesbrough	96	35	26	35	135	125
Middlesbrough Ironopolis	2	1	1	0	8	3
Millwall	18	5	4	9	19	25
Newport County	3	2	0	1	21	4

	P	W	D	L	F	A
Northampton	9	4	2	3	16	11
Northwich Victoria	2	1	0	1	6	5
Norwich City	41	17	12	12	63	47
Nottingham Forest	96	43	24	29	147	117
Notts. County	64	32	15	17	134	75
Oldham Athletic	39	17	12	10	62	42
Oxford United	17	6	5	6	30	30
Pecsi Dozsa	2	1	0	1	2	2
Peterborough United	7	3	1	3	10	7
Plymouth Argyle	33	19	8	6	64	34
Portsmouth	56	25	12	19	85	90
Port Vale	18	9	5	4	35	26
Preston North End	78	34	12	32	124	124
Queens Park Rangers	36	15	6	15	53	58
Reading	6	4	1	1	18	8
Real Zaragoza	2	1	0	1	4	4
Rendal	1	1	0	0	5	0
Rotherham United	21	11	6	4	49	23
Scunthorpe United	10	4	2	4	16	14
Sheffield United	117	40	29	48	169	172
Sheffield Wednesday	113	50	26	37	178	152
Shrewsbury Town	10	4	2	4	12	9
Southampton	60	22	15	23	82	81
Southend United	4	2	1	1	7	9
Southport	5	3	2	0	19	2
Sporting Lisbon	2	1	1	0	2	1
Stockport County	3	2	1	0	7	1
Stockton	1	1	0	0	4	1
Stoke City	74	37	16	21	127	85
Sunderland	125	44	40	41	187	191
Swansea City	31	19	3	9	61	38
Swindon Town	17	7	6	4	36	17
Torquay United	1	1	0	0	3	1
Tottenham Hotspur	107	35	25	47	148	177
Tow Law Town	1	1	0	0	4	0
Tranmere Rovers	6	4	0	2	16	7
Ujpesti Dozsa	2	2	0	0	6	2
Vitoria Setubal	2	1	0	1	6	4
Walsall	14	11	0	3	32	12
Watford	29	10	11	8	39	33
West Bromwich Albion	102	35	26	41	166	175

	P	W	D	L	F	A
West Ham United	93	37	27	29	142	134
West Hartlepool NER	1	1	0	0	8	0
Wigan Athletic	2	1	1	0	5	4
Willington Athletic	1	1	0	0	6	0
Wimbledon	11	3	1	7	14	21
Wolverhampton Wanderers	84	28	19	37	133	139
Wrexham	10	3	3	4	12	14
York City	4	2	2	0	6	3

Players' Career Records

The figures show all appearances in the FA Premiership, Football League, FA Cup and the various guises of the Football League Cup. Test matches and play-off games are included, as is the annulled fixture v Nottingham Forest in 1974. Other matches include Anglo-Scottish and Anglo-Italian Cup matches, Texaco, Zenith Data Systems, Simod and Full Members Cup matches as well as Wartime Cup and League games. The figures do not include friendlies or abandoned games.

* Indicates players who only appeared as wartime guests.

+ Indicates players who only appeared while on loan from another club.

Player	FAPL App	FAPL Goals	League App	League Goals	FACup App	FACup Goals	LgeCup App	LgeCup Goals	Europe App	Europe Goals	Others App	Others Goals	Totals App	Totals Goals
G Adams (1896/97)			13	1									13	1
WB Agnew (1902/04)			43	0	1	0							44	0
A Aitken (1895/1906)			312	33	33	8					4	1	349	42
RS Aitken (1990/92)			54	1	6	0	2	0			3	0	65	1
WJ Aitken (1920/24)			104	10	6	0							110	10
JT Alderson (1913/19)			1	0									1	0
S Alderson (1965/67)			3	0			1	0					4	0
SJ Allan (1908/11)			15	5									15	5
IJ Allchurch (1958/62)			143	46	8	4	3	1					154	51
GB Allen (1964/70)			22	1	1	0	1	0	2	0			26	1
J Allen (1898/1901)			5	0									5	0
JWA Allen (1931/34)			81	34	9	7							90	41
M Allen (1993-)	9	5					3	2					12	7
R Allen (1897/98)			24	4	5	0							29	4
JB Allon (1984/87)			9	2			1	0					10	2
RFD Ancell (1936/44)			97	1	5	0					53	0	155	1
AL Anderson (1908/12)			61	5	6	2							67	7
JCP Anderson (1982/91)			283/16	14	14	0	17	1			8/1	0	322/17	15
*RJ Anderson (1940)											3	1	3	1
S Anderson (1963/65)			81	13	2	1	1	0					84	14
WR Anderson (1946/48)			1	0									1	0
M Appleby (1990-)	1	0	17/2	0	2	0	3	0			2/2	0	25/4	0
RD Appleby (**-)											2	0	2	0
W Appleyard (1903/08)			128	71	17	16							145	87
J Archibald (1922/23)			1	0									1	0

Player	FAPL App	FAPL Goals	League App	League Goals	FACup App	FACup Goals	LgeCup App	LgeCup Goals	Europe App	Europe Goals	Others App	Others Goals	Totals App	Totals Goals
P Arentoft (1969/71)			46/4	2	3	0			10/1	1			59/5	3
W Askew (1990)			6	0							2	0	8	0
JR Auld (1896/97)			14	3	1	0							15	3
JA Bailey (1985/88)			39/1	0	1	0	1	0					41/1	0
*R Bainbridge (1943)											1	0	1	0
IJ Baird (1984/85)			4/1	1									4/1	1
*J Balmer (1941)											6	1	6	1
T Bamlett (1901/04)			2	0									2	0
S Barber (1925/28)			1	0									1	0
MA Barker (1973/79)			21/2	0	4	0	1	0			1	0	27/2	0
JW Barr (1893/4)			1	0									1	0
*J Barron (1944)											1	0	1	0
SJ Barrowclough (1970/78)			201/18	3	15/7	2	14/3	1	4	0	27	4	261/28	10
T Bartlett (1893/94 & 1896/97)			3	3									3	3
D Barton (1975/83)			101/1	5	2/1	0	5	1					108/2	6
*NR Batey (1942)											8	0	8	0
RR Batty (1945/58)			161	1	20	0							182	1
PA Beardsley (1983/87 & 1993-)	35	21	146/1	61	9	2	13	1	1	0	1	0	204/1	85
D Beasant (1988/89)			20	0	2	0	2	0			3	0	27	0
H Bedford (1930/32)			30	17	2	1							32	18
A Bell (1973/75)			1	0							1	0	2	0
D Bell (1930/34)			21	1	2	0							23	1
DS Bell (1981/83)			3/1	0									3/1	0
GA Bell (1918/20)											3	3	3	3
JR Bell (1956/62)			111	8	6	0							117	8

Player	FAPL		League		FACup		LgeCup		Europe		Others		Totals	
	App	Goals	App	Goals	App	Goals	App	Goals	App	Goals	App	Goals	App	Goals
*W Bell (1942)	-	-	-	-	-	-	-	-	-	-	2	0	2	0
A Bennett (1965/69)	-	-	85	22	1	0	3	1	0/1	0	-	-	89/1	23
RB Bennie (1901/04)	-	-	33	0	4	0	-	-	-	-	-	-	37	0
RW Benson (1902/04)	-	-	1	0	-	-	-	-	-	-	-	-	1	0
RTF Bentley (1946/48)	-	-	48	22	6	3	-	-	-	-	-	-	54	25
J Beresford (1992-)	32	0	42	1	7	0	7	0	-	-	2	0	90	1
W Bertram (1920/21)	-	-	3	0	-	-	-	-	-	-	-	-	3	0
J Best (1919/20)	-	-	2	0	1	0	-	-	-	-	-	-	3	0
A Betton (1931/34)	-	-	61	1	2	0	-	-	-	-	-	-	63	1
*HJR Billington (1940)	-	-	-	-	-	-	-	-	-	-	4	3	4	3
J Bird (1975/80)	-	-	84/3	5	4	1	4	0	1/1	0	2	0	95/4	6
RJE Birkett (1938/41)	-	-	23	3	3	0	-	-	-	-	40	12	66	15
EL Birnie (1898/1905)	-	-	19	0	1	0	-	-	-	-	-	-	20	0
M Blackburn (1939/45)	-	-	-	-	-	-	-	-	-	-	12	1	12	1
R Blackburn (1906/08)	-	-	5	0	-	-	-	-	-	-	-	-	5	0
R Blackhall (1974/78)	-	-	25/12	0	5/1	2	0/1	0	1	0	1/1	0	32/15	2
JH Blackley (1977/79)	-	-	46	0	5	0	1	0	-	-	-	-	52	0
S Blake (1905 & 1909/14)	-	-	14	0	1	0	-	-	-	-	-	-	15	0
R Blanthorne (1908/10)	-	-	1	1	-	-	-	-	-	-	-	-	1	1
J Blyth (1896/97)	-	-	1	1	-	-	-	-	-	-	-	-	1	1
S Boam (1979/81)	-	-	69	1	5	0	3	1	-	-	-	-	77	2
P Bodin (1992)	-	-	6	0	-	-	-	-	-	-	-	-	6	0
I Bogie (1985/89)	-	-	7/7	0	1/2	0	0/1	0	-	-	3/1	1	11/11	1
H Bolton (1905)	-	-	1	0	-	-	-	-	-	-	-	-	1	0
C Booth (1913/20)	-	-	34	6	-	-	-	-	-	-	8	5	42	11

Player	FAPL		League		FACup		LgeCup		Europe		Others		Totals	
	App	Goals	App	Goals	App	Goals	App	Goals	App	Goals	App	Goals	App	Goals
W Bott (1934/36)			37	11	7	4							44	15
AE Bottom (1958)			11	10									11	10
ER Bowden (1937/40)			48	6	4	0					3	3	55	9
J Bowman (1892/93)			1	0									1	0
J Boyd (1925/35)			198	58	16	5							214	63
*W Boyes (1941)													2	0
P Bracewell (1992-)	32	1	19/6	2	3/1	0	3	1			2	0	59/7	4
GJ Bradley (1938/46)			1	0							20	1	21	1
R Bradley (1927/29)			1	0									1	0
W Bradley (1914/27)			133	0	10	0					4	0	147	0
DS Bradshaw (1989/92)			32/6	0	2/1	0	3	0			3	0	40/7	0
GM Brander (1952/54)			5	2									5	2
GN Brazil (1989/**)			7/16	2	0/1	0	1/1	1			0/1	0	8/19	3
F Brennan (1946/56)			318	3	29	0							347	3
IA Broadis (1953/55)			42	15	9	3							51	18
PK Broady (1939/45)											1		1	0
KS Brock (1988/93)			135/10	13	11		7	1			9/1	1	162/11	16
+A Brown (1981/82)			5	3									5	3
EC Brown (1945/47)			24	8							12	4	12	4
H Brown (1906/07)											24	24	8	
J Brown (1918/19)											1			
M Brown (1983/85)			39	0	2	0	4	0				1	45	1
N Brown (1907/08)											1	0	1	0
J Brownlie (1978/82)			124	2	7/1	1	4	0					135/1	3
AR Bruce (1974/75)			16/4	3							4	1	20/4	4

Player	FAPL App	FAPL Goals	League App	League Goals	FACup App	FACup Goals	LgeCup App	LgeCup Goals	Europe App	Europe Goals	Others App	Others Goals	Totals App	Totals Goals
HC Bulloch (1935/36)	-	-	5	0	-	-	-	-	-	-	-	-	5	0
C Burgess (1900/01)	-	-	30	0	1	0	-	-	-	-	-	-	31	0
R Burke (1946/47)	-	-	15	0	2	0	-	-	-	-	-	-	17	0
MS Burleigh (1968/74)	-	-	11	0	-	-	-	-	-	-	4	0	15	0
ME Burns (1974/78)	-	-	143/2	39	17	5	14	4	4	0	11	3	189/2	51
MT Burns (1927/36)	-	-	104	0	3	0	-	-	-	-	-	-	107	0
J Burridge (1989/**)	-	-	67	0	7	0	4	0	-	-	6	0	84	0
AD Burton (1963/73)	-	-	181/7	6	9	0	7/1	2	18/1	0	5	0	220/9	8
+V Busby (1971/72)	-	-	4	2	1	0	-	-	-	-	-	-	5	2
JW Butler (1960/65)	-	-	3	0	-	-	1	0	-	-	-	-	4	0
T Cahill (1951/55)	-	-	4	0	-	-	-	-	-	-	-	-	4	0
A Caie (1901/03)	-	-	31	1	4	0	-	-	-	-	-	-	35	1
T Cairns (1914/1916)	-	-	1	0	-	-	-	-	-	-	-	-	1	0
WH Cairns (1933/44)	-	-	87	51	3	2	-	-	-	-	23	14	113	67
NA Calder (1939/45)	-	-	-	-	-	-	-	-	-	-	1	0	1	0
R Callachan (1977/78)	-	-	9	0	-	-	-	-	2	0	-	-	11	0
T Campbell (1894/95)	-	-	2	0	-	-	-	-	-	-	-	-	2	0
HG Cameron (1951/52)	-	-	2	0	-	-	-	-	-	-	-	-	2	0
JM Campbell (1897/88)	-	-	23	9	3	2	-	-	-	-	3	1	29	12
P Cannell (1972/78)	-	-	48/1	13	5	2	7/1	4	3	1	5/1	2	68/3	20
JP Cape (1930/34)	-	-	51	18	2	2	-	-	-	-	-	-	53	20
W Carlton (1926/29)	-	-	5	1	1	0	-	-	-	-	-	-	6	1
S Carney (1979/85)	-	-	125/9	1	9	0	6	0	-	-	-	-	140/9	1
*EM Carr (1942)	-	-	-	-	-	-	-	-	-	-	70	56	70	56
F Carr (**-93)	-	-	20/5	3	-	-	2/2	0	-	-	3/1	0	25/8	3

187

Player	FAPL		League		FACup		LgeCup		Europe		Others		Totals	
	App	Goals	App	Goals	App	Goals	App	Goals	App	Goals	App	Goals	App	Goals
J Carr (1899/1912)	-	-	252	5	25	0	-	-	-	-	-	-	277	5
JR Carr (1894/98)	-	-	4	0	-	-	-	-	-	-	-	-	4	0
K Carr (1976/85)	-	-	173	0	13	0	9	0	-	-	-	-	195	0
P Cartwright (1979/83)	-	-	57/8	3	1	0	0/3	1	-	-	-	-	58/11	4
J Carver (1936/39)	-	-	70	0	6	0	-	-	-	-	-	-	76	0
T Casey (1952/58)	-	-	116	8	16	2	-	-	-	-	-	-	132	10
T Cassidy (1970/80)	-	-	170/10	22	22/1	1	17/2	3	3	3	13/1	2	225/14	28
W Chalmers (1928/31)	-	-	41	13	1	0	-	-	-	-	-	-	42	13
C Chambers (1975/78)	-	-	-	-	-	-	-	-	-	-	1	0	1	0
A Chandler (1925/26)	-	-	33	0	3	0	-	-	-	-	-	-	36	0
MR Channon (1982)	-	-	4	1	-	-	-	-	-	-	-	-	4	1
*AC Chilton (1942)	-	-	-	-	-	-	-	-	-	-	2	0	2	0
AH Clark (1948/49)	-	-	1	0	-	-	-	-	-	-	-	-	1	0
FA Clark (1962/75)	-	-	388/1	0	26	0	19	1	23	0	29	1	485/1	1
JR Clark (1921/24)	-	-	11	2	-	-	-	-	-	-	-	-	11	2
L Clark (1990-)	29	2	84/10	16	9	-	10	0	-	-	4	1	136/7	20
RJ Clark (1923/28)	-	-	77	16	-	-	-	-	-	-	-	-	77	16
JD Clarke (1982/87)	-	-	124	4	5	0	5	1	-	-	-	-	134	5
R Clarke (1980/81)	-	-	14	2	4	1	-	-	-	-	-	-	18	3
H Clifton (1938/46)	-	-	29	15	6	2	-	-	-	-	42	27	77	44
C Clish (1961/63)	-	-	20	0	2	0	1	0	-	-	-	-	23	0
A Cole (1992-)	40	34	11/1	12	3	1	2	6	-	-	-	-	56/1	53
J Collins (1892/93 & 1895/97)	-	-	34	9	8	2	-	-	-	-	-	-	42	11
J Connell (1896/97)	-	-	24	3	1	0	-	-	-	-	-	-	25	3
E Connelly (1935/38)	-	-	25	8	5	1	-	-	-	-	-	-	30	9

Player	FAPL App	FAPL Goals	League App	League Goals	FACup App	FACup Goals	LgeCup App	LgeCup Goals	Europe App	Europe Goals	Others App	Others Goals	Totals App	Totals Goals
J Connolly (1978/80)	-	-	42/7	10	0/1	0	1	0	-	-	-	-	43/8	10
*J Connor (1942)	-	-	-	-	-	-	-	-	-	-	2	0	2	0
J Cook (1919/20)	-	-	-	-	-	-	-	-	-	-	1	0	1	0
E Copeland (1939/45)	-	-	-	-	-	-	-	-	-	-	20	3	20	3
E Cooper (1913/20)	-	-	45	2	1	0	-	-	-	-	10	2	56	4
J Cooper (1952/59)	-	-	6	0	-	-	-	-	-	-	-	-	6	0
R Corbett (1943/51)	-	-	46	1	14	0	-	-	-	-	62	0	122	1
JA Cornwell (1987/89)	-	-	28/5	1	1	0	3	0	-	-	4/2	0	36/7	1
W Coulson (1971/73)	-	-	-	-	-	-	-	-	-	-	1	0	1	0
J Cowan (1967/73)	-	-	6/3	0	-	-	0/1	0	-	-	-	-	6/4	0
WD Cowan (1923/26)	-	-	87	23	14	5	-	-	-	-	-	-	101	28
RG Cowell (1943/56)	-	-	289	0	38	0	-	-	-	-	81	0	408	0
*N Coyde (1942)	-	-	-	-	-	-	-	-	-	-	7	1	7	1
JE Craggs (1964/71 & 1982/83)	-	-	60/4	1	2	0	1/1	0	5	0	-	-	68/5	1
AH Craig (1987/89)	-	-	6/4	0	1/1	0	-	-	-	-	2	0	9/5	0
B Craig (1938/50)	-	-	66	0	1	0	-	-	-	-	55	0	122	0
DJ Craig (1962/78)	-	-	346/5	8	22	3	17/1	1	21	0	23	1	429/6	13
DM Craig (1969/75)	-	-	-	-	-	-	-	-	-	-	1	0	1	0
TB Craig (1974/78)	-	-	122/2	22	13	3	11	2	4	2	5	0	155/2	29
T Crate (1891/95)	-	-	39	14	2	1	-	-	-	-	-	-	41	15
R Crielly (1889/95)	-	-	54	1	5	0	-	-	-	-	-	-	59	1
+AJ Cropley (1980)	-	-	3	0	-	-	-	-	-	-	-	-	3	0
D Crosson (1972/75)	-	-	6	0	-	-	0/1	0	-	-	3	0	9/1	0
CA Crowe (1944/57)	-	-	178	5	14	1	-	-	-	-	24	1	216	7
L Crown (1926/27)	-	-	2	0	-	-	-	-	-	-	-	-	2	0

Player	FAPL		League		FACup		LgeCup		Europe		Others		Totals	
	App	Goals	App	Goals	App	Goals	App	Goals	App	Goals	App	Goals	App	Goals
RJ Crumley (1900/07)	-	-	4	0	-	-	-	-	-	-	-	-	4	0
*DS Cumming (1943)	-	-	-	-	-	-	-	-	-	-	56	0	56	0
H Cummings (1918/19)	-	-	-	-	-	-	-	-	-	-	1	0	1	0
R Cummings (1954/56 & 1963/65)	-	-	43/1	14	1	0	-	-	-	-	-	-	44/1	14
A Cunningham (1929/30)	-	-	12	2	3	0	-	-	-	-	-	-	15	2
AE Cunningham (1985/87)	-	-	37/10	4	1	0	2	2	-	-	-	-	40/10	6
T Curry (1912/29)	-	-	221	5	14	0	-	-	-	-	13	0	248	5
WM Curry (1953/59)	-	-	80	36	8	4	-	-	-	-	-	-	88	40
G Dalton (1958/67)	-	-	85	2	2	0	7	0	-	-	-	-	94	2
DL Davidson (1930/37)	-	-	128	0	16	0	-	-	-	-	-	-	144	0
T Davidson (1901/03)	-	-	38	0	5	0	-	-	-	-	-	-	43	0
A Davies (1985/87)	-	-	20/1	1	2/1	0	-	-	-	-	-	-	22/2	1
ER Davies (1951/58)	-	-	157	49	13	1	-	-	-	-	-	-	170	50
IC Davies (1979/82)	-	-	74/1	3	1	0	6	1	-	-	-	-	81/1	4
RW Davies (1966/71)	-	-	181	40	8	3	3	0	24	10	-	-	216	53
W Day (1962/63)	-	-	13	0	1	1	-	-	-	-	-	-	14	1
J Denmark (1937/46)	-	-	51	0	-	-	-	-	-	-	54	0	105	0
RS Dennison (1929/34)	-	-	11	2	-	-	-	-	-	-	-	-	11	2
W Deswart (1939/45)	-	-	-	-	-	-	-	-	-	-	1	0	1	0
J Devine (1930/31)	-	-	22	11	-	-	-	-	-	-	-	-	22	11
*S Diamond (1942)	-	-	-	-	-	-	-	-	-	-	1	1	1	1
C Dickson (1894/95)	-	-	21	12	2	0	-	-	-	-	-	-	23	12
K Dillon (1989/91)	-	-	62	0	6/1	0	3/1	0	-	-	-	-	71/2	0
ES Dixon (1914/23)	-	-	49	7	4	3	-	-	-	-	8	0	61	10
JT Dixon (1943/44)	-	-	-	-	-	-	-	-	-	-	38	13	38	13

Player	FAPL		League		FACup		LgeCup		Europe		Others		Totals	
	App	Goals	App	Goals	App	Goals	App	Goals	App	Goals	App	Goals	App	Goals
SH Docking (1934/38)	-	-	21	3	-	-	-	-	-	-	-	-	21	3
JT Dodds (1906/08)	-	-	5	0	-	-	-	-	-	-	-	-	5	0
N Dodgin (1940/50)	-	-	84	1	2	0	-	-	-	-	46	1	132	2
A Donaldson (1943/49)	-	-	19	6	-	-	-	-	-	-	12	3	31	9
RS Donaldson (1939/47)	-	-	-	-	-	-	-	-	-	-	87	2	87	2
Donaldson (1894/95)	-	-	2	0	-	-	-	-	-	-	-	-	2	0
J Donnachie (1905/06)	-	-	2	0	-	-	-	-	-	-	-	-	2	0
JW Donnelly (1918/19)	-	-	-	-	-	-	-	-	-	-	5	1	5	1
J Doran (1918/19)	-	-	-	-	-	-	-	-	-	-	4	1	4	1
A Douglas (1913/19)	-	-	49	2	7	0	-	-	-	-	-	-	56	2
J Dowsey (1924/26)	-	-	3	0	-	-	-	-	-	-	-	-	3	0
J Dryden (1932/34)	-	-	5	1	1	0	-	-	-	-	-	-	6	1
A Duffy (1966/70)	-	-	2/2	0	-	-	-	-	-	-	-	-	2/2	0
CF Duffy (1906/08)	-	-	16	1	-	-	-	-	-	-	-	-	16	1
*R Duffy (1944)	-	-	-	-	-	-	-	-	-	-	0	21	-	-
ASM Duncan (1908/13)	-	-	73	10	8	1	-	-	-	-	-	-	81	11
JG Duncan (1950/53)	-	-	5	3	-	-	-	-	-	-	-	-	5	3
*L Duns (1939)	-	-	-	-	-	-	-	-	-	-	20	8	20	8
K Dyson (1968/71)	-	-	74/2	22	4	1	1/1	1	13/1	2	0/2	0	92/6	26
GE Eastham (1956/60)	-	-	124	29	5	5	-	-	-	-	-	-	129	34
*H Eastham (1941)	-	-	-	-	-	-	-	-	-	-	1	0	-	0
E Edgar (1973/76)	-	-	-	-	1	0	-	-	-	-	-	-	1	0
D Elliott (1966/71)	-	-	78/2	4	2/1	0	3	0	3/1	-	-	-	86/4	-
R Elliott (1990-)	13/2	0	14/1	0	2	0	1	0	0	-	1	0	31/3	0
R Ellison (1968/73)	-	-	5	0	2	0	-	-	-	-	-	-	7	0

Player	FAPL App	Goals	League App	Goals	FACup App	Goals	LgeCup App	Goals	Europe App	Goals	Others App	Goals	Totals App	Goals
A English (1939/45)	-	-	-	-	-	-	-	-	-	-	23	6	23	6
R Evans (1956/59)	-	-	4	0	-	-	-	-	-	-	-	-	4	0
TJ Evans (1927/30)	-	-	13	1	-	-	-	-	-	-	-	-	13	1
*W Fagan (1942)	-	-	-	-	-	-	-	-	-	-	2	0	2	0
J Fairbrother (1947/52)	-	-	132	0	12	0	-	-	-	-	-	-	144	0
DL Fairhurst (1929/46)	-	-	266	2	18	0	-	-	-	-	-	-	284	2
C Fairier (1918/19)	-	-	-	-	-	-	-	-	-	-	7	0	7	0
J Fashanu (1991)	-	-	-	-	-	-	0/1	0	-	-	-	-	0/1	0
WT Feeney (1930/32)	-	-	4	1	-	-	-	-	-	-	-	-	4	1
JI Fell (1962/63)	-	-	49	16	2	0	2	1	-	-	-	-	53	17
W Fereday (1989/90)	-	-	27/6	0	1	0	3/1	0	-	-	1/2	0	32/9	0
BJ Ferguson (1979/80)	-	-	4/1	1	-	-	-	-	-	-	-	-	4/1	1
RB Ferguson (1955/62)	-	-	11	0	1	0	-	-	-	-	-	-	12	0
PJ Ferris (1981/86)	-	-	1/10	0	-	-	0/2	1	-	-	-	-	1/12	1
A Fidler (1929/30)	-	-	5	0	-	-	-	-	-	-	-	-	5	0
J Findlay (1905/06)	-	-	2	0	-	-	-	-	-	-	-	-	2	0
J Finlay (1909/27)	-	-	153	8	8	0	-	-	-	-	12	1	173	9
*T Finney (1942)	-	-	-	-	-	-	-	-	-	-	6	3	6	3
D Flannigan (1928/29)	-	-	3	0	-	-	-	-	-	-	-	-	3	0
JBM Fleming (1911/13)	-	-	4	0	-	-	-	-	-	-	-	-	4	0
A Foggon (1967/71)	-	-	54/7	14	4	0	1/1	0	10/3	2	-	-	69/11	16
D Ford (1969/71)	-	-	24/2	3	1/1	0	-	-	3	0	-	-	28/3	3
JC Ford (1931/34)	-	-	1	-	-	-	-	-	-	-	-	-	1	-
*LG Forster (1942)	-	-	-	-	-	-	-	-	-	-	13	0	13	0
WB Forster (1932/38)	-	-	3	0	-	-	-	-	-	-	-	-	3	0

Player	FAPL App	FAPL Goals	League App	League Goals	FACup App	FACup Goals	LgeCup App	LgeCup Goals	Europe App	Europe Goals	Others App	Others Goals	Totals App	Totals Goals
WI Foulkes (1951/54)	-	-	58	8	10	1	-	-	-	-	-	-	68	9
R Fox (1994-)	14	2	-	-	-	-	-	-	-	-	-	-	14	2
R Foyers (1895/97)	-	-	34	0	5	0	-	-	-	-	-	-	39	0
AJ Franks (1953/60)	-	-	72	4	3	0	-	-	-	-	-	-	75	4
J Fraser (1899/1901)	-	-	49	9	3	0	-	-	-	-	-	-	52	9
R Fraser (1946/50)	-	-	26	0	1	0	-	-	-	-	-	-	27	0
AD Frost (1939)	-	-	5	1	-	-	-	-	-	-	-	-	5	1
HK Gallacher (1925/30)	-	-	160	133	14	10	-	-	-	-	-	-	174	143
J Gallacher (1989/90)	-	-	22/7	6	2	0	3	1	-	-	3	1	30/7	8
*P Gallacher (1939)	-	-	-	-	-	-	-	-	-	-	1	0	1	0
WL Gallantree (1931/36)	-	-	9	0	-	-	-	-	-	-	-	-	9	0
EJE Garbutt (1939/51)	-	-	52	0	1	0	-	-	-	-	-	-	53	0
Alex Gardner (1899/1910)	-	-	279	22	34	4	-	-	-	-	-	-	313	26
Andrew Gardner (1902/03)	-	-	9	3	1	0	-	-	-	-	-	-	10	3
DR Gardner (1899/1902)	-	-	76	2	2	1	-	-	-	-	-	-	78	3
P Garland (1991/92)	-	-	0/2	0	-	-	-	-	-	-	0/1	0	0/3	0
A Garnham (1934/39)	-	-	45	0	5	0	-	-	-	-	1	0	51	0
HA Garrow (1960/63)	-	-	4	1	-	-	-	-	-	-	-	-	4	1
PJ Gascoigne (1985/88)	-	-	83/9	21	4	3	8	1	-	-	4/1	0	99/10	25
A Gaskell (1953/54)	-	-	1	0	-	-	-	-	-	-	-	-	1	0
H Gayle (1982/83)	-	-	8	2	-	-	-	-	-	-	-	-	8	2
+T Gaynor (1990)	-	-	4	1	-	-	-	-	-	-	-	-	4	1
T Ghee (1897/1902)	-	-	130	2	10	1	-	-	-	-	4	1	144	4
T Gibb (1968/75)	-	-	190/9	12	8/3	0	12	1	24	3	17/5	3	251/17	19
CH Gibson (1948/49)	-	-	23	5	1	0	-	-	-	-	-	-	24	5

Player	FAPL App	FAPL Goals	League App	League Goals	FACup App	FACup Goals	LgeCup App	LgeCup Goals	Europe App	Europe Goals	Others App	Others Goals	Totals App	Totals Goals
J Gibson (1959/61)	-	-	2	1	-	-	-	-	-	-	-	-	2	1
R Gibson (1918/19)	-	-	-	-	-	-	-	-	-	-	1	0	1	0
RJ Gibson (1911/12)	-	-	-	-	-	-	-	-	-	-	-	-	-	0
WM Gibson (1923/29)	-	-	124	2	18	2	-	-	-	-	-	-	142	4
R Gilfillan (1959/61)	-	-	7	2	-	-	-	-	-	-	-	-	7	2
T Gilhespy (1893/94)	-	-	4	0	-	-	-	-	-	-	-	-	4	0
A Gilhome (1939/45)	-	-	-	-	-	-	-	-	-	-	21	3	21	3
WF Gillespie (1927/29)	-	-	9	0	-	-	-	-	-	-	-	-	9	0
*JR Glassey (1943)	-	-	-	-	-	-	-	-	-	-	2	0	2	0
P Goddard (1986/88)	-	-	61	19	6	3	5	1	-	-	-	-	72	23
W Golding (1939/45)	-	-	-	-	-	-	-	-	-	-	2	0	2	0
T Goodwill (1913/16)	-	-	52	4	8	3	-	-	-	-	-	-	60	7
J Gordon (1935/45)	-	-	132	2	11	1	-	-	-	-	111	18	254	21
M Gorry (1976/78)	-	-	0/1	0	-	-	-	-	-	-	-	-	0/1	0
AA Gosnell (1904/10)	-	-	106	15	18	3	-	-	-	-	-	-	124	18
AM Gourlay (1988/92)	-	-	2/2	-	-	-	0/1	0	-	-	-	-	2/3	0
AE Gowling (1975/78)	-	-	91/1	30	15	8	9	7	3	3	4	4	122/1	52
D Graham (1940/50)	-	-	71	0	3	0	-	-	-	-	90	1	164	1
JR Graham (1901/03)	-	-	6	0	-	-	-	-	-	-	-	-	6	0
S Graham (1902/05)	-	-	5	0	1	0	-	-	-	-	-	-	6	0
W Graham (1892/98)	-	-	88	10	11	1	-	-	-	-	-	-	99	11
AM Graver (1947/50)	-	-	1	0	-	-	-	-	-	-	-	-	1	0
AD Gray (1920/21)	-	-	2	-	-	-	-	-	-	-	-	-	2	0
*R Gray (1939)	-	-	-	-	-	-	-	-	-	-	2	0	2	0
*TD Gray (1944)	-	-	-	-	-	-	-	-	-	-	1	0	1	0

Player	FAPL App	FAPL Goals	League App	League Goals	FACup App	FACup Goals	LgeCup App	LgeCup Goals	Europe App	Europe Goals	Others App	Others Goals	Totals App	Totals Goals
A Green (1971/73)	-	-	33	3	2	0	-	-	-	-	3/1	0	38/1	3
S Green (1939/45)	-	-	-	-	-	-	-	-	-	-	2	0	2	0
R Greener (1951/55)	-	-	3	0	-	-	-	-	-	-	-	-	3	0
T Grey (1911/19)	-	-	1	0	-	-	-	-	-	-	-	-	1	0
AJ Grundy (1936/44)	-	-	2	0	-	-	-	-	-	-	-	-	2	0
CW Guthrie (1970/72)	-	-	3	0	-	-	1	0	-	-	-	-	4	0
RG Guthrie (1963/73)	-	-	52/3	2	2	0	0/1	0	3/2	0	3	0	60/6	2
A Guy (1975/79)	-	-	3/1	0	2	0	1	0	-	-	1	0	7/1	0
PM Haddock (1978/86)	-	-	53/4	3	3	0	2	0	-	-	3	0	61/4	3
A Hagan (1919/23)	-	-	21	5	-	-	-	-	-	-	4	1	25	6
G Hair (1943/49)	-	-	23	7	3	1	-	-	-	-	51	14	77	22
KO Hale (1956/62)	-	-	30	15	1	0	4	1	-	-	-	-	35	16
AN Hall (1907/08)	-	-	6	2	-	-	-	-	-	-	-	-	6	2
E Hall (1933/37)	-	-	2	0	-	-	-	-	-	-	-	-	2	0
T Hall (1913/20)	-	-	54	15	4	1	-	-	-	-	-	-	58	16
B Halliday (1979/82)	-	-	32	1	4	0	2	0	-	-	-	-	38	1
W Halliday (1927/28)	-	-	1	0	-	-	-	-	-	-	-	-	1	0
DS Hamilton (1939/46)	-	-	-	-	-	-	-	-	-	-	10	2	10	2
W Hampson (1914/27)	-	-	163	1	11	0	-	-	-	-	-	-	174	1
GL Hannah (1949/57)	-	-	167	41	8	2	-	-	-	-	-	-	175	43
HTW Hardinge (1905/07)	-	-	9	1	-	-	-	-	-	-	-	-	9	1
S Hardwick (1976/83)	-	-	92	1	4	0	3	0	2	0	-	-	101	1
S Hardy (1911/18)	-	-	3	1	-	-	-	-	-	-	-	-	3	1
MG Harford (1980/81 & 1982)	-	-	18/1	4	-	-	-	-	-	-	-	-	18/1	4
CJ Harker (1955/61)	-	-	1	0	-	-	-	-	-	-	-	-	1	0

Player		FAPL		League		FACup		LgeCup		Europe		Others		Totals	
		App	Goals	App	Goals	App	Goals	App	Goals	App	Goals	App	Goals	App	Goals
DR	Harnby (1939/47)	–	–	–	–	–	–	–	–	–	–	8	0	8	0
A	Harris (1935/36)	–	–	12	4	–	–	–	–	–	–	–	–	12	4
J	Harris (1925/31)	–	–	149	2	8	0	–	–	–	–	–	–	157	2
NL	Harris (1920/25)	–	–	174	87	20	14	–	–	–	–	–	–	194	101
J	Harrower (1961/62)	–	–	5	0	1	0	–	–	–	–	–	–	6	0
WR	Hart (11940/45)	–	–	–	–	–	–	–	–	–	–	38	1	38	1
BR	Harvey (1958/61)	–	–	86	0	4	0	1	0	–	–	–	–	91	0
Jn	Harvey (1897/99)	–	–	26	6	5	2	–	–	–	–	4	2	35	10
Jo	Harvey (1945/53)	–	–	224	12	23	0	–	–	–	–	33	1	280	13
J	Hay (1911/19)	–	–	132	8	17	0	–	–	–	–	–	–	149	8
	Haynes (1894/95)	–	–	1	0	–	–	–	–	–	–	–	–	1	0
PT	Heard (1984/85)	–	–	34	2	2	0	–	–	–	–	–	–	36	2
G	Hedley (1908 & 1910)	–	–	1	0	–	–	–	–	–	–	–	–	1	0
R	Hedley (1894/95 & 1895)	–	–	3	1	–	–	–	–	–	–	–	–	3	1
C	Hedworth (1982/86)	–	–	8/1	0	–	–	1	0	–	–	–	–	9/1	0
HB	Henderson (1939/45)	–	–	–	–	–	–	–	–	–	–	5	0	5	0
Jason	Henderson (1919/20)	–	–	6	1	–	–	–	–	–	–	–	–	6	1
John	Henderson (1895/97)	–	–	30	0	5	0	–	–	–	–	–	–	35	0
JG	Hendrie (1988/89)	–	–	34	4	4	0	2	1	–	–	3	0	43	5
*A	Herd (1940)	–	–	–	–	–	–	–	–	–	–	4	3	4	3
GW	Heslop (1959/62)	–	–	27	0	1	0	4	0	–	–	–	–	32	0
HA	Heward (1932/34)	–	–	5	0	–	–	–	–	–	–	–	–	5	0
R	Hewison (1908/14 & 1919/20)—	–	–	67	0	3	0	–	–	–	–	–	–	70	0
G	Heywood (1900/02)	–	–	13	3	–	–	–	–	–	–	–	–	13	3
W	Hibbert (1911/20)	–	–	139	46	16	3	–	–	–	–	4	1	159	50

Player	FAPL App	FAPL Goals	League App	League Goals	FACup App	FACup Goals	LgeCup App	LgeCup Goals	Europe App	Europe Goals	Others App	Others Goals	Totals App	Totals Goals
TA Hibbitt (1971/75 & 1978/81)	-	-	227/1	12	15	1	16	0	-	-	33	5	291/1	18
A Higgins (1905/19)	-	-	126	36	24	5	-	-	-	-	-	-	150	41
W Higgins (1898/1900)	-	-	35	3	4	0	-	-	-	-	-	-	39	3
GW Highmoor (1939/45)	-	-	-	-	-	-	-	-	-	-	3	0	3	0
JH Hill (1928/31)	-	-	74	2	4	0	-	-	-	-	-	-	78	2
JM Hill (1957/58)	-	-	11	2	-	-	-	-	-	-	-	-	11	2
D Hiley (1962/67)	-	-	194	31	8	1	7	1	-	-	-	-	209	33
E Hindmarsh (1939/45)	-	-	-	-	-	-	-	-	-	-	6	0	6	0
G Hindson (1968/71)	-	-	7	1	-	-	-	-	0/1	0	-	-	7/1	1
T Hockey (1963/65)	-	-	52	3	2	0	2	0	-	-	-	-	56	3
GP Hodges (1987)	-	-	7	0	-	-	-	-	-	-	-	-	7	0
G Hodgson (1971/74)	-	-	8/1	0	1	0	-	-	-	-	-	-	1/2	0
K Hodgson (1959/61)	-	-	6	0	1	0	-	-	-	-	-	-	7	0
C Holland (1994-)	2/1	0	-	-	-	-	-	-	-	-	-	-	2/1	0
DM Hollins (1961/67)	-	-	112	0	3	0	6	0	-	-	-	-	121	0
M Hooper (1993-)	19	0	-	-	3	0	2	0	-	-	-	-	24	0
G Hope (1972/75)	-	-	6	1	-	-	-	-	-	-	-	-	6	1
GL Hope (1939/45)	-	-	-	-	-	-	-	-	-	-	1	0	1	0
JWM Hope (1969/71)	-	-	1	0	-	-	-	-	-	-	-	-	1	0
A Horsfield (1969)	-	-	7/2	3	-	-	-	-	1	0	-	-	8/2	3
FC Houghton (1948/53)	-	-	55	10	2	0	-	-	-	-	-	-	57	10
P Howard (1971/76)	-	-	182/2	7	23	0	19	0	-	-	37	1	261/2	9
S Howden (1939/45)	-	-	-	-	-	-	-	-	-	-	10	1	10	1
*D Howe (1939)	-	-	-	-	-	-	-	-	-	-	1	5	1	5
SN Howey (1986-)	13/1	0	57/17	3	6/2	0	6/2	1	-	-	5	0	87/22	4

Player	FAPL App	FAPL Goals	League App	League Goals	FACup App	FACup Goals	LgeCup App	LgeCup Goals	Europe App	Europe Goals	Others App	Others Goals	Totals App	Totals Goals
J Howie (1903/10)	-	-	198	69	37	14	-	-	-	-	-	-	235	83
L Hubble (1939/45)	-	-	-	-	-	-	-	-	-	-	2	0	2	0
J Hudson (1939/45)	-	-	-	-	-	-	-	-	-	-	3	0	3	0
R Hudson (1973/78)	-	-	16/4	1	3	1	1	0	-	-	4	0	24/5	2
FC Hudspeth (1910/29)	-	-	430	34	42	3	-	-	-	-	10	1	482	38
G Hughes (1956/63)	-	-	133	18	9	2	-	-	-	-	1	0	143	20
J Hughes (1932/35)	-	-	5	0	-	-	-	-	-	-	-	-	5	0
J Hughes (1939/45)	-	-	-	-	-	-	-	-	-	-	2	0	2	0
T Hughes (1912/14)	-	-	2	0	-	-	-	-	-	-	-	-	2	0
WJ Hughes (1908/09)	-	-	1	0	-	-	-	-	-	-	-	-	1	0
A Hunt (1991/93)	-	-	34/9	11	2	2	3	1	-	-	3	0	42/9	14
I Hunter (1918/19)	-	-	-	-	-	-	-	-	-	-	1	0	1	0
JA Hunter (1919 & 1924/25)	-	-	10	0	2	0	-	-	-	-	-	-	12	0
*JB Hunter (1941)	-	-	-	-	-	-	-	-	-	-	8	0	8	0
D Hutchison (1929/32)	-	-	40	16	6	5	-	-	-	-	-	-	46	21
R Hutchinson (1919/20)	-	-	-	-	-	-	-	-	-	-	1	0	1	0
TO Hutton (1939/45)	-	-	-	-	-	-	-	-	-	-	3	0	3	0
W Hynd (1894/95)	-	-	9	0	-	-	-	-	-	-	-	-	9	0
J Iley (1962/69)	-	-	227/5	15	9	0	7	1	0/1	0	-	-	243/6	16
WN Imrie (1934/38)	-	-	125	24	3	0	-	-	-	-	-	-	128	24
R Inglis (1893/94)	-	-	3	0	-	-	-	-	-	-	-	-	3	0
W Innerd (1900/03)	-	-	3	0	-	-	-	-	-	-	-	-	3	0
D Jackson (1986/88)	-	-	53/16	7	5	1	5	1	-	-	4	0	67/16	9
J Jackson (1897/99)	-	-	58	0	6	2	-	-	-	-	4	1	68	3
PA Jackson (1986/88)	-	-	60	3	6	0	3	0	-	-	3	0	72	3

Player	FAPL App	FAPL Goals	League App	League Goals	FACup App	FACup Goals	LgeCup App	LgeCup Goals	Europe App	Europe Goals	Others App	Others Goals	Totals App	Totals Goals
H Jeffrey (1892/97)	-	-	45	3	3	0	-	-	-	-	-	-	48	3
M Jeffrey (1993-)	2	0	-	-	-	-	-	-	-	-	-	-	2	0
G Jobey (1906/13)	-	-	47	2	6	0	-	-	-	-	-	-	53	2
H Johnson (1933/37)	-	-	5	0	-	-	-	-	-	-	-	-	5	0
PE Johnson (1980/83)	-	-	16	0	4	0	-	-	-	-	-	-	20	0
R Jones (1976/77)	-	-	5	0	-	-	-	-	-	-	2	0	7	0
*AL Juliussen (1943)	-	-	-	-	-	-	-	-	-	-	1	0	1	0
AE Keating (1923/25)	-	-	12	3	-	-	-	-	-	-	-	-	12	3
VAW Keeble (1952/57)	-	-	104	56	16	11	-	-	-	-	-	-	120	67
JK Keegan (1982/84)	-	-	74	48	3	0	4	1	-	-	-	-	85	49
GM Keeley (1974/76)	-	-	43/1	2	8	0	10	2	-	-	11	0	72/1	4
ERL Keen (1927/30)	-	-	1	0	-	-	-	-	-	-	-	-	1	0
JE Keen (1922/25)	-	-	2	0	-	-	-	-	-	-	-	-	2	0
S Keery (1952/57)	-	-	19	1	1	0	-	-	-	-	-	-	20	1
M Keir (1893/94)	-	-	1	0	-	-	-	-	-	-	-	-	1	0
RM Keith (1956/64)	-	-	208	2	11	0	4	0	-	-	-	-	223	2
D Kelly (1938/45)	-	-	1	0	-	-	-	-	-	-	8	0	9	0
David Kelly (**-93)	-	-	70	35	5	1	4	2	-	-	4	1	83	39
G Kelly (1985/89)	-	-	53	0	3	0	4	0	-	-	4	0	64	0
J Kelly (1933/35)	-	-	5	1	-	-	-	-	-	-	-	-	5	1
PA Kelly (1974/81)	-	-	31/2	0	-	-	3	0	1	0	1	0	36/2	0
WB Kelly (1911)	-	-	6	0	-	-	-	-	-	-	-	-	6	0
WJ Kelsey (1906/07)	-	-	2	0	-	-	-	-	-	-	-	-	2	0
AP Kennedy (1971/78)	-	-	155/3	9	21/2	0	16	0	2	0	16/1	1	210/6	10
KV Kennedy (1970/72)	-	-	1	0	-	-	-	-	-	-	-	-	1	0

Player	FAPL App	FAPL Goals	League App	League Goals	FACup App	FACup Goals	LgeCup App	LgeCup Goals	Europe App	Europe Goals	Others App	Others Goals	Totals App	Totals Goals
JR Kerray (1962/63)	-	-	38	10	1	0	1	0	-	-	-	-	40	10
KF Kettleborough (1966)	-	-	30	0	2	0	1	0	-	-	-	-	33	0
B Kilcline (1992/94)	1	0	19/12	0	1/2	0	3/2	0	-	-	5	0	29/16	0
G King (1946/48)	-	-	2	0	-	-	-	-	-	-	-	-	2	0
J King (1913/20)	-	-	54	8	7	2	-	-	-	-	-	-	61	10
R King (1942/46)	-	-	-	-	2	0	-	-	-	-	31	0	33	0
*WJD Kinghorn (1941)	-	-	-	-	-	-	-	-	-	-	2	0	2	0
M Kingsley (1898/1904)	-	-	180	0	9	0	-	-	-	-	-	-	189	0
J Kinsella (1897)	-	-	2	0	-	-	-	-	-	-	-	-	2	0
JW Kirkaldy (1904/07)	-	-	11	1	-	-	-	-	-	-	-	-	11	1
AJ Kirkman (1963)	-	-	5		-	-	-	-	-	-	-	-	5	1
T Knox (1965/67)	-	-	24/1	1	-	-	1	0	-	-	-	-	25/1	1
FLA Koenan (1980/81)	-	-	11/1	1	-	-	2	0	-	-	-	-	13/1	1
B Kristensen (1989/93)	-	-	69/10	4	6	0	3	0	-	-	8/1	1	86/11	5
G Lackenby (1950/56)	-	-	19	0	-	-	-	-	-	-	-	-	19	0
J Laidlaw (1900/01)	-	-	10	3	1	0	-	-	-	-	-	-	11	3
T Lang (1926/34)	-	-	215	53	14	5	-	-	-	-	-	-	229	58
M Larnach (1977/78)	-	-	12/1	0	-	-	-	-	-	-	-	-	12/1	0
D Laughton (1973/75)	-	-	7	0	-	-	0/1	0	-	-	1/1	0	8/2	0
J Laverick (1893/95)	-	-	4	0	-	-	-	-	-	-	-	-	4	0
JA Law (1939/45)	-	-	-	-	-	-	-	-	-	-	1	0	1	0
JH Law (1893/94)	-	-	8	2	2	0	-	-	-	-	-	-	10	2
J Lawrence (1904/22)	-	-	432	0	64	0	-	-	-	-	9	0	505	0
T Leach (1934/36)	-	-	51	2	2	0	-	-	-	-	-	-	53	2
PH Leaver (1980/82)	-	-	-	-	-	-	1	0	-	-	-	-	1	0

Player	FAPL App	FAPL Goals	League App	League Goals	FACup App	FACup Goals	LgeCup App	LgeCup Goals	Europe App	Europe Goals	Others App	Others Goals	Totals App	Totals Goals
R Lee (1939/45)											2	0	2	0
Robert Lee (1992–)	41	7	36	10	7	2	6	2					90	21
K Leek (1961)			13	6			1	0					14	6
WA Leighton (1932/38)			39	8	1	0							40	8
M Lennox (1895/98)			46	17	3	1							49	18
*DG Lewis (1943)											1	0	1	0
R Lidell (1904/11)			14	2									14	2
L Lightfoot (1939/45)											10	0	10	0
DM Lindsay (1930/31)			19	12									19	12
J Lindsay (1899/1900)			2	0									2	0
W Lindsay (1888/90)			59	1	1	0					2	0	62	1
EB Litchfield (1939/45)											2	0	2	0
J Little (1927/28)			3	0									3	0
R Little (1912/19)			3	0							3	1	6	1
J Littlefair (1900/02)			2	0									2	0
A Livingstone (1935/38)			33	5									33	5
J Lockey (1895/99)			1	0							2	0	3	0
*AJ Lockie (1940)											1	0	1	0
J Logan (1895/96)			7	5	2	3							9	8
A Lormor (1987/90)			6/2	3									6/2	3
J Loughlin (1924/27)			12	5									12	5
J Low (1921/28)			108	8	13	1							121	9
WL Low (1909/24)			324	9	43	0					11	0	378	9
J Lowery (1947/52)			6	0							6	0	12	0
W Lowery (1893/95)			28	0	2	0							30	0

Player	FAPL App	FAPL Goals	League App	League Goals	FACup App	FACup Goals	LgeCup App	LgeCup Goals	Europe App	Europe Goals	Others App	Others Goals	Totals App	Totals Goals
T Lowes (1910/19)	-	-	16	3	-	-	-	-	-	-	-	-	16	3
G Lowrie (1948/49)	-	-	12	5	-	-	-	-	-	-	-	-	12	5
GT Luke (1950/53 & 1959/61)	-	-	27	4	2	0	-	-	-	-	-	-	29	4
McBain (1932)	-	-	1	0	-	-	-	-	-	-	-	-	1	0
A McCaffery (1975/78)	-	-	57/2	4	5	1	3/1	0	3	0	-	-	68/3	5
W McCall (1948)	-	-	16	4	-	-	-	-	-	-	-	-	16	4
J McClarence (1904/08)	-	-	30	13	2	0	-	-	-	-	-	-	32	13
RS McColl (1901/04)	-	-	64	18	3	2	-	-	-	-	-	-	67	20
A McCombie (1904/10)	-	-	113	0	18	0	-	-	-	-	-	-	131	0
*CJ McCormack (1944)	-	-	-	-	-	-	-	-	-	-	1	0	1	0
JA McCormack (1906/09)	-	-	2	1	-	-	-	-	-	-	-	-	2	1
JH McCormack (1939/45)	-	-	-	-	-	-	-	-	-	-	2	2	2	2
WR McCracken (1904/23)	-	-	377	6	55	0	-	-	-	-	11	0	443	8
D McCreery (1982/89)	-	-	237/6	2	2	0	15	0	-	-	4	0	266/7	2
A McCulloch (1908)	-	-	1	0	-	-	-	-	-	-	-	-	1	0
J McCurley (1927/30)	-	-	43	8	2	0	-	-	-	-	-	-	45	8
R McDermidd (1895/97)	-	-	56	2	8	0	-	-	-	-	-	-	64	2
T McDermott (1973/74 & 1982/84)	-	-	129/1	18	13	4	7	2	-	-	18	0	167/1	24
J McDonald (1912/14)	-	-	37	6	5	0	-	-	-	-	-	-	42	6
MI MacDonald (1971/76)	-	-	187	95	23	14	18	12	-	-	29/1	17	257/1	138
NR McDonald (1982/88)	-	-	163/17	24	10/1	1	12	3	-	-	5	0	190/18	28
R McDonald (1988/89)	-	-	6/4	1	1/3	0	-	-	-	-	1	1	8/7	2
TH McDonald (1921/31)	-	-	341	100	26	13	-	-	-	-	1	-	367	113
D McDonough (1991/92)	-	-	2/1	0	-	-	-	-	-	-	-	-	2/1	0
A MacFarlane (1898/1901)	-	-	84	16	2	0	-	-	-	-	-	-	86	16

Player	FAPL App	FAPL Goals	League App	League Goals	FACup App	FACup Goals	LgeCup App	LgeCup Goals	Europe App	Europe Goals	Others App	Others Goals	Totals App	Totals Goals
WS McFaul (1966/75)	-	-	290	0	23	0	18	0	24	0	32	0	387	0
RJ McGarry (1962/67)	-	-	118/3	41	6	3	5	2	-	-	-	-	129/3	46
ME McGhee (1977/79 & 1989/91)	-	-	84/11	29	8/1	6	5/1	1	-	-	5	0	102/13	36
R McGough (1914/15)	-	-	2	0	-	-	-	-	-	-	2	0	4	0
JT McGrath (1961/68)	-	-	169/1	2	5	0	6	0	-	-	-	-	180/1	2
JJ McGuigan (1958/62)	-	-	50	15	3	1	2	1	-	-	-	-	55	17
*JS McInnes (1941)	-	-	-	-	-	-	-	-	-	-	1	0	1	0
A McInroy (1929/34)	-	-	143	0	17	0	-	-	-	-	-	-	160	0
*A McIntosh (1940)	-	-	-	-	-	-	-	-	-	-	3	2	3	2
RA McIntosh (1920/24)	-	-	101	2	2	0	-	-	-	-	-	-	103	2
E McIntyre (1900/06)	-	-	6	0	-	-	-	-	-	-	-	-	6	0
J McKane (1891/95)	-	-	41	0	3	0	-	-	-	-	-	-	44	0
R McKay (1926/28)	-	-	62	22	4	1	-	-	-	-	-	-	66	23
W McKay (1895/97)	-	-	18	6	3	1	-	-	-	-	-	-	21	7
+D McKellar (1986)	-	-	10	0	-	-	-	-	-	-	-	-	10	0
RR McKenzie (1922/35)	-	-	238	6	18	1	-	-	-	-	-	-	256	7
*D McKerrell (1941)	-	-	-	-	-	-	2	0	-	-	-	-	2	0
W McKinney (1957/65)	-	-	85	6	7	2	-	-	-	-	2	0	94	8
R McKinnon (1984/86)	-	-	1	0	-	-	-	-	-	-	-	-	1	0
D MacClean (1975/78)	-	-	7/2	0	-	-	1	0	1	0	-	-	9/2	0
H McMenemy (1931/37)	-	-	138	34	10	1	-	-	-	-	-	-	148	35
A McMichael (1949/63)	-	-	402	8	25	0	4	0	-	-	-	-	431	8
J McNamee (1966/71)	-	-	115/2	8	6	0	7/1	0	1	0	-	-	129/3	8
J McNee (1894/95)	-	-	21	4	2	0	-	-	-	-	-	-	23	4
MA McNeil (1949/51)	-	-	9	0	2	0	-	-	-	-	-	-	11	0

Player	FAPL		League		FACup		LgeCup		Europe		Others		Totals	
	App	Goals	App	Goals	App	Goals	App	Goals	App	Goals	App	Goals	App	Goals
WP McPhillips (1930/38)	–	–	33	0	1	0	–	–	–	–	–	–	34	0
G McQuade (1939/45)	–	–	–	–	–	–	–	–	–	–	1	0	1	0
JK McTavish (1912/13)	–	–	34	6	5	1	–	–	–	–	–	–	39	7
TL McVay (1939/45)	–	–	–	–	–	–	–	–	–	–	–	–	1	0
P McWilliam (1902/11)	–	–	199	11	41	1	–	–	–	–	–	–	240	12
Maguire (/**)	–	–	3	0	–	–	–	–	–	–	–	–	3	0
MJ Mahoney (1975/78)	–	–	108	0	12	0	13	0	2	0	3	0	138	0
AE Maitland (1924/30)	–	–	156	0	7	0	–	–	–	–	–	–	163	0
L Makel (1990/92)	–	–	6/6	1	–	–	1	0	–	–	0/1	0	7/7	1
WGL Malcolm (1957/60)	–	–	1	0	–	–	–	–	–	–	–	–	1	0
P Manners (1977/79)	–	–	2	0	–	–	–	–	–	–	–	–	2	0
J Markie (1962/64)	–	–	2	0	–	–	–	–	–	–	–	–	2	0
G Marshall (1963/68)	–	–	177	0	6	0	4	0	–	–	–	–	187	0
TWJ Marshall (1958/62)	–	–	5	1	–	–	–	–	–	–	–	–	5	1
DW Martin (1977/78)	–	–	9/2	2	–	–	–	–	–	–	–	–	9/2	2
MP Martin (1978/83)	–	–	139/8	5	10	1	6	0	–	–	–	–	155/8	6
A Mathie (1993-)	0/15	3	–	–	1	0	–	–	–	–	–	–	1/15	3
G Mathison (1926/33)	–	–	20	0	2	0	–	–	–	–	–	–	22	0
*J Meek (1941)	–	–	–	–	–	–	–	–	–	–	2	2	2	2
GJ Megson (1984/86)	–	–	21/3	1	2	1	1/1	0	–	–	–	–	24/4	2
W Mellor (1914/20)	–	–	23	2	2	0	–	–	–	–	1	0	26	2
A Metcalf (1909/12)	–	–	12	2	–	–	–	–	–	–	–	–	12	2
JET Milburn (1943/57)	–	–	353	177	44	23	–	–	–	–	95	38	492	238
JN Milburn (1939/41)	–	–	–	–	–	–	–	–	–	–	1	0	1	0
J Miller (1890/94)	–	–	9	0	1	0	–	–	–	–	–	–	10	0

Player	FAPL App	FAPL Goals	League App	League Goals	FACup App	FACup Goals	LgeCup App	LgeCup Goals	Europe App	Europe Goals	Others App	Others Goals	Totals App	Totals Goals
W Miller (1895/97)	-	-	42	2	6	0	-	-	-	-	-	-	48	2
DJ Mills (+1982 & 1983/84)	-	-	33/6	9	-	-	0/2	0	-	-	-	-	33/8	9
W Milne (1894/95 & 1897)	-	-	6	-	-	-	-	-	-	-	-	-	6	-
Mirandinha (1987/90)	-	-	47/7	20	4/1	1	4	2	-	-	5/1	1	60/9	24
+** Mitchell (1991)	-	-	2	1	-	-	-	-	-	-	-	-	2	1
I Mitchell (1970/71)	-	-	2/1	1	1	-	-	-	0/1	0	-	-	3/2	1
K Mitchell (1975/81)	-	-	61/5	2	5	0	-	-	-	-	1	0	67/6	2
RC Mitchell (1949/61)	-	-	367	95	41	18	-	-	-	-	-	-	408	113
SA Mitchell (1953/63)	-	-	45	0	3	0	-	-	-	-	-	-	48	0
TM Mitchell (1920/26)	-	-	60	5	1	0	-	-	-	-	-	-	61	5
J Mitten (1958/61)	-	-	9	3	-	-	-	-	-	-	1	0	10	3
G Mole (1900)	-	-	-	-	1	-	-	-	-	-	-	-	1	-
R Moncur (1960/74)	-	-	293/3	3	18	1	10	0	22	4	15	2	358/3	10
AW Monkhouse (1953/56)	-	-	21	9	2	2	-	-	-	-	-	-	23	11
E Mooney (1919/27)	-	-	121	3	14	1	-	-	-	-	-	-	135	4
T Mooney (1936/44)	-	-	75	17	5	2	-	-	-	-	1	0	81	19
+P Moran (1991)	-	-	1	0	-	-	-	-	-	-	-	-	1	0
T Mordue (1925/26)	-	-	5	2	-	-	-	-	-	-	-	-	5	2
*SH Mortensen (1942)	-	-	-	-	-	-	-	-	-	-	5	2	5	2
G Moses (1939/46)	-	-	-	-	-	-	-	-	-	-	9	6	9	6
A Mowatt (1891/99 & 1900)	-	-	1	0	-	-	-	-	-	-	-	-	1	0
T Mulgrew (1952/54)	-	-	14	1	1	0	-	-	-	-	-	-	15	1
K Mulgrove (1977/80)	-	-	0/1	0	-	-	-	-	-	-	-	-	0/1	0
*J Mullen (1942)	-	-	-	-	-	-	-	-	-	-	15	4	15	4
JJ Murray (1932/36)	-	-	92	10	4	0	-	-	-	-	-	-	96	10

Player	FAPL		League		FACup		LgeCup		Europe		Others		Totals	
	App	Goals	App	Goals	App	Goals	App	Goals	App	Goals	App	Goals	App	Goals
A Mutch (1922/24)	-	-	36	0	7	0	-	-	-	-	-	-	43	0
J Myers (1939/45)	-	-	-	-	-	-	-	-	-	-	1	1	1	1
CRA Napier (1965/66)	-	-	8	0	-	-	-	-	-	-	-	-	8	0
I Nattrass (1970/79)	-	-	226/12	16	23	1	22	3	-	-	25/1	2	300/13	22
J Naylor (1930/32)	-	-	30	0	2	-	-	-	-	-	-	-	32	0
DF Neale (1959/63)	-	-	88	8	6	3	4	1	-	-	-	-	98	12
A Neilson (1991-)	10/4	0	20/2	1	-	-	2	0	-	-	5	0	37/6	1
J Nelson (1930/35)	-	-	146	0	13	0	-	-	-	-	-	-	159	0
A Nesbit (1985/87)	-	-	1/2	-	-	-	-	-	0/1	-	-	-	1/3	0
J Nesbitt (1955/59)	-	-	3	0	-	-	-	-	-	-	-	-	3	0
GW Nevin (1928/30)	-	-	6	0	-	-	-	-	-	-	-	-	6	0
L Nevins (1939/47)	-	-	-	-	-	-	-	-	-	-	33	5	33	5
TB Niblo (1898/1902 & 1907/08)	-	-	60	5	-	-	-	-	-	-	-	-	60	5
B Nicholson (1905/07)	-	-	1	0	-	-	-	-	-	-	-	-	1	0
GA Nicholson (1978/81)	-	-	7/5	0	1	0	3	0	-	-	-	-	11/5	0
*WE Nicholson (1942)	-	-	-	-	-	-	-	-	-	-	19	0	19	0
P Noble (1964/68)	-	-	22/3	7	-	-	-	-	-	-	-	-	22/3	7
GO Nulty (1974/78)	-	-	101	11	10	1	10	2	2	0	4	0	127	14
G Oates (1976/78)	-	-	26/9	2	-	-	3	1	-	-	4	0	33/9	3
LF O'Brien (1988/94)	4/2	0	127/18	19	10	1	9	1	2	0	9/2	1	161/24	22
PG O'Brien (1895/96)	-	-	9	2	2	0	-	-	-	-	-	-	11	2
LA O'Neil (1961/65)	-	-	1	0	-	-	-	-	-	-	-	-	1	0
TH O'Neil (1942/48)	-	-	-	-	-	-	-	-	-	-	1	0	1	0
MA O'Neil (1987/89)	-	-	36/12	15	3/2	1	2	0	-	-	4/1	1	45/15	17
R Orr (1901/08)	-	-	160	60	20	9	-	-	-	-	-	-	180	69

Player	FAPL		League		FACup		LgeCup		Europe		Others		Totals	
	App	Goals	App	Goals	App	Goals	App	Goals	App	Goals	App	Goals	App	Goals
*F Osborne (1940)	-	-	-	-	-	-	-	-	-	-	1	0	1	0
J Ostler (1896/1900)	-	-	67	3	7	0	-	-	-	-	4	0	78	3
M Owens (1975/78)	-	-	-	-	-	-	-	-	-	-	1	0	1	0
R Pailor (1914/15)	-	-	11	2	5	3	-	-	-	-	-	-	16	5
N Papavasiliou (1993-)	7	0	-	-	-	-	-	-	-	-	-	-	7	0
JB Parks (1936/40)	-	-	60	11	1	1	-	-	-	-	12	2	73	14
O Park (1924/31)	-	-	42	0	1	0	-	-	-	-	-	-	43	0
W Parker (1939/45)	-	-	-	-	-	-	-	-	-	-	1	0	1	0
*J Parr (1943)	-	-	-	-	-	-	-	-	-	-	1	0	1	0
A Parkinson (1978/79)	-	-	0/3	0	-	-	-	-	-	-	-	-	0/3	0
T Paterson (1950/52)	-	-	2	0	-	-	-	-	-	-	-	-	2	0
WAK Paterson (1954/58)	-	-	22	1	5	1	-	-	-	-	-	-	27	2
HD Paton (1921/22)	-	-	13	0	-	-	-	-	-	-	-	-	13	0
JT Patten (1892/94)	-	-	1	0	-	-	-	-	-	-	-	-	1	0
D Pattinson (1900/02)	-	-	1	1	-	-	-	-	-	-	-	-	1	1
LJ Payne (1988/89)	-	-	6/1	0	-	-	-	-	-	-	-	-	6/1	0
D Peacock (1994-)	9	0	-	-	-	-	-	-	-	-	-	-	9	0
G Peacock (1990/93)	-	-	102/3	35	6	2	6	5	-	-	3	4	117/3	46
W Pears (1936/41)	-	-	2	0	-	-	-	-	-	-	-	-	2	0
J Pearson (1978/80)	-	-	11	3	0/1	0	2	1	-	-	-	-	13/1	4
*SC Pearson (1941)	-	-	-	-	-	-	-	-	-	-	5	0	5	0
TU Pearson (1933/48)	-	-	212	46	16	6	-	-	-	-	51	10	279	62
JG Peart (1912/13)	-	-	17	6	-	-	-	-	-	-	-	-	17	6
JH Peddie (1897/1902)	-	-	125	73	10	5	-	-	-	-	1	0	136	78
WST Penman (1963/66)	-	-	62/1	18	2	0	-	-	-	-	-	-	64/1	18

Player	FAPL App	FAPL Goals	League App	League Goals	FACup App	FACup Goals	LgeCup App	LgeCup Goals	Europe App	Europe Goals	Others App	Others Goals	Totals App	Totals Goals
*S Peppitt (1941)											2	0	2	0
TW Philipson (1919/21)			14	4	1	0							15	4
F Pingel (1989)			13/1	1									13/1	1
L Porter (1944/49)											16	2	16	2
A Price (1940/45)											43	1	43	1
KG Prior (1952/54 & 1956/57)			10	3									10	3
R Pudan (1906/09)			24	0	6	0							30	0
K Pugh (1977/82)			0/1	0									0/1	0
WH Punton (1954/58)			23	1	2	0							25	1
GW Pyke (1913/22)			13	3									13	3
C Quinn (1893/96)			42/4	12	2	0					1	3	46/4	15
M Quinn (1989/92)			92/1	52	7	4	6/2	2			7/1	3	112/4	61
WH Rafferty (1979/80)			34/5	6	1	0	2	2					37/5	8
JE Raine (1905/06)			4	0									4	0
A Rainnie (1919/20)			1	0									1	0
Alex Ramsay (1919/21)			34	2	3	0					5	3	42	5
And. Ramsay (1890/93)			1	0									1	0
CE Randall (1908/11)			18	6	1	0							19	6
R Ranson (1988/92)			78/5	1	10	0	4	0			4/1	0	96/6	1
J Reay (1892/93)					1	1							1	1
WS Redhead (1954/59)			1	0									1	0
F Reed (1919)											2	0	2	0
AD Reed (1971/73)			15/8	0	0/2	0					1	0	16/10	0
O Reid (1894/96)			2	0									2	0
J Reid (1899/1900)			4	1									4	1

Player	FAPL		League		FACup		LgeCup		Europe		Others		Totals	
	App	Goals	App	Goals	App	Goals	App	Goals	App	Goals	App	Goals	App	Goals
GG Reilly (1985)	-	-	31	10	-	-	2	0	-	-	-	-	33	10
T Rendell (1894/95)	-	-	23	0	2	2	-	-	-	-	-	-	25	2
E Richardson (1922/24)	-	-	2	0	-	-	-	-	-	-	-	-	2	0
J Richardson (1929/45)	-	-	208	1	15	0	-	-	-	-	114	0	337	1
JR Richardson (1928/34 & 1937/38)	-	-	150	46	13	7	-	-	-	-	-	-	163	53
O Richardson (1902/03)	-	-	1	0	-	-	-	-	-	-	-	-	1	0
J Ridley (1907/11)	-	-	2	0	-	-	-	-	-	-	-	-	2	0
RJ Roberts (1901/04)	-	-	51	17	4	0	-	-	-	-	-	-	55	17
J Robertson (1988)	-	-	7/5	0	-	-	0/2	0	-	-	2	0	9/7	0
D Robinson (1989/91)	-	-	0/8	0	0/1	1	0/1	0	-	-	-	-	0/10	1
*JA Robinson (1941)	-	-	-	-	-	-	-	-	-	-	1	0	1	0
JW Robinson (1931)	-	-	1	0	-	-	-	-	-	-	-	-	1	0
M Robinson (1993-)	11/4	0	2/7	0	1	0	-	-	-	-	-	-	14/11	0
Ray Robinson (1919/20)	-	-	27	4	2	0	-	-	-	-	-	-	29	4
Rob. Robinson (1952/54)	-	-	5	0	-	-	-	-	-	-	-	-	5	0
S Robinson (1975/80)	-	-	11/1	2	2	1	-	-	-	-	-	-	13/1	3
EO Robledo (1949/53)	-	-	37	0	8	0	-	-	-	-	-	-	45	0
GO Robledo (1949/53)	-	-	146	82	18	9	-	-	-	-	-	-	164	91
BS Robson (1962/71)	-	-	205/1	82	10	4	4	2	24	9	-	-	243/1	97
K Robson (1971/74)	-	-	14	3	-	-	1	2	-	-	3	1	18	6
R Robson (1939/45)	-	-	-	-	-	-	-	-	-	-	5	1	5	1
TH Robson (1966/68)	-	-	46/2	11	1	0	1	0	-	-	-	-	48/2	11
D Roche (1988/93)	-	-	23/9	0	1	0	2	0	-	-	1/2	0	27/11	0
GV Roeder (1983/88)	-	-	193	8	11	1	11	1	-	-	4	0	219	10
E Rogers (1936/69)	-	-	56	10	2	0	-	-	-	-	-	-	58	10

Player	FAPL App	FAPL Goals	League App	League Goals	FACup App	FACup Goals	LgeCup App	LgeCup Goals	Europe App	Europe Goals	Others App	Others Goals	Totals App	Totals Goals
J Rogers (1898/1900)			54	10	3	1							57	11
T Rogers (1892/94)			22	0	2	0							24	0
EW Ross (1967/69)			2	0			2	0					4	0
TS Rowlandson (1905/07)			1	0									1	0
R Roxburgh (1920/24)			24	0									24	0
G Rushton (1939/45)											1	0	1	0
SR Russell (1920/26)			28	0	3	0							31	0
T Russell (1934/37)			7	0									7	0
J Rutherford (1902/13)			290	78	44	14							334	92
R Rutherford (1939/45)											19	2	19	2
RE Rutherford (1905/06)			1	0									1	0
TV Rutherford (1939/45)											25	0	25	0
JB Ryan (1983/84)			28	1	1	0	2	0					31	1
I Ryder (1893/94)			1	0									1	0
J Ryder (1892/96)			2	0									2	0
RD Sales (1942/47)											42	0	42	0
W Salthouse (1939/45)											1	0	1	0
KG Sansom (1988/89)			20	0			4	0					24	0
W Saunders (1981/85)			79	1	6	0	8	0					93	1
AJ Scanlon (1960/62)			22	5	4	1	1	0					27	6
R Scarr (1939/45)											7	0	7	0
*FH Scott (1944)											6	1	6	1
G Scott (1929/30)			3	1	3	0							6	1
J Scott (1967/70)			7	2	3	0							10	2
JA Scott (1976/80)			70/4	6	4/1	1	14/1	5			4	0	92/6	12
			9/1	0									9/1	0

Player	FAPL App	FAPL Goals	League App	League Goals	FACup App	FACup Goals	LgeCup App	LgeCup Goals	Europe App	Europe Goals	Others App	Others Goals	Totals App	Totals Goals
JG Scott (1910/13)			8	1									8	1
KW Scott (1984/94)	18	0	209	8	6/1	1	18	0			12/2	2	263/3	4
ME Scott (1955/61)			25	2	1	0							26	2
MM Scott (1900/01)			5	0									5	0
W Scott (1938/46)			6	2	3	0					10	4	19	6
WH Scott (1923/26)			4	0									4	0
J Scoular (1953/61)			247	6	24	0							271	6
S Sellars (1992-)	29/1	4	13	2	3	0	1/1	1			3	0	46/2	7
C Seymour (1939/43)													3	0
GS Seymour (1920/29)			242	73	24	11							266	84
LF Shackleton (1946/48)			57	26	7	3							64	29
R Shankley (1934/35)			6	0									6	0
K Sheedy (1992/93)	36/1	4			2/1	1	4	1			4	1	46/2	7
A Shepherd (1908/14)			104	76	19	16							123	92
J Shiel (1936/38)			1	0									1	0
RT Shinton (1980/82)			41/1	10	3/1	0	3	0					47/2	10
*JD Short (1940)											43	35	43	35
A Shoulder (1978/82)			99/8	35	3/1	1	4/2	2					106/11	38
A Sibley (1947/50)			31	6	1	0							32	6
W Simm (1893/94)			1	0									1	0
RC Simpson (1951/60)			262	0	33	0							295	0
TG Simpson (1939/45)											4	0	4	0
** Simpson (1990)			1/4	0									1/4	0
JEW Sinclair (1967/69)			42/1	6	1/1	0	1	1	4/2	1			48/4	8
TS Sinclair (1907/12)			8	0									8	0

211

Player	FAPL		League		FACup		LgeCup		Europe		Others		Totals	
	App	Goals	App	Goals	App	Goals	App	Goals	App	Goals	App	Goals	App	Goals
J Sloan (1945/46)											7	0	7	0
** Sloan (1990/91)			11/5	1	1	0					1	0	13/5	1
A Smailes (1919/22)			73	30	4	0							77	30
*F Smallwood (1942)											2	0	2	0
R Smellie (1896/97)			26	15	1	0							27	15
*AH Smirk (1940)											1	0	1	0
A Smith (1975/79)			1/2	0							1	0	2/2	0
D Smith (1935/36)			1	0							1	0	2	0
Jason SMith (1969/76)			124/5	13	14/1	0	9/1	0	5	0	18/2	3	170/9	16
Jack Smith (1934/38)			104	69	8	4							112	73
John Smith (1887/89 & 1894/96)			25	10	2	0							27	10
S Smith (1918/19)											1	0	1	0
T Smith (1941/52)			8	0	2	0					145	0	155	0
W Smith (1898/99)			15	4							4	2	19	6
*F Soo (1941)											2	0	2	0
J Sorley (1891/93)			1	1	1	0							2	1
J Soulsby (1914/15)			1	0									1	0
J Soye (1906/09)			7	2									7	2
FB Speedie (1906/08)			52	13	7	1							59	14
CW Spencer (1921/28)			161	1	14	0							175	1
S Spike (1939/45)											3	0	3	0
*JO Spuhler (1943)											3	0	3	0
J Spink (1913/19)			20	0	4	0							24	0
P Srnicek (1990-)	23	0	52	0	5	0	2	0			6	0	88	0
RW Starling (1930/32)			51	8	2	0							53	8

Player	FAPL App	FAPL Goals	League App	League Goals	FACup App	FACup Goals	LgeCup App	LgeCup Goals	Europe App	Europe Goals	Others App	Others Goals	Totals App	Totals Goals
Stell (1939/45)	-	-	-	-	-	-	-	-	-	-	1	0	1	0
H Stenhouse (1902/05)	-	-	6	0	-	-	-	-	-	-	-	-	6	0
P Stephenson (1984/88)	-	-	58/3	1	2	0	3/1	0	-	-	3/1	0	66/5	1
J Stevenson (1898/1900)	-	-	33	12	4	1	-	-	-	-	-	-	37	13
*AV Stewart (1943)	-	-	-	-	-	-	-	-	-	-	2	0	2	0
I Stewart (1985/87)	-	-	34/8	3	2/1	0	4/1	0	-	-	-	-	40/10	3
J Stewart (1908/13)	-	-	121	49	17	4	-	-	-	-	-	-	138	53
T Stewart (1896/98)	-	-	17	0	1	0	-	-	-	-	-	-	18	0
WG Stewart (1901/03)	-	-	47	4	6	1	-	-	-	-	-	-	53	5
M Stimson (1989/**)	-	-	59/4	1	4	0	5	0	-	-	5	0	73/4	1
GC Stobart (1946/49)	-	-	66	21	6	1	-	-	-	-	-	-	72	22
R Stokoe (1947/61)	-	-	261	4	26	1	-	-	-	-	-	-	287	5
J Stott (1895/99)	-	-	113	9	14	2	-	-	-	-	4	0	131	11
A Stubbins (1937/46)	-	-	27	5	3	1	-	-	-	-	188	231	218	237
A Suddick (1961/66)	-	-	144	41	4	1	-	-	-	-	-	-	152	43
C Suggett (1978/81)	-	-	20/3	0	-	-	-	-	-	-	-	-	21/3	0
*J Surtees (1941)	-	-	-	-	-	-	-	-	-	-	2	2	2	2
CS Swan (1919/24)	-	-	4	0	-	-	-	-	-	-	-	-	4	0
P Sweeney (1989/90)	-	-	28/8	0	3	0	2/1	0	-	-	2	0	35/9	0
TA Swinburne (1934/47)	-	-	77	0	7	0	-	-	-	-	51	0	135	0
A Tait (1952/60)	-	-	32	8	2	2	-	-	-	-	-	-	34	10
NH Tapken (1933/38 & *1942)	-	-	106	0	7	0	-	-	-	-	9	0	122	0
IH Tait (1923/27)	-	-	4	0	-	-	-	-	-	-	-	-	4	0
A Taylor (1925/26)	-	-	1	0	-	-	-	-	-	-	-	-	1	0
C Taylor (1963/64)	-	-	33	7	-	-	3	0	-	-	-	-	36	7

Player	FAPL App	FAPL Goals	League App	League Goals	FACup App	FACup Goals	LgeCup App	LgeCup Goals	Europe App	Europe Goals	Others App	Others Goals	Totals App	Totals Goals
E Taylor (1942/51)	-	-	107	19	10	2	-	-	-	-	26	7	143	28
JE Taylor (1939/45)	-	-	-	-	1	-	-	-	-	-	1	2	2	2
JH Taylor (1952/60)	-	-	28	5	1	0	-	-	-	-	-	-	29	5
*PH Taylor (1941)	-	-	-	-	-	-	-	-	-	-	7	0	7	0
RB Templeton (1903/04)	-	-	51	4	1	1	-	-	-	-	-	-	52	5
JW Thain (1921/22)	-	-	1	0	-	-	-	-	-	-	-	-	1	0
CA Theaker (1938/47)	-	-	13	0	3	0	-	-	-	-	65	0	81	0
AM Thomas (1986/88)	-	-	24/7	6	3	1	1	0	-	-	1	2	29/7	9
BE Thomas (1962/64)	-	-	73	48	2	1	3	1	-	-	-	-	78	50
JW Thomas (1911/12)	-	-	1	0	-	-	-	-	-	-	-	-	1	0
MR Thomas (1983/88)	-	-	118	0	5	0	7	0	-	-	1	0	131	0
A Thompson (**–93)	-	-	13/3	-	1	0	-	-	-	-	3	0	17/3	0
F Thompson (1923/25)	-	-	2	-	-	-	-	-	-	-	-	-	2	-
G Thompson (1903/05)	-	-	1	0	1	0	-	-	-	-	-	-	2	0
H Thompson (1908/10)	-	-	2	0	-	-	-	-	-	-	-	-	2	0
JH Thompson (1950/57)	-	-	8	0	-	-	-	-	-	-	-	-	8	0
M Thompson (1939/45)	-	-	-	-	-	-	-	-	-	-	2	0	2	0
T Thompson (1946/50)	-	-	20	6	-	-	-	-	-	-	-	-	20	6
W Thompson (1957/67)	-	-	79/1	1	6	0	3	0	-	-	-	-	88/1	1
WK Thompson (1892/97)	-	-	80	33	11	7	-	-	-	-	-	-	91	40
WN Thompson (1939/45)	-	-	-	-	-	-	-	-	-	-	1	0	1	0
JA Thomson (1968/71)	-	-	4/1	0	-	-	-	-	-	-	-	-	4/1	0
RW Thomson (1928/34)	-	-	73	0	7	0	-	-	-	-	-	-	80	0
A Thorn (1988/89)	-	-	36	2	4	1	-	-	-	-	3	0	43	3
J Tildesley (1903/06)	-	-	21	0	1	0	-	-	-	-	-	-	22	0

Player	FAPL App	FAPL Goals	League App	League Goals	FACup App	FACup Goals	LgeCup App	LgeCup Goals	Europe App	Europe Goals	Others App	Others Goals	Totals App	Totals Goals
B Tinnion (1985/89)			30/2	2			5	0			3/1	0	38/3	2
K Todd (1981/82)			5/2	3	2/1	0	1	0					8/3	3
J Trewick (1980/84)			76/2	8	7	0	2	0					85/2	8
J Tudor (1971/76)			161/3	53	15	4	8	1			32/1	15	216/4	73
G Tulthorpe (1918/19)											6	1	6	1
T Tuohy (1960/63)			38	9	1	0	3	0					42	9
AD Turner (1903/04)			13	1									13	1
DJ Turner (1960/63)			2	0			1	0					3	0
T Urwin (1924/30)			188	23	12	1							200	24
I Varadi (1981/83)			81	39	5	2	4	1					90	42
TH Varty (1939/45)											1	0	1	0
CCM Veitch (1899/1915)			276	43	45	6							321	49
B Venison (1992-)	38/1	0	44	0	6	0	7	0			3	0	98/1	0
CR Waddle (1980/85)			169/1	46	12	4	9	2					190/1	52
HW Wake (1919/23)			3	0	1	0							4	0
L Walker (1963/64)			1	0			1	0					2	0
NS Walker (1977/82)			65/5	3	3	0	1	0					69/5	3
TJ Walker (1941/54)			184	35	20	3					29	2	233	40
** Walker (**/**)			2	0							1	0	3	0
G Wall (1919)											1	0	1	0
J Wallace (1890/95)			42	19	3	2							45	21
*JL Wallace (1942)											1	0	1	0
*K Walshaw (1941)											4	0	4	0
T Warburton (1895/96)			3	0									3	0
E Ward (1920/22)			21	5	4	0							25	5

Player	FAPL		League		FACup		LgeCup		Europe		Others		Totals	
	App	Goals	App	Goals	App	Goals	App	Goals	App	Goals	App	Goals	App	Goals
W A Ward (1894/96)	-	-	18	0	3	0	-	-	-	-	-	-	21	0
W Wardrope (1895/1900)	-	-	127	43	14	7	-	-	-	-	4	1	145	51
H Ware (1935/37)	-	-	44	9	5	0	-	-	-	-	-	-	49	9
G Watkin (1962/63)	-	-	1	0	-	-	-	-	-	-	-	-	1	0
J Watson (1902/03)	-	-	3	0	-	-	-	-	-	-	-	-	3	0
John Watson (1990/93)	-	-	0/1	0	-	-	-	-	-	-	0/1	0	0/2	0
*JT Watson (1941)	-	-	-	-	-	-	-	-	-	-	1	0	1	0
S Watson (1990-)	30/3	2	46/8	1	7/1	0	3	0	-	-	3/1	0	89/13	3
*J Watters (1941)	-	-	-	-	-	-	-	-	-	-	2	1	2	1
C Watts (1896/1906)	-	-	89	0	8	0	-	-	-	-	4	0	101	0
K Waugh (1952/56)	-	-	7	0	-	-	-	-	-	-	-	-	7	0
R Waugh (1908/12)	-	-	11	1	-	-	-	-	-	-	-	-	11	1
C Wayman (1941/47)	-	-	47	32	6	4	-	-	-	-	71	35	124	71
S Weaver (1929/36)	-	-	204	41	25	2	-	-	-	-	-	-	229	43
*RW Westwood (1939)	-	-	-	-	-	-	-	-	-	-	1	3	1	3
K Wharton (1979/89)	-	-	268/22	26	22	0	13/2	1	-	-	8	0	311/24	27
J White (1896/98)	-	-	48	1	5	0	-	-	-	-	-	-	53	1
LR White (1953/62)	-	-	244	142	22	11	3	0	-	-	-	-	269	153
R Whitehead (1954/62)	-	-	20	0	-	-	-	-	-	-	-	-	20	0
W Whitehurst (1985/86)	-	-	28	7	1	0	1/1	0	-	-	-	-	30/1	7
A Whitson (1905/19)	-	-	124	0	21	0	-	-	-	-	-	-	145	0
E Whittle (1939/45)	-	-	-	-	-	-	-	-	-	-	1	0	1	0
D Whitton (1892/93)	-	-	-	-	1	0	-	-	-	-	-	-	1	0
Jack Wilkinson (1930/32)	-	-	30	7	2	0	-	-	-	-	-	-	32	7
John Wilkinson (1927/29)	-	-	27	11	-	-	-	-	-	-	-	-	27	11

Player	FAPL		League		FACup		LgeCup		Europe		Others		Totals	
	App	Goals	App	Goals	App	Goals	App	Goals	App	Goals	App	Goals	App	Goals
R Williams (1933/35)	-	-	35	14	1	0	-	-	-	-	-	-	36	14
DL Willis (1907/13)	-	-	95	3	12	1	-	-	-	-	-	-	107	4
R Willis (1893/95)	-	-	34	19	2	0	-	-	-	-	-	-	36	19
J Willitts (1939/45)	-	-	-	-	-	-	-	-	-	-	1	0	1	0
T Wills (1903/06)	-	-	18	0	1	0	-	-	-	-	-	-	19	0
CA Wilson (1958/59)	-	-	1	0	-	-	-	-	-	-	-	-	1	0
GW Wilson (1907/19)	-	-	176	25	41	8	-	-	-	-	-	-	217	33
J Wilson (1959/62)	-	-	12	2	-	-	1	0	-	-	-	-	13	2
JA Wilson (1933/36)	-	-	28	5	2	0	-	-	-	-	-	-	30	5
JH Wilson (1912/14)	-	-	3	0	1	0	-	-	-	-	-	-	4	0
JT Wilson (1919/21)	-	-	7	2	-	-	-	-	-	-	2	1	9	3
JW Wilson (1927/30)	-	-	1	0	-	-	-	-	-	-	-	-	1	0
W Wilson (1925/29)	-	-	127	0	7	0	-	-	-	-	-	-	134	0
W Wilson (1900/03)	-	-	4	0	-	-	-	-	-	-	-	-	4	0
WA Wilson (1918/19)	-	-	-	-	-	-	-	-	-	-	2	0	2	0
WS Wilson (1960/62)	-	-	-	-	-	-	1	0	-	-	1	0	2	0
** Wilson (1992)	-	-	2	0	-	-	-	-	-	-	-	-	2	0
G Winstanley (1964/59)	-	-	5/2	0	1	0	-	-	1	0	-	-	7/2	0
C Withe (1980/83)	-	-	2	0	-	-	-	-	-	-	-	-	2	0
P Withe (1978/80)	-	-	76	25	4	2	3	0	-	-	-	-	83	27
EE Wood (1928/30)	-	-	9	0	-	-	-	-	-	-	-	-	9	0
GA Wood (1939/48)	-	-	-	-	-	-	-	-	-	-	7	0	7	0
J Woodburn (1938/48)	-	-	44	4	3	0	1	0	-	-	49	4	96	8
CMP Woods (1959/52)	-	-	26	7	3	3	1	0	-	-	-	-	30	10
H Woods (1922/23)	-	-	14	2	2	0	-	-	-	-	-	-	16	2

Player	FAPL App	FAPL Goals	League App	League Goals	FACup App	FACup Goals	LgeCup App	LgeCup Goals	Europe App	Europe Goals	Others App	Others Goals	Totals App	Totals Goals
PB Woods (1939/45)	-	-	-	-	-	-	-	-	-	-	16	0	16	0
AJ Woolard (1952/56)	-	-	8	0	2	0	-	-	-	-	-	-	10	0
C Woollett (1942/46)	-	-	-	-	-	-	-	-	-	-	75	13	75	13
BG Wright (1956/63)	-	-	45	1	1	0	1	0	-	-	-	-	47	1
JD Wright (1938/48)	-	-	72	1	10	0	-	-	-	-	24	0	106	1
TJ Wright (1988/93)	0/1	0	70	3	4	0	6	0	-	-	1	0	81/1	3
WJ Wright (1958/59)	-	-	5	3	-	-	-	-	-	-	-	-	5	3
J Wrightson (1986/87)	-	-	3/1	0	-	-	-	-	-	-	-	-	3/1	0
J Yeats (1940/45)	-	-	-	-	-	-	-	-	-	-	2	0	2	0
D Young (1964/73)	-	-	41/2	2	-	-	4	0	5/1	0	2/1	0	52/4	2

1886/87 *as Newcastle West End*

	v Sunderland	(a)	1-2	
	(match replayed after being declared void)			
Replay	v Sunderland	(h)	1-0	Angus
	v Gainsborough Town	(h)	2-6	Aitken, Dobson

1887/88

	v Redcar	(h)	5-1	Angus 2, Barker, McDonald, Nicholson
	v Sunderland	(a)	1-3	McColl

1888/89

	v Bishop Auckland	(h)	7-2	Nicholson 3, Kelso, McColl, McDonald, AN Other
	v Sunderland Albion	(h)	3-5	
	(match replayed after being declared void)			
Replay	v Sunderland Albion	(h)	1-2	Nicholson

1889/90

	v Port Clarence	(h)	9-1	Not Known
	v Birtley	(a)	2-1	Not Known
	v South Bank	(h)	5-2	Not Known
	v Stockton	(a)	1-0	Not Known
	v Grimsby Town	(h)	1-2	McColl

1890/91

	v Elswick Rangers	(a)	5-2	Not Known
	v Southwick	(h)	8-1	Not Known
	v Sunderland Albion	(h)	0-3	

1891/92

	v Newcastle East End	(h)	0-3	

1887/88 *as Newcastle East End*

	v South Bank	(a)	2-3	W. Muir 2

1888/89

	v Port Clarence	(h)	3-1	Raylstone, Muir, White
	v Stockton	(h)	2-1	Hoban, AN Other
	v Sunderland	(a)	0-2	

1889/90

	v Shankhouse BW	(h)	4-0	Not Known
	v St Augustine's	(a)	1-2	Not Known

1890/91

	v Bishop Auckland Town	(a)	2-1	Not Known
	v Shankhouse BW	(h)	5-0	Not Known
	v Sunderland Albion	(h)	2-2	Not Known
	v Sunderland Albion	(h)	0-2	

1891/92

	v Tow Law	(a)	5-1	Not Known
	v Newcastle West End	(a)	3-0	Not Known
	v Shankhouse BW	(h)	3-2	Not Known
	v Bishop Auckland Town	(h)	7-0	Not Known
	v Nottingham Forest	(a)	1-2	Not Known

1892/93 *as Newcastle East End/Newcastle United*

	v Middlesbrough	(h)	2-3	Reay, Thompson

1893/4 *as Newcastle United*

1st Round	v Sheffield United	(h)	2-0	Wallace 2
2nd Round	v Bolton Wanderers	(h)	1-2	Crate

1894/5

1st Round	v Burnley	(h)	2-1	Rendell 2
2nd Round	v Aston Villa	(a)	1-7	Thompson

1895/6

Qualifying	v Leadgate Exiles	(a)	Walk Over	
	v West Hartlepool NER	(a)	8-0	Logan 2, Thompson, Collins 2, Stott, Graham, o.g.
	v Middlesbrough	(h)	4-1	Wardrope 2, McKay, AN Other
	v Rendal	(h)	5-0	Wardrope, Aitken 2, Logan, Thompson
	v Tow Law Town	(h)	4-0	Wardrope, Thompson, Lennox, Stott
1st Round	v Chesterfield	(a)	4-0	Wardrope 2, Aitken, Thompson
2nd Round	v Bury	(h)	1-3	Thompson

1896/7

1st Round	v Aston Villa	(a)	0-5	

1897/8

Qualifying	*v* Willington A	(h)	6-0	Aitken 4, Campbell, Jackson
	v Stockton	(a)	4-1	Campbell, Harvey, Ghee, Jackson
	v Middlesbrough	(a)	2-0	Wardrope, Harvey
1st Round	*v* Preston North End	(a)	2-1	Peddie 2
2nd Round	*v* Southampton St Mary's	(a)	0-1	

1898/9

1st Round	*v* Glossop	(a)	1-0	Peddie
2nd Round	*v* Liverpool	(a)	1-3	Peddie

1899/00

1st Round	*v* Reading	(h)	2-1	Stevenson, Rogers
2nd Round	*v* Southampton	(a)	1-4	Peddie

1900/01

1st Round	*v* Middlesbrough	(a)	1-3	Aitken

1901/02

1st Round	*v* Woolwich Arsenal	(a)	2-0	Veitch, A. Gardner
2nd Round	*v* Sunderland	(h)	1-0	Orr
3rd Round	*v* Sheffield United	(h)	1-1	Stewart
Replay	*v* Sheffield United	(a)	1-2	McColl

1902/03

1st Round	*v* Grimsby Town	(a)	1-2	McColl

1903/04

1st Round	*v* Bury	(a)	1-2	Templeton

1904/05

1st Round	*v* Plymouth Argyle	(h)	1-1	Gosnell
Replay	*v* Plymouth Argyle	(a)	1-1	Gosnell
2nd Replay	*v* Plymouth Argyle	(n)	2-0	Orr 2 (1 pen)
2nd Round	*v* Tottenham Hotspur	(a)	1-1	Howie
Replay	*v* Tottenham Hotspur	(h)	4-0	Orr 2, Appleyard, Howie
3rd Round	*v* Bolton Wanderers	(a)	2-0	Appleyard, Howie
Semi-Final	*v* Sheffield Wednesday	(n)	1-0	Howie
Final	*v* Aston Villa	(n)	0-2	

1905/06

1st Round	*v* Grimsby	(h*)	6-0	Gosnell, Orr 2, Appleyard 2, J Rutherford
2nd Round	*v* Derby County	(a)	0-0	

Replay	v Derby County	(h)	2-1	Appleyard, J. Rutherford
3rd Round	v Blackpool	(h)	5-0	Orr 2, Appleyard, Gardner, o.g.
4th Round	v Birmingham	(a)	2-2	Veitch 2 (1 pen)
Replay	v Birmingham	(h)	3-0	Appleyard 2, Howie
Semi-Final	v Woolwich Arsenal	(n)	2-0	Veitch, Howie
Final	v Everton	(n)	0-1	

Grimsby drawn at home, but game played at Newcastle

1906/07

| 1st Round | v Crystal Palace | (h) | 0-1 | |

1907/08

1st Round	v Nottingham Forest	(h)	2-0	Appleyard, Rutherford
2nd Round	v West Ham United	(h)	2-0	Appleyard 2
3rd Round	v Liverpool	(h)	3-1	Speedie, Appleyard, Rutherford
4th Round	v Grimsby Town	(h)	5-1	Appleyard 3, Gardner, o.g.
Semi-Final	v Fulham	(n)	6-0	Appleyard, Gardner, Howie 2, Rutherford 2
Final	Wolverhampton Wand.	(n)	1-3	Howie

1908/09

1st Round	v Clapton Orient	(h)	5-0	Anderson, Shepherd, Wilson 3
2nd Round	v Blackpool	(h)	2-1	Howie, Rutherford
3rd Round	v West Ham United	(a)	0-0	
Replay	v West Ham United	(h)	2-1	Anderson, Shepherd (pen)
4th Round	v Sunderland	(h)	2-2	Rutherford, Wilson
Replay	v Sunderland	(a)	3-0	Shepherd 2, Wilson
Semi-Final	v Manchester United	(n)	0-1	

1909/10

1st Round	v Stoke	(a)	1-1	Howie
Replay	v Stoke	(h)	2-1	Higgins, Howie
2nd Round	v Fulham	(h)	4-0	Higgins 2, Rutherford, McCracken (pen)
3rd Round	v Blackburn Rovers	(h)	3-1	Higgins, Howie, Rutherford
4th Round	v Leicester F	(h)	3-0	Wilson, Shepherd, Howie

Semi-Final	v Swindon Town	(n)	2-0	Stewart, Rutherford
Final	v Barnsley	(n)	1-1	Rutherford
Replay	v Barnsley	(n)	2-0	Shepherd 2 (1 pen)

1910/11

1st Round	v Bury	(h)	6-1	Shepherd 3, Stewart, Duncan, McWilliam
2nd Round	v Northampton Town	(h)	1-1	Higgins
Replay	v Northampton Town	(h*)	1-0	Shepherd (pen)

Scheduled for Northampton, but played at Newcastle

3rd Round	v Hull City	(h)	3-2	Shepherd 2, Veitch
4th Round	v Derby County	(h)	4-0	Shepherd, Stewart, Rutherford, Willis
Semi-Final	v Chelsea	(n)	3-0	Wilson, Shepherd, Stewart
Final	v Bradford City	(n)	0-0	
Replay	v Bradford City	(n)	0-1	

1911/12

| 1st Round | v Derby County | (a) | 0-3 | |

1912/13

1st Round	v Bradford City	(h)	1-0	G. Wilson
2nd Round	v Hull City	(a)	0-0	
Replay	v Hull City	(h)	3-0	Hibbert, Rutherford, Hudspeth (pen)
3rd Round	v Liverpool	(a)	1-1	Shepherd
Replay	v Liverpool	(h)	1-0	Hudspeth (pen)
4th Round	v Sunderland	(a)	0-0	
Replay	v Sunderland	(h)	2-2	McTavish, Veitch
2nd Replay	v Sunderland	(h)	0-3	

1913/14

| 1st Round | v Sheffield United | (h) | 0-5 | |

1914/15

1st Round	v West Ham United	(a)	2-2	Goodwill 2
Replay	v West Ham United	(h)	3-2	Pailor 2, Hibbert
2nd Round	v Swansea Town	(h)	1-1	McCracken (pen)
Replay	v Swansea Town	(a)	2-0	King, Pailor
3rd Round	v Sheffield Wednesday	(a)	2-1	King, Hibbert
4th Round	v Chelsea	(a)	1-1	Goddwill
Replay	v Chelsea	(h)	0-1	

1919/20

| 1st Round | v Crystal Palace | (h) | 2-0 | Dixon, Hall |
| 2nd Round | v Huddersfield Town | (h) | 0-1 | |

1920/21

1st Round	v Nottingham Forest	(h*)	1-1	Harris
Replay	v Nottingham Forest	(h)	2-0	Seymour, Harris
2nd Round	v Liverpool	(h)	1-0	Harris
3rd Round	v Everton	(a)	0-3	

1921/22

1st Round	v Newport County	(h)	6-0	McDonald 2, Harris, Dixon 2, Mooney
2nd Round	v Preston North End	(a)	1-3	Seymour

1922/23

1st Round	v Southampton	(h)	0-0	
Replay	v Southampton	(a)	1-3	Harris

1923/24

1st Round	v Portsmouth	(a)	4-2	Seymour, Harris, J. Low, Gibson
2nd Round	v Derby County	(a)	2-2	McDonald 2
Replay	v Derby County	(h)	2-2	Harris, Cowan
2nd Replay	v Derby County	(n)	2-2	Seymour, Hudspeth (pen)
3rd Replay	v Derby County	(h)	5-3	Seymour, Harris 3, Cowan
3rd Round	v Watford	(a)	1-0	Seymour
4th Round	v Liverpool	(h)	1-0	McDonald
Semi-Final	v Manchester City	(n)	2-0	Harris 2
Final	v Aston Villa	(n)	2-0	Seymour, Harris

1924/25

1st Round	v Hartlepool United	(h)	4-1	Cowan, Harris, McDonald, McKenzie
2nd Round	v Leicester City	(h)	2-2	McDonald (pen), Cowan
Replay	v Leicester City	(a)	0-1	

1925/26

3rd Round	v Aberdare A	(h)	4-1	Cowan, Gallacher 2, Gibson
4th Round	v Cardiff City	(a)	2-0	Seymour 2
5th Round	v Clapton Orient	(a)	0-2	

1926/27

3rd Round	v Notts. County	(h)	8-1	Gallacher 3, McDonald 3, Seymour, Urwin
4th Round	v Corinthians	(a)	3-1	McDonald 2, McKay
5th Round	v Southampton	(a)	1-2	McDonald (pen)

1927/28

3rd Round	v Blackburn Rovers	(a)	1-4	Seymour

1928/29

3rd Round	v Swindon Town	(a)	0-2	

1929/30

3rd Round	v York City	(h)	1-1	Gallacher
Replay	v York City	(a)	2-1	Gallacher, Hutchinson
4th Round	v Clapton Orient	(h)	3-1	J.R. Richardson 3
5th Round	v Brighton & Hove Albion	(h)	3-0	Gallacher 3
6th Round	v Hull City	(h)	1-1	Lang
Replay	v Hull City	(a)	0-1	

1930/31

3rd Round	v Nottingham Forest	(h)	4-0	Bedford, Hutchinson 3
4th Round	v Leeds United	(a)	1-4	Hutchinson (pen)

1931/32

3rd Round	v Blackpool	(a)	1-1	Lang
Replay	v Blackpool	(h)	1-0	Boyd
4th Round	v Southport	(h)	1-1	Boyd
Replay	v Southport	(a)	1-1	Boyd
2nd Replay	v Southport	(n)	9-0	Lang, McMenemy, Cape 2, Weaver, Boyd, J.R. Richardson 3
5th Round	v Leicester City	(h)	3-1	Allen, Lang, Weaver
6th Round	v Watford	(h)	5-0	Allen 3, Boyd, J.R. Richardson
Semi-Final	v Chelsea	(n)	2-1	Allen, Lang
Final	v Arsenal	(n)	2-1	Allen 2

1932/33

3rd Round	v Leeds United	(h)	0-3	

1933/34

3rd Round	v Wolverhampton Wanderers	(a)	0-1	

1934/35

3rd Round	v Hull City	(a)	5-1	Bott 2, Cairns, Pearson, o.g.
4th Round	v Tottenham Hotspur	(**)	0-2	

1935/36

3rd Round	v Walsall	(a)	2-0	Connelly, J. Smith
4th Round	v Sheffield Wednesday	(a)	1-1	Pearson

Replay	v Sheffield Wednesday	(h)	3-1	Bott 2, J. Smith
5th Round	v Arsenal	(h)	3-3	Pearson, J. Smith 2
Replay	v Arsenal	(a)	0-3	

1936/37

3rd Round	v Preston North End	(a)	0-2	

1937/38

3rd Round	v West Bromwich Albion	(a)	0-1	

1938/39

3rd Round	v Brentford	(a)	2-0	Clifton, Mooney
4th Round	v Cardiff City	(a)	0-0	
Replay	v Cardiff City	(h)	4-1	Clifton, Gordon, Mooney, Park
5th Round	v Preston North End	(h)	1-2	Cairns

1946/47

3rd Round	v Crystal Palace	(h)	6-2	Bentley, Pearson, Shackleton 2, Stobbart, Wayman
4th Round	v Southampton	(h)	3-1	Wayman
5th Round	v Leicester City	(h)	1-1	Shackleton
Replay	v Leicester City	(a)	2-1	Bentley, Pearson
6th Round	v Sheffield United	(a)	2-0	Bentley (pen), Milburn
Semi-Final	v Charlton Athletic	(n)	0-4	

1947/48

3rd Round	v Charlton Athletic	(a)	1-2	Pearson

1948/49

3rd Round	v Bradford	(h)	0-2	

1949/50

3rd Round	v Oldham Athletic	(a)	7-2	Milburn 3, Mitchell, Walker 2, o.g.
4th Round	v Chelsea	(a)	0-3	

1950/51

3rd Round	v Bury	(h)	4-1	Milburn, G. Robledo, Taylor, Walker
4th Round	v Bolton Wanderers	(h)	3-2	Milburn 2, Mitchell
5th Round	v Stoke City	(a)	4-2	Milburn, Mitchell, G. Robledo 2
6th Round	v Bristol Rovers	(h)	0-0	
Replay	v Bristol Rovers	(a)	3-1	Crowe, Milburn, Taylor

Semi-Final	v Wolverhampton Wand.	(n)	0-0	
Replay	v Wolverhampton Wand.	(n)	2-1	Milburn, Mitchell
Final	v Blackpool	(n)	2-0	Milburn 2

1951/52

3rd Round	v Aston Villa	(h)	4-2	Foulkes, Mitchell 2, G. Robledo
4th Round	v Tottenham Hotspur	(a)	3-0	Mitchell, G. Robledo 2
5th Round	v Swansea Town	(a)	1-0	Mitchell
6th Round	v Portsmouth	(a)	4-2	Milburn 3, G. Robledo
Semi-Final	v Blackburn Rovers	(n)	0-0	
Replay	v Blackburn Rovers	(n)	2-1	Mitchell (pen), G. Robledo
Final	v Arsenal	(n)	1-0	G. Robledo

1952/53

3rd Round	v Swansea Town	(h)	3-0	Davies, Keeble, Mitchell
4th Round	v Rotherham United	(h)	1-3	Keeble

1953/54

3rd Round	v Wigan Athletic	(h)	2-2	Broadis, Milburn
Replay	v Wigan Athletic	(a)	3-2	Broadis, Keeble, White
4th Round	v Burnley	(a)	1-1	Broadis
Replay	v Burnley	(h)	1-0	Mitchell (pen)
5th Round	v West Bromwich Albion	(a)	2-3	Milburn, Mitchell

1954/55

3rd Round	v Plymouth Argyle	(a)	1-0	Keeble
4th Round	v Brentford	(h)	3-2	Curry, Hannah, R. Mitchell
5th Round	v Nottingham Forest	(a)	1-1	Milburn
Replay	v Nottingham Forest	(h)	2-2	Keeble, R. Mitchell
2nd Replay	v Nottingham Forest	(h)	2-1	Monkhouse 2
6th Round	v Huddersfield Town	(a)	1-1	White
Replay	v Huddersfield Town	(h)	2-0	Keeble, R. Mitchell
Semi-Final	v York City	(n)	1-1	Keeble
Replay	v York City	(n)	2-0	Keeble, White
Final	v Manchester City	(n)	3-1	Hannah, Milburn, R. Mitchell

1955/56

3rd Round	v Sheffield Wednesday	(a)	3-1	Curry, Keeble, Milburn
4th Round	v Fulham	(a)	5-4	Casey, Keeble 2, Milburn, Stokoe
5th Round	v Stoke City	(h)	2-1	Curry, Mitchell
6th Round	v Sunderland	(h)	0-2	

1956/57

3rd Round	v Manchester City	(h)	1-1	White
Replay	v Manchester City	(a)	5-4	Curry, Tait, White 2, Casey (pen)
4th Round	v Millwall	(a)	1-2	Tait

1957/58 /

3rd Round	v Plymouth Argyle	(a)	6-1	Eastham 2, R. Mitchell, White 3
4th Round	v Scunthorpe United	(h)	1-3	Paterson

1958/59

3rd Round	v Chelsea	(h)	1-4	Eastham

1959/60

3rd Round	v Wolverhampton Wand.	(h)	2-2	Allchurch, Eastham
Replay	v Wolverhampton Wand.	(a)	2-4	Eastham, White

1960/61

3rd Round	v Fulham	(h)	5-0	Allchurch, Neale 3, Woods
4th Round	v Stockport County	(h)	4-0	Allchurch, White, Woods 2
5th Round	v Stoke City	(h)	3-1	Scanlon, Allchurch, McKinley (pen)
6th Round	v Sheffield United	(h)	1-3	McGuigan

1961/62

3rd Round	v Peterborough United	(h)	0-1	

1962/63

3rd Round	v Bradford City	(a)	6-1	McGarry 2, Thomas, Hilley, Hughes 2
4th Round	v Norwich City	(a)	0-5	

1963/64

3rd Round	v Bedford Town	(h)	1-2	Anderson

1964/65

3rd Round	v Swansea Town	(a)	0-1	

1965/66

3rd Round	v Chester City	(a)	3-1	Robson, McGarry, Craig
4th Round	v Sheffield Wednesday	(h)	1-2	Suddick

1966/67

3rd Round	v Coventry City	(a)	4-3	Davies 3, B. Robson
4th Round	v Nottingham Forest	(a)	0-3	

1967/68

3rd Round	v Carlisle United	(h)	0-1	

1968/69

3rd Round	v Reading	(h)	4-0	Craig, Dyson, B. Robson, Scott
4th Round	v Manchester City	(h)	0-0	
Replay	v Manchester City	(a)	0-2	

1969/70

3rd Round	v Southampton	(a)	0-3	

1970/71

3rd Round	v Ipswich Town	(h)	1-1	Mitchell
Replay	v Ipswich Town	(a)	1-2	Robson

1971/72

3rd Round	v Hereford United	(h)	2-2	Tudor, MacDonald
Replay	v Hereford United	(a)	1-2	MacDonald

1972/73

3rd Round	v Bournemouth	(h)	2-0	MacDonald, o.g.
4th Round	v Luton Town	(h)	0-2	

1973/74

3rd Round	v Hendon	(h)	1-1	Howard
Replay	v Hendon	(a*)	4-0	Hibbit, Tudor, MacDonald, McDermott (pen)

* Played at Vicarage Road, Watford

4th Round	v Scunthorpe United	(h)	1-1	McDermott
Replay	v Scunthorpe United	(a)	3-0	MacDonald 2, Barrowclough
5th Round	v West Bromwich Albion	(a)	3-0	Tudor, MacDonald, Barrowclough
6th Round	v Nottingham Forest	(h)	4-3+	Tudor, Moncur, McDermott (pen), D.J. Craig

+ Match annulled by order of FA

6th Round	v Nottingham Forest	(n)	0-0	
Replay	v Nottingham Forest	(n)	1-0	MacDonald

Semi-Final	v Burnley	(n)	2-0	MacDonald
Final	v Liverpool	(n)	0-3	

1974/75

3rd Round	v Manchester City	(a*)	2-0	Nulty, Burns

* Scheduled for Newcastle, but played at Manchester by order of FA

4th Round	v Walsall	(a)	0-1	

1975/76

3rd Round	v Queens Park Rangers	(a)	0-0	
Replay	v Queens Park Rangers	(h)	2-1	T. Craig (pen), Gowling
4th Round	v Coventry City	(a)	1-1	Gowling
Replay	v Coventry City	(h)	5-0	Gowling, MacDonald 2, Cassidy, Burns
5th Round	v Bolton Wanderers	(a)	3-3	Gowling, MacDonald 2
Replay	v Bolton Wanderers	(h)	0-0	
2nd Replay	v Bolton Wanderers	(n)	2-1	Gowling, Burns
6th Round	v Derby County	(a)	2-4	Gowling 2

1976/77

3rd Round	v Sheffield United	(a)	0-0	
Replay	v Sheffield United	(h)	3-1	T. Craig, Burns, McCaffery
4th Round	v Manchester City	(h)	1-3	Gowling

1977/78

3rd Round	v Peterborough United	(a)	1-1	Hudson
Replay	v Peterborough United	(h)	2-0	T. Craig (pen), Blackhall
4th Round	v Wrexham	(h)	2-2	Bird, Blackhall
Replay	v Wrexham	(a)	1-4	Burns

1978/79

3rd Round	v Torquay United	(h)	3-1	Robinson, Withe, Nattrass (pen)
4th Round	v Wolverhampton Wand.	(h)	1-1	Withe
Replay	v Wolverhampton Wand.	(a)	0-1	

1979/80

3rd Round	v Chester City	(h)	0-2	

1980/81

3rd Round	v Sheffield Wednesday	(h)	2-1	Waddle 2
4th Round	v Luton Town	(h)	2-1	Clarke, Martin
5th Round	v Exeter City	(h)	1-1	Shoulder
Replay	v Exeter City	(a)	0-4	

1981/82

3rd Round	v Colchester United	(h)	1-1	Varadi
Replay	v Colchester United	(a)	4-3	Waddle, Varadi, Saunders, Brownlie
4th Round	v Grimsby Town	(h)	1-2	o.g.

1982/83

3rd Round	v Brighton & Hove Albion	(a)	1-1	McDermott
4th Round	v Brighton & Hove Albion	(h)	0-1	

1983/84

3rd Round	v Liverpool	(a)	0-4	

1984/85

3rd Round	v Nottingham Forest	(a)	1-1	Megson
Replay	v Nottingham Forest	(h)	1-3	Waddle

1985/86

3rd Round	v Brighton & Hove Albion	(h)	0-2	

1986/87

3rd Round	v Northampton Town	(h)	2-1	A. Thomas, Goddard
4th Round	v Preston North End	(h)	2-0	Roeder, Goddard
5th Round	v Tottenham Hotspur	(a)	0-1	

1987/88

3rd Round	v Crystal Palace	(h)	1-0	Gascoigne
4th Round	v Swindon Town	(h)	5-0	D. Jackson, Goddard, Gascoigne 2 (1 pen), O'Neill
5th Round	v Wimbledon	(h)	1-3	McDonald

1988/89

3rd Round	v Watford	(h)	0-0	
Replay	v Watford	(a)	2-2	Brock, Mirandinha (pen)
2nd Replay	v Watford	(h)	0-0	
3rd Replay	v Watford	(a)	0-1	

1989/90

3rd Round	v Hull City	(a)	1-0	O'Brien
4th Round	v Reading	(a)	3-3	McGhee 2, Quinn
Replay	v Reading	(h)	4-1	McGhee 2, Quinn, Robinson
5th Round	v Manchester United	(h)	2-3	McGhee (pen), Scott

1990/91

3rd Round	v Derby County	(h)	2-0	Quinn, Stimson
4th Round	v Nottingham Forest	(h)	2-2	Quinn, McGhee
Replay	v Nottingham Forest	(a)	0-3	

1991/92

3rd Round	v Bournemoouth	(a)	0-0	
Replay	v Bournemouth	(h)	0-0*	
	Abandoned after 17 min – fog			
Replay	v Bournemouth	(h)	2-2	Hunt 2
	aet Bournemouth won 4-3 on penalties			

1992/93

3rd Round	v Port Vale	(h)	4-0	Peacock 2, Lee, Sheedy
4th Round	v Rotherham United	(a)	1-1	Lee
Replay	v Rotherham United	(h)	2-0	Kelly, Clark
5th Round	v Blackburn Rovers	(a)	0-1	

1993/94

3rd Round	v Coventry City	(h)	2-0	Cole, Beardsley
4th Round	v Luton Town	(h)	1-1	Beardsley
Replay	v Luton Town	(a)	0-2	

Full Record in Domestic Cup Competitions – *League Cup*

1960/61

1st Round	v Colchester United	(a)	1-4	Neale

1961/62

1st Round	v Scunthorpe United	(h)	2-0	Hale, Allchurch
2nd Round	v Sheffield United	(a)	2-2	McGuigan, McKinney
Replay	v Sheffield United	(h)	0-2	

1962/63

2nd Round	v Leyton Orient	(h)	1-1	
Replay	v Leyton Orient	(a)	2-4	Suddick og

1963/64

2nd Round	v Preston North End	(h)	3-0	McGarry (pen), Thomas, Burton
3rd Round	v Bournemouth	(a)	1-2	McGarry (pen)

1964/65

2nd Round	v Blackpool	(a)	0-3	

1965/66

2nd Round	v Peterborough United	(h)	3-4	Hiley, Bennett, Iley

1966/67

2nd Round	v Leeds United	(a)	0-1	

1967/68

2nd Round	v Lincoln City	(a)	1-2	Burton

1968/69

2nd Round	v Southport	(a)	2-0	B. Robson (pen), Sinclair
3rd Round	v Southampton	(a)	1-4	B. Robson

1969/70

2nd Round	v Sheffield United	(a)	0-2	

1970/71

2nd Round	v Bristol Rovers	(a)	1-2	Dyson

1971/72

2nd Round	v Halifax Town	(h)	2-1	MacDonald, Cassidy
3rd Round	v Arsenal	(a)	0-4	

1972/73

2nd Round	v Port Vale	(a)	3-1	MacDonald, Barrowclough, Craig
3rd Round	v Blackpool	(h)	0-3	

1973/74

2nd Round	v Doncaster Rovers	(h)	6-0	Robson 2, MacDonald 3, Clark
3rd Round	v Birmingham City	(a)	2-2	Gibb, McDermott
Replay	v Birmingham City	(h)	0-1	

1974/75

2nd Round	v Nottingham Forest	(a)	1-1	MacDonald
Replay	v Nottingham Forest	(h)	3-0	MacDonald, Burns, Keeley
3rd Round	v Queens Park Rangers	(a)	4-0	Tudor, MacDonald 3
4th Round	v Fulham	(h)	3-0	Cannell, MacDonald, Cassidy
5th Round	v Chester City	(h)	0-0	
Replay	v Chester City	(a)	0-1	

1975/76

2nd Round	v Southport	(h*)	6-0	Gowling 4, Cannell 2
Drawn for Southport, but switched to Newcastle				
3rd Round	v Bristol Rovers	(a)	1-1	Gowling
Replay	v Bristol Rovers	(h)	2-0	T. Craig (pen),

				Nattrass
4th Round	v Queens Park Rangers	(a)	3-1	MacDonald, Burns, Nulty
5th Round	v Notts. County	(h)	1-0	o.g.
Semi-Final (1)	v Tottenham Hotspur	(a)	0-1	
Semi-Final (2)	v Tottenham Hotspur	(h)	3-1	Gowling, Keeley, Nulty
Final	v Manchester City	(Wem)	1-2	Gowling

1976/77

2nd Round	v Gillingham	(a)	2-1	Cassidy, Cannell
3rd Round	v Stoke City	(h)	3-0	T. Craig (pen), Burns, Nattrass
4th Round	v Manchester United	(a)	2-7	Burns. Nattrass

1977/78

2nd Round	v Millwall	(h)	0-2	

1978/79

2nd Round	v Watford	(a)	1-2	Pearson

1979/80

2nd Round (1)	v Sunderland	(a)	2-2	Davies, Cartwright
2nd Round (2)	v Sunderland	(h)	2-2*	Shoulder, Boam

(*aet Sunderland won on penalties)

1980/81

2nd Round (1)	v Bury	(h)	3-2	Rafferty 2, Shoulder
2nd Round (2)	v Bury	(a)	0-1	

1981/82

2nd Round (1)	v Fulham	(h)	1-2	Barton
2nd Round (2)	v Fulham	(a)	0-2	

1982/83

2nd Round (1)	v Leeds United	(a)	1-0	Varadi
2nd Round (2)	v Leeds United	(h)	1-4	Clarke

1983/84

2nd Round (1)	v Oxford United	(h)	1-1	McDermott
2nd Round (2)	v Oxford United	(a)	1-2	Keegan

1984/85

2nd Round (1)	v Bradford City	(h)	3-1	Wharton, McDonald, Ferris
2nd Round (2)	v Bradford City	(a)	1-0	Waddle
3rd Round	v Ipswich Town	(a)	1-1	McDonald
Replay	v Ipswich Town	(h)	1-2	Waddle

1985/86

2nd Round (1)	*v* Barnsley	(h)	0-0	
2nd Round (2)	*v* Barnsley	(a)	1-1	Cunningham

Newcastle won on away goals rule

3rd Round	*v* Oxford United		1-3	Cunningham

1986/87

2nd Round (1)	*v* Bradford City	(a)	0-2	
2nd Round (2)	*v* Bradford City	(h)	1-0	Roeder

1987/88

2nd Round (1)	*v* Blackpool	(a)	0-1	
2nd Round (2)	*v* Blackpool	(h)	4-1	D. Jackson, Gascoigne, Goddard, Mirandinha
3rd Round	*v* Wimbledon	(a)	1-2	McDonald (pen)

1988/89

2nd Round (1)	*v* Sheffield United	(a)	0-3	
2nd Round (2)	*v* Sheffield United	(h)	2-0	Hendrie, Mirandinha

1989/90

2nd Round (1)	*v* Reading	(a)	1-3	Gallacher
2nd Round (2)	*v* Reading	(h)	4-0	Brazil (pen), Brock, Thorn, McGhee
3rd Round	*v* West Bromwich Albion	(h)	0-1	

1990/91

2nd Round (1)	*v* Middlesbrough	(a)	0-2	
2nd Round (2)	*v* Middlesbrough	(h)	1-0	Anderson

1991/92

2nd Round (1)	*v* Crewe Alexandra	(a)	4-3	Hunt, Peacock 3
2nd Round (2)	*v* Crewe Alexandra	(h)	1-0	Howey
3rd Round	*v* Peterborough United	(a)	0-1	

1992/93

1st Round (1)	*v* Mansfield Town	(h)	2-1	Peacock 2
1st Round (2)	*v* Mansfield Town	(a)	0-0	
2nd Round (1)	*v* Middlesbrough	(h)	0-0	
2nd Round (2)	*v* Middlesbrough	(a)	3-1	Kelly 2, O'Brien
3rd Round	*v* Chelsea	(a)	1-2	Lee

1993/94

2nd Round (1)	v Notts. County	(h)	4-1	Cole 3, Bracewell
2nd Round (2)	v Notts. County	(a)	7-1	Allen 2, Beardsley, Cole 3, Lee
3rd Round	v Wimbledon	(a)	1-2	Sellars

Cup Final Squads – *FA Cup*

Date	Opponents	Venue	Score	Att.
15/4/05	v Aston Villa	Crystal Palace	Lost 0-2	101.117

Team: Lawrence, McCombie, Carr, Gardner, Aitken, McWilliam, Rutherford, Howie, Appleyard, Veitch, Gosnell

21/4/06	v Everton	Crystal Palace	Lost 0-1	75,609

Team: Lawrence, McCombie, Carr, Gardner, Aitken, McWilliam, Rutherford J, Howie, Veitch, Orr, Gosnell

Ten of the eleven players who appeared in Newcastle's first Cup Final side were also there for the second, the only change being Orr for Appleyard. Appleyard was, however, United's leading scorer in the 05/06 competition with 6 goals.

25/4/08	v Wolverhampton Wanderers	Crystal Palace	Lost 1-3	65,000

Team: Lawrence, McCracken, Pudan, Gardner, Veitch, McWilliam, Rutherford, Howie, Appleyard, Speedie, Wilson. Scorer: Howie

23/4/10	v Barnsley	Crystal Palace	Drew 1-1	76,980

Team: Lawrence, McCracken, Whitson, Veitch, Low, McWilliam, Rutherford, Howie, Shepherd, Higgins, Wilson. Scorer: Rutherford

28/4/10	v Barnsley	Goodison Park	Won 2-0	55,364

Team: Lawrence, McCracken, Carr, Veitch, Low, McWilliam, Rutherford, Howie, Shepherd, Higgins, Wilson. Scorer: Shepherd 2 (1 pen)

So Lawrence, Carr, Veitch, Rutherford, McWilliam and Howie had all survived the five years since that first Cup Final, most playing in all five games before finally collecting winners medals.

22/4/11	v Bradford City	Crystal Palace	Drew 0-0	69,800

Team: Lawrence, McCracken, Whitson, Veitch, Low, Willis, Rutherford, Stewart, Jobey, Higgins, Wilson.

This Final was Jobey's first appearance in the competition

26/4/11	v Bradford City	Old Trafford	Lost 0-1	66,646

Team: Lawrence, McCracken, Whitson, Veitch, Low, Willis, Rutherford, Stewart, Jobey, Higgins, Wilson

27/4/24 *v* Aston Villa   Wembley   Won 2-0   91,695
Team: Bradley, Hampson, Hudspeth, Mooney, Spencer, Gibson, J Low, Cowan, Harris, McDonald, Seymour. Scorers: Seymour, Harris

23/4/32 *v* Arsenal   Wembley   Won 2-1   92,298
Team: McInroy, Nelson, Fairhurst, McKenzie, Davidson, Weaver, Boyd, JR Richardson, Allen, McMenemy, Lang. Scorer: Allen 2
This same team played in very nearly every game of the 31/32 Competition. The one change was when Cape played at No 9 instead of Allen, in the 4th Round, 2nd Replay against Southport.

28/4/51 *v* Blackpool   Wembley   Won 2-0   100,000
Team: Fairbrother, Cowell, Corbett, Harvey, Brennan, Crowe, Walker, Taylor, Milburn, G Robledo, Mitchell. Scorer: Milburn 2

3/5/52 *v* Arsenal   Wembley   Won 1-0   100,000
Team: Simpson, Cowell, McMichael, Harvey, Brennan, E Robledo, Walker, Foulkes, Milburn, G Robledo, Mitchell. Scorer: G Robledo

7/5/55 *v* Manchester City   Wembley   Won 3-1   100,000
Team: Simpson, Cowell, Batty, Scoular, Stokoe, Casey, White, Milburn, Keeble, Hannah, R Mitchell. Scorers: Hannah, Milburn, R Mitchell

4/5/74 *v* Liverpool   Wembley   Lost 0-3   100,00
Team: McFaul, Clark, Kennedy, McDermott, Howard, Moncur, Smith (Gibb), Cassidy, MacDonald, Tudor, Hibbitt.

Cup Final Squad – *League Cup*

28/2/76 *v* Manchester City   Wembley   Lost 1-2   100,000
Team: Mahoney, Nattrass, Kennedy, Barrowclough, Keeley, Howard, Burns, Cassidy, MacDonald, Gowling – T Craig, Sub not used: Cannell. *Scorer:* Gowling

Cup Final Squads – *FA Charity Shield*

28/4/09 *v* Northampton Town   (Stamford Bridge)   2-0   7,000
Team: Lawrence, McCracken, Whitson, Willis, Veitch, McWilliam, Rutherford, Howie, Allan. Wilson, Anderson. *Scorers* : Allan, Rutherford

12/10/32 *v* Everton   (h)   3-5   15,000
Team: Burns, Nelson, Fairhurst, Bell, Davidson, Weaver, Boyd, Richardson, Allen, McMenemy, Lang. *Scorers:* Boyd, McMenemy 2

24/9/51 *v* Tottenham Hotspur   (a)   1-2   27.760
Team: Simpson, Duncan, McMichael, Harvey, Brennan, E Robledo, Walker, G Robledo, Milburn, Hannah, Mitchell. *Scorers:* Milburn

24/9/52   v Manchester United   (a)   2-4   11,381

Team: Simpson, Cowell, Batty, E Robledo, Stokoe, Casey, Walker, G Robledo, Keeble, Black, Mitchell. *Scorer:* Keeble 2

14/9/55   v Chelsea   (a)   0-3   12,802

Team: Thompson, Lackenby, McMichael, Scoular, Brennan, Casey, White, Davies, Milburn, Hannah, Punton

Other Competitions – *Texaco Cup*

1971/72

1st Round (1)	v Hearts	(a)	0-1	
1st Round (2)	v Hearts	(h)	2-1*	MacDonald 2
	(2-2 on aggregate; Newcastle won on penalties)			
2nd Round (1)	v Coventry City	(a)	1-1	Howard
2nd Round (2)	v Coventry City	(h)	5-1	MacDonald, Tudor 2, Nattrass (og)
Semi-Final (1)	v Derby County	(a)	0-1	
Semi-Final (2)	v Derby County	(h)	2-3	MacDonald, Barrowclough

1972/73

1st Round (1)	v Ayr United	(a)	0-0	
1st Round (2)	v Ayr United	(h)	2-0	Smith, Tudor
2nd Round (1)	v West Bromwich Alb	(a)	1-2	Hibbitt
2nd Round (2)	v West Bromwich Alb	(h)	3-1	Tudor, Gibb Hibbitt
Semi-Final (1)	v Ipswich Town	(h)	1-1	MacDonald
Semi-Final (2)	v Ipswich Town	(a)	0-1	

1973/74

1st Round (1)	v Morton	(a)	2-1	Tudor, Smith
1st Round (2)	v Morton	(h)	1-1	o.g.
2nd Round (1)	v Birmingham City	(a)	1-1	MacDonald (pen)
2nd Round (2)	v Birmingham City	(h)	1-1*	Tudor
	(Abandoned during extra time due to bad light)			
2nd Round (2)	v Birmingham City	3-1	(h)	Tudor 2, Clark
Semi-Final (1)	v Dundee United	(a)	0-2	
Semi-Final (2)	v Dundee United	(h)	4-1	Robson, Tudor, MacDonald, Cassidy
Final	v Burnley	(h)	2-1	MacDonald, Moncur

1974/75

Group Matches	v Sunderland	(a)	1-2	Tudor

	v Carlisle United	(a)	2-2	Burns 2
	v Middlesbrough	(h)	4-0	MacDonald, Cassidy, Tudor, Burns
2nd Round (1)	v Aberdeen	(a)	1-1	MacDonald
2nd Round (2)	v Aberdeen	(h)	3-2	MacDonald 2, Hibbitt
Semi-Final (1)	v Birmingham City	(h)	1-1	MacDonald
Semi-Final (2)	v Birmingham City	(a)	4-1	Kennedy, Nattrass, Cannell, o.g.
Final (1)	v Southampton	(a)	0-1	
Final (2)	v Southampton	(h)	3-0	Tudor, Bruce, Cannell

(Newcastle won 3-1 on aggregate)

Full Members/Simod/Zenith Data Systems Cup

1986/87
| 1st Round | v Everton | (a) | 2-5 | A. Thomas 2 |

1987/88
| 1st Round | v Shrewsbury Town | (h) | 2-1 | Mirandinha, Bogie |
| 2nd Round | v Bradford City | (a) | 1-2 | Scott |

1988/89
| 1st Round | v Watford | (a) | 1-2 | McDonald |

1989/90
2nd Round	v Oldham Athletic	(h)	2-0	Quinn 2
3rd Round	v Derby County	(h)	3-2	O'Brien, Gallacher, og
Semi-Final	v Middlesbrough	(a)	0-1	

1990/91
| 2nd Round | v Nottingham Forest | (a) | 1-2 | Scott |

1991/92
| 1st Round | v Tranmere Rovers | (a) | 6-6 | Quinn 3 (1 pen), Peacock 2, Clark |

aet Tranmere won 4-3 on penalties

Other Competitions – *Anglo Scottish Cup*

1975/76

Group Matches	v Carlisle United	(a)	0-2	
	v Sunderland	(h)	0-2	
	v Middlesbrough	(h)	2-2	Hibbitt, Gowling

1976/77

Group Matches	v Sheffield United	(**)	1-0	Gowling
	v Hull City	(a)	0-0	
	v Middlesbrough	(h)	3-0	Gowling 2, Barrowclough
2nd Round (1)	v Ayr United	(a)	0-3	

Newcastle were disqualified for fielding an under strength side at Ayr, without the second leg being played

Other Competitions – *Anglo Italian Cup*

1972/73

League Matches	v Roma	(a)	2-0	Tudor 2
	v Bologna	(h)	1-0	Gibb
	v Como	(a)	2-0	Moncur, Tudor
	v Torino	(h)	5-1	Tudor, MacDonald, Smith, Hibbitt, og
Semi-Final (1)	v Crystal Palace	(a)	0-0	
Semi-Final (2)	v Crystal Palace	(h)	5-1	MacDonald 3, Barrowclough, Gibb
Final	v Fiorentina	(a)	2-1	D Craig, o.g.

Team: McFaul, D Craig, Clark, McDermott, Howard, Moncur, Cassidy, Smith, Tudor, Gibb, Hibbitt, Subs not used: Steele, Robson, Nattrass

1992/93

Group Matches	v Grimsby Town	(a)	2-2	Quinn, Kelly
	v Leicester City	(h)	4-0	Brock, Quinn 2 (1 pen), Sheedy
International Stage	v Lucchese	(a)	1-1	Kristensen
	v Ascoli	(h)	0-1	
	v Bari	(a)	0-3	
	v Cesena	(h)	2-2	Peacock 2

European Cup Competitions – *Inter-Cities Fairs Cup*

1968/69

1st Round	v Feyenoord	(h)	4-0	Davies, Gibb, B. Robson, Scott
	v Feyenoord	(a)	0-2	
2nd Round	v Sporting Lisbon	(a)	1-1	Scott
	v Sporting Lisbon	(h)	1-0	B. Robson
3rd Round	v Real Zaragoza	(a)	2-3	Davies, B. Robson
	v Real Zaragoza	(h)	2-1	Gibb, B. Robson
4th Round	v Vitoria Setubal	(h)	5-1	Davies, Foggon, Gibb, B. Robson
	v Vitoria Setubal	(a)	1-3	Davies
Semi-Final	v Glasgow Rangers	(a)	0-0	
	v Glasgow Rangers	(h)	2-0	Scott, Sinclair
Final	v Ujpesti Dozsa	(h)	3-0	Moncur 2, Scott
	v Ujpesti Dozsa	(a)	3-2	Arentoft, Foggon, Moncur

European Cup Competitions – *European Fairs Cup*

1969/70

1st Round	v Dundee United	(a)	2-1	Davies 2
	v Dundee United	(h)	1-0	Dyson
2nd Round	v FC Porto	(a)	0-0	
	v FC Porto	(h)	1-0	Scott
3rd Round	v Southampton	(h)	0-0	
	v Southampton	(a)	1-1	Robson
4th Round	v Anderlecht	(a)	0-2	
	v Anderlecht	(h)	3-1	Dyson, Robson 2

1970/71

1st Round	v Inter Milan	(a)	1-1	Davies
	v Inter Milan	(h)	2-0	Davies, Moncur
2nd Round	v Pecsi Dozsa	(h)	2-0	Davies 2
	v Pecsi Dozsa	(a)	0-2*	

*Pecsi Dozsa won on penalties

European Cup Competitions – *UEFA Cup*

1977/78

1st Round	v Bohemians	(a)	0-0	
	v Bohemians	(h)	4-0	T. Craig 2, Gowling 2
2nd Round	v Bastia	(a)	1-2	Cannell
	v Bastia	(h)	1-3	Gowling

Cup Final Squads – *Fairs Cup*

29/5/69   v Ujpesti Dozsa   (h)   Won 3-0   59,234
Team: McFaul, Craig, Clark, Gibb, Burton, Moncur, Scott, B Robson, Davies, Arentoft, Sinclair (Foggon), Subs not used: Hope, Craggs. *Scorers:* Moncur 2, Scott

11/6/69   v Ujpesti Dozsa   (a)   Won 3-2   34,000
Team: McFaul, Craig, Clark, Gibb, Burton, Moncur, Scott (Foggon), B Robson, Davies, Arentoft, Sinclair, Subs not used: Hope, McNamee. *Scorers:* Arentoft, Foggon, Moncur

Miscellaneous

Managers

Frank G. Watt – Secretary-Manager 1896-1930

Known as the Governor, Frank Watt was arguably the most influential figure in the club's history. Born in Edinburgh, Watt was a former referee who built the team into the dominant force in Edwardian football.

Honours

League Championship:	1905,1907,1909, 1927
2nd Division Promotion:	1898
FA Cup Winners:	1910, 1924
FA Cup Runners Up:	1905, 1906, 1908, 1911
FA Charity Shield Winners:	1909

Andy Cunningham – 1930-1935

After one year as a player, Andy Cunningham became United's first manager in January 1930, possibly the First Division's first player-manager. Born in Kilmarnock and 12 times a Scottish International, he had signed from Glasgow Rangers for £2,300. He took over an ailing team and with the sale of Hughie Gallacher he had a big rebuilding job on his hands. He succeeded to start with, winning the FA Cup in 1932, but he presided over the relegation squad of 1934 and finally left at the end of the 1935 season. He was later manager of Dundee and, after the war, a sports journalist. He died in 1973.

Honours

FA Cup Winner:	1932

Tom Mather – 1935-1939

Mather was appointed as replacement to Cunningham in June 1935, after having been a successful manager at Stoke City, taking the Potters to a Second Division title. His four seasons in charge saw United fail to get out of the Second Division, nearly being relegated to the Third in 1938. After the war he was manager of Leicester City and Kilmarnock, before retiring back to Stoke, where he died in 1957.

Stan Seymour – 1939-47 and 1950-1954

Seymour played more than 250 games for the Magpies between 1920 and 1929, before being elected to the board when he retired as a player. He took charge of team affairs during the Second World War and for the first league season afterwards, steered the side to an FA Cup Semi-Final. He took over the reins again in 1950 when George Martin moved on and was behind the back to back FA Cup winning teams of the fifties. Born in County Durham, his early playing career took in Bradford City and Greenock Morton. One of the most devoted and influential figures in the club's history, he remained as a director of the club until his death in 1973. His son, also called Stan, was a Chairman of the Club.

Honours

As Player

FA Cup Winner:	1924
League Championship:	1927

As Manager

FA Cup Winner:	1951, 1952

George Martin – 1947-1950

Born in Bathgate, Scotland, Martin had a playing career which took in Hull City, Everton, Middlesbrough and Luton. He became Luton manager during the war. He took over at St James' Park in 1947, taking the team back to the First Division in his first season. Late in 1950 he moved to Aston Villa and was to be scout and caretaker manager for Luton again. He died in 1972.

Honours

Second Division Promotion:	1948

Duggie Livingstone – 1954-1956

Duggie Livingstone was a highly experienced manager when he came to Tyneside but, despite the FA Cup success, his tenure was not a happy one. He first dropped and was then ordered to reinstate Jackie Milburn, before he left to join Fulham in January 1956.

Born near Dumbarton, Livingstone was a player with Celtic and Everton and became a coach with Exeter City. He then spent ten years with Sheffield United before moving into management with Sheffield Wednesday. He had spells as manager of Sparta Rotterdam and both the Republic of Ireland and Belgium national sides. After Newcastle and Fulham he finished his career at Chesterfield. He died in 1981 while living in Marlow in Buckinghamshire.

Honours

FA Cup Winner:	1955

Charlie Mitten – 1958-61

Mitten took over after the club had been without a manager for two years. He spent just over three seasons with the club, with little success. Born in Rangoon – his parents were in the Army – Mitten played for Manchester United and England and finished his career with Fulham and then Mansfield. After building a promising squad, United suffered relegation during his third season in charge and he was dismissed in October 1961. His son, John, later played for the Magpies.

Norman Smith – 1961-1962

Smith led the team for less than one season, finishing 11th in the Second Division after taking over as manager following Mitten's departure. He had been the team's trainer for the previous 23 years. He was 64 when he took over and it was never intended to be a long term appointment.

He was born in Newcastle and had a playing career with Huddersfield – with whom he won three Championship medals – Sheffield Wednesday and Queens Park Rangers. He retired after the 1962 season and died in Newcastle in 1978.

Joe Harvey – 1962-1975

Joe Harvey was a Newcastle man through and through. The Yorkshire born right-half had his first taste of League football before the War with Bradford City, but signed for United in 1945 for £4,250. He became Captain and won promotion from the Second Division and two FA Cups. He became player-coach in 1953, but soon left to be manager of first Workington, then Barrow. He came back to Newcastle in 1962 and his 13 years in charge saw a Second Division Championship, victory in Europe and an FA Cup Final. He retired in 1975, but later became assistant manager and scout. He died in 1989.

Honours

As Player

FA Cup Winner:	1951, 1952
2nd Division Promotion:	1948

As Manager

Inter-Cities Fairs Cup Winner:	1969
2nd Division Champions:	1965
FA Cup Runners-Up:	1974

Gordon Lee – 1975-77

Gordon Lee built a good Newcastle team during his brief reign, but he won few fans, selling star striker Malcolm MacDonald to the dismay of the Gallowgate faithful.

Lee's playing career took in Aston Villa and Shrewsbury Town, where he later became coach. His first managerial post was at Port Vale, where he won the Fourth Division title and he came to Newcastle the season after steering Blackburn Rovers to the Third Division title. In his first full year he took United to the League Cup Final, but in January 1977 he left suddenly. He was later manager of Preston, Reykjavik of Iceland and Leicester City.

Honours

League Cup Runners-Up:	1976

Richard Dinnis – 1977

Dinnis took over Lee's prospering side and finished the 1976/77 season in 5th place but by the time of his dismissal in November they were struggling at the foot of the league. He had arrived as assistant to Lee, who he had also worked with at Blackburn. The Lancashire-born Dinnis was never a professional player but moved into coaching with Burnley. After Newcastle he went to the States, later returning to Blackburn. He also had spells at Bristol City, Middlesbrough and in Saudi Arabia.

Bill McGarry – 1977-80

McGarry's playing career took in Port Vale and Huddersfield, where he became an England international. He became player-manager of Bournemouth, before moving on to Watford and Ipswich. He had eight years as manager of Wolves before trying his luck in Saudi Arabia. He became Newcastle manager after Dinnis' dismissal but couldn't save United from relegation. In his two full seasons in charge he couldn't quite build a promotion winning team and he was sacked soon after the start of the 1980/81 season. His later career saw him take several coaching jobs around the globe, in Africa and the Middle East, as well as working at Brighton and Wolves. He died in 1991.

Arthur Cox – 1980-1984

Midlands born Cox's playing career was stopped in its tracks through injury at the age of 18. He began coaching in 1958 with Coventry, later working with Walsall, Aston Villa, Preston and Halifax. He became assistant manager at Blackpool and was Bob Stokoe's assistant at Sunderland when they won the FA Cup in 1973. He briefly worked in Turkey before becoming Chesterfield manager from where he joined Newcastle.

He built a fine side, including Kevin Keegan, which won promotion in 1984 but surprisingly quit before the the start of the next season, to join the then Third Division Derby County. He took County back to the First, but was sacked in 1993. He has recently rejoined Newcastle as part of Kevin Keegan's management team.

Honours

2nd Division Promotion: 1984

Jack Charlton – 1984-1985

A hugely successful player with Leeds United and England, Jack Charlton was part of the 1966 World Cup winning team. He retired from playing in 1972 to become manager of Middlesbrough with whom he won the Second Division title in 1974. He had another successful spell as boss of Sheffield Wednesday, but then drifted away from the game to concentrate on his television and fishing careers. He was tempted out of retirement by Newcastle but although he had a reasonably successful season in charge, his appetite was not in the club game. He left suddenly just before the 1985 season, and in 1986 became manager of the Republic of Ireland, who he has now taken to the final stages of two World Cups.

Willie McFaul – 1985-1988

The Northern Irish goalkeeper was brought to United in 1966 by Joe Harvey and went on to play 355 games for the Magpies. He also won six international caps. He retired as a player in 1975 and became coach of Newcastle's juniors, remaining at the club until his appointment as manager. His first season in charge showed plenty of promise but by the time he left in October 1988 the team was on its way back to the Second Division

Jim Smith – 1988-1991

Smith took over at Newcastle when first choice Howard Kendall turned the job down. A player with a string of lower division clubs he became manager of Colchester United in 1972. He had spells at Blackburn, Birmingham City, Oxford and Queens Park Rangers, never quite achieving the success he deserved. He had a similar experience at Newcastle, suffering relegation in his 1989 and finally losing his place in 1991. He moved on to become boss at Portsmouth, where he remains.

Ossie Ardiles – 1991-1992

Ossie was a World Cup winner with Argentina, before he brought his South American skills to Tottenham, with whom he won an FA Cup Winners medal. He became player manager at Swindon, before moving to St James' Park, but despite building an attractive team, results were poor and he was dismissed after little more than a year. He became boss at West Bromwich Albion, taking them back to the First Division, and is now in charge at Tottenham.

Kevin Keegan – 1992-

Keegan had a glorious playing career which took in Liverpool, SV Hamburg, Southampton and Newcastle, winning numerous honours and 63 caps for England. When he finished playing he left the game, but was tempted back to St James' Park in 1992 where success was almost immediate. He saved the team from relegation, then took them to the First Division title, third place in the Premiership and – hopefully – back into Europe.

Honours
1st Division Champions: 1993

The History of Newcastle United

In the late nineteenth century, Newcastle was just becoming one of the most important industrial centres in Britain and with the growth of the city came serious football. The first organised matches were played in 1877, with the earliest clubs of the region including Tyne Association and Newcastle Rangers. However, it was only in November 1881 that the team that was to become United was born. Stanley Cricket Club, based in South Byker, formed their own Football team and in October 1882 this team became known as Newcastle East End. Rosewood FC, also from Byker, merged with East End to make it into one of the strongest teams in the area.

In August 1882, on the other side of the city, a team called West End was formed, again by an existing cricket club and were soon playing their football at a place called St. James' Park. Both teams prospered, especially West End whose side included the Scottish Internationals Ralph Aitken and Bob Kelso. Then their Secretary-Manager Tom Watson was lured across the city to East End, now playing their football in Heaton, and the balance of power swung. East End turned professional in 1889 and also became a Limited Company, with £1,000 worth of shares issued.

Both teams became members of the Northern League in 1889, West End finishing runners up in their first season, but by spring 1892 the team was in decline and the club had severe financial problems. West End's directors approached East End to negotiate a take-over and by the start of the 1892/93 season, East End were in place at St. James' Park to begin the Northern League campaign – West End were no more. In an effort to revitalise the club a new name was adopted and on December 22nd, 1892, Newcastle United was born.

At this time the Football League was beginning to flourish, and the new club wanted to be a part of it. They applied for membership of the First Division before the 1892 season but were only offered a place in the newly formed Second Division, which they declined. The next season they were again only offered Second Division status but his time they accepted, joining the league along with Liverpool, Rotherham, Woolwich Arsenal and Middlesbrough Ironopolis. The first league game was the long away trip to Plumstead in London, the then home of Woolwich Arsenal and it ended in a 2-2 draw. This was also the year that the famous black and white stripes were first worn.

United's crowds were initially small, but they grew steadily and by 1896 there were 14,000 in attendance for the FA Cup tie against Bury. Then Frank G Watt was appointed as Secretary-Manager and under his 36 year reign United went through perhaps their most glorious years. It started in 1898 with promotion to the First Division after finishing as runners-up to Burnley. The Magpies were to lose their first game in the top flight, 4-2 to Wolves, and the first few seasons were a struggle, but soon a squad had been built that was to become the dominant force in English football.

Players such as the record appearance holder Jimmy Lawrence in goal, Veitch and McCracken in defence and Rutherford and Appleyard up front led the team to their first League Championship in 1905, pipping Everton to the title by one point, and narrowly missing out on doing the 'double', losing their first ever FA Cup Final 2-0 to Aston Villa. The following year they finished fourth in the league and again lost the Cup Final, 1-0 against Everton.

In the 1906/07 season, United again took the league title, equalling the then record points total of 51, but went out of the FA Cup in a shock First Round defeat by then non-league Crystal Palace. There was a third losing Cup Final appearance the following season, 3-1 to Wolves and fourth place in the league, but in 1909 a third League title was claimed, with another record points total.

1910 saw the FA Cup finally arrive on Tyneside at last, following a replay against Barnsley, and there was another Final appearance a year later, this time going down to Bradford City. In those seven seasons, the Magpies had appeared in five FA Cup finals, won three League titles and finished outside the top four only once – a period of success that has been matched by few other teams in the history of the game.

After the devastation of the First World War, Newcastle rebuilt quickly, but were never to quite regain their pre-war dominance. With the new team based around the solid defence of Frank Hudspeth and the flair of Stan Seymour, good league runs in 1920 and 1921 were followed by a second Cup success in 1924. In just the second final to be played at the new Wembley stadium, Seymour and Neil Harris got the goals that beat Aston Villa 2-0.

Then along came Hughie Gallacher, signed from Airdrie, and he was to be United's leading scorer for the next five seasons. The tactical nous of United's Billy McCracken had led to a change in the offside rule, and this gave forwards that much more freedom, which Gallacher exploited to the full. The 1926/27 season, with Gallacher as skipper, saw United run away with the title, winning by a clear five points from reigning champions Huddersfield.

But the bubble burst. The team declined and then, in the close season of 1930, Gallacher was controversially sold to Chelsea and Andy Cunningham was appointed the Magpies' first full time manager. The first home game of the new season saw the still record crowd of 68,386 watch Gallacher's new team lose 1-0 to his old one. After a slow start, Cunningham steadily built a new team culminating in the third FA Cup triumph in 1932 with the controversial 2-1 win over Arsenal.

Cunningham's team was not to prosper and by 1934, United's thirty six year reign in the top flight was over, a run of just one win in the last 14 games resulting in relegation to the Second Division. Cunningham left and Tom Mather took over as manager, but the team struggled in the Second Division, in the 1937/38 season only avoiding relegation to the Third Division North on goal difference.

During the War, however, with former player Stan Seymour now in charge, United rebuilt, bringing a string of players including Jackie Milburn to the club. In the 1946/47 season, Newcastle had a great cup run and narrowly missed promotion, while in 1948 they finally did go back up, and amassed a record average home gate of almost 57,000. Players like Joe Harvey, Frank Brennan and Chilean International George Robledo breathed new life into the team and they just missed the Championship in 1949, but earned their deserved glory with FA Cup wins in 1951, 1952 and 1955.

Despite the arrival of players such as Ivor Allchurch and George Eastham, that third Cup win of the fifties was a peak and the team went into decline. Charlie Mitten took over as boss in 1958 but by 1961 United had been relegated once more and the old crowd favourite Joe Harvey replaced him. Harvey was to remain as manager for the next thirteen years.

His reign saw United slowly build themselves into a solid team, returning to the First Division in 1965, consolidating for a couple of years and then qualifying for Europe for the first time. A team based around the talents of favourites such as Wyn Davies, Bryan Robson and 'keeper Ian McFaul was not expected to do well on the Continent, but surprised everybody by bringing the Inter-Cities Fairs trophy to Tyneside, beating Feyenoord, Sporting Lisbon and Rangers on the way to the final against the Hungarians, Ujpest Dozsa.

United played another two seasons in Europe, but by the end of the 1971 season the team was beginning to age and Harvey brought in new blood. Malcolm MacDonald was the supreme example of the Seventies footballer, and in his five years at St James' Park, Supermac was to win the hearts of the fans.

But it was a bad start to the 1971/72 season, with poor league form and an FA Cup defeat by the then non-league Hereford United, but the team stayed up and by 1974 were at Wembley again, losing to a Kevin Keegan inspired Liverpool.

Harvey gave up the manager's seat in 1975 and Gordon Lee arrived and although he built an effective team, it was not an exciting one and he was unpopular with the fans. He did earn a Wembley appearance in his first season, Newcastle losing the League Cup Final to Manchester City, but MacDonald was sold and Lee's popularity declined even further. He left mid-way through the next season to be replaced by his assistant Richard Dinnis, but these were not happy days. The team collapsed amid a player revolt, crowds dropped below 8,000 and Newcastle were relegated again to the Second Division.

Bill McGarry, then Arthur Cox, led the team through a difficult few seasons. Promotion was never on the cards, there were no great Cup runs and the team's finances were in a parlous state. By 1982 however, a new team was emerging. Peter Beardsley and David McCreery were signed. Chris Waddle graduated from the Juniors and most importantly Kevin Keegan arrived to play out his career with the Magpies. United finished fourth in 1983, then won promotion in 1984 playing attractive, attacking football.

It seemed as if this team could go on to great things, but Cox surprisingly left to join the then Third Division Derby County, before he had taken Newcastle into a First Division game.

Jack Charlton was the new manager and, even with Keegan now retired, his one season in charge saw the team earn a respectable place in the league. Still, Charlton's heart was not in the league game and he left after just the one season, having sold Chris Waddle to Spurs, and Willie McFaul took charge. The team still prospered, with Beardsley in great form for both United and England and the young Paul Gascoigne began to make a mark from the Juniors.

The fans were unhappy when Beardsley was sold to Liverpool, but McFaul appeased them by bringing the exciting Brazilian International Mirandinha to Tyneside. The team was fun to watch but never came close to winning anything and by the time Gascoigne had been sold to Spurs, relegation started to loom again.

Big name signings such as 'keeper Dave Beasant and striker Paul Goddard failed to improve things and McFaul was sacked in October 1988. New manager Jim Smith arrived from QPR, but he couldn't halt the slide and by the end of the season United were back down.

Smith carried on in charge for another two years but he never built a team strong enough to win promotion, although United did finish 3rd in 1990. The play-offs, however, were a disaster, United losing embarrassingly to rivals Sunderland, who had only managed to finish 6th but ended up being promoted. Ossie Ardiles took over in 1991, with terrible results. Towards the end of the 1991/92 season, with relegation looking probable rather than just possible, he was out and the saviour Kevin Keegan arrived. With right-hand man Terry McDermott by his side, he guided the team to safety on the last day of the season and, with Chairman Sir John Hall's bank balance to back him up, built a new team that would run away with the divisional title the following year.

There have been many false dawns for the Magpies in the years since the team's Edwardian dominance. Will Keegan's men – Cole and Beardsley, Lee, Fox, Peacock and co – really go on to achieve greatness? Can you wait for the start of the new season?

Newcastle's Full League Record

Year	P	Home					Away					Pts	Pos	Cup Comps	
		W	D	L	F	A	W	D	L	F	A			FA	Lge
Newcastle East End															
Northern League															
1889/90	18	6	2	1	18	9	3	1	5	14	19	21	2nd	Q	
1890/91	14	5	0	2	20	5	0	2	5	5	34	20	5th	Q	
1891/92	16	6	0	2	24	7	3	2	3	13	12	20	4th		1st
Newcastle West End															
Northern League															
1889/90	18	7	1	1	29	11	5	1	3	15	12	26	2nd	1st	
1890/91	14	2	3	2	15	15	1	1	5	6	23	10	7th	Q	
1891/92	16	3	0	5	13	22	1	0	7	8	34	8	8th	Q	
Newcastle East End/Newcastle United															
Northern League															
1892/93	10	3	0	2	16	6	2	1	2	15	14	11	2nd		1st
Newcastle United															
Division Two															
1893/94	28	12	1	1	44	10	3	5	6	22	29	36	4th	2nd	
1894/95	30	11	1	3	51	28	1	2	12	21	56	27	10th	2nd	
1895/96	30	14	0	1	57	14	2	0	11	16	36	34	5th	2nd	
1896/97	30	13	1	1	42	13	4	0	11	14	39	35	5th	1st	
1897/98	30	14	0	1	43	10	7	3	5	21	22	45	2nd	2nd	

Year	P	W	D	L	F	A	W	D	L	F	A	Pts	Pos	FA	Lge
			Home						*Away*					*Cup Comps*	
Division 1															
1898/99	34	9	3	5	33	18	2	5	10	16	30	30	13th	2nd	
1899/00	34	10	5	2	34	15	3	5	9	19	28	36	5th	2nd	
1900/01	34	10	5	2	27	13	4	5	8	15	24	38	6th	1st	
1901/02	34	11	3	3	41	14	2	6	8	7	20	37	3rd	3rd	
1902/03	34	12	1	4	31	11	2	3	12	10	40	32	14th	1st	
1903/04	34	12	3	2	31	13	6	3	8	27	32	42	4th	1st	
1904/05	34	14	1	2	41	12	6	1	7	31	21	48	1st	F	
1905/06	38	12	4	2	49	23	6	3	10	25	25	43	4th	F	
1906/07	38	18	1	0	51	12	4	6	9	23	34	51	1st	1st	
1907/08	38	11	4	4	41	24	4	8	7	24	30	42	4th	F	
1908/09	38	14	1	4	32	20	10	4	5	33	21	53	1st	S-F	
1909/10	38	14	3	2	33	22	8	3	7	37	34	45	4th	W	
1910/11	38	8	7	4	37	18	7	4	9	24	25	40	8th	F	
1911/12	38	10	4	5	37	25	8	4	7	27	25	44	3rd	1st	
1912/13	38	8	5	6	30	23	5	3	11	17	24	34	14th	4th	
1913/14	38	8	6	4	27	18	4	5	10	12	30	37	11th	1st	
1914/15	38	8	4	7	29	23	3	6	10	17	25	32	15th	4th	
1919/20	42	11	5	5	31	13	6	4	11	13	26	43	8th	2nd	
1920/21	42	14	3	4	43	18	6	7	8	23	27	50	5th	3rd	
1921/22	42	11	5	5	36	19	7	5	9	23	26	46	7th	2nd	
1922/23	42	13	6	2	31	11	5	5	10	14	26	48	4th	1st	
1923/24	42	11	5	5	40	21	4	9	12	20	33	44	9th	W	
1924/25	42	11	6	4	43	18	5	6	10	18	24	48	6th	2nd	
1925/26	42	13	3	5	59	33	3	7	11	25	42	42	10th	5th	
1926/27	42	19	1	1	64	20	6	5	10	32	38	56	1st	5th	

Year	P	W	D	Home L	F	A	W	D	Away L	F	A	Pts	Pos	Cup Comps FA	Lge
1927/28	42	9	7	5	49	41	6	6	9	30	40	43	9th	3rd	
1928/29	42	15	2	4	48	29	4	4	13	22	43	44	10th	3rd	
1929/30	42	13	4	4	52	32	2	3	16	19	60	37	19th	6th	
1930/31	42	9	2	10	41	45	6	4	11	37	42	36	17th	4th	
1931/32	42	13	5	3	52	31	5	1	15	28	56	42	11th	W	
1932/33	42	15	2	4	44	24	7	3	11	27	39	49	5th	3rd	
1933/34	42	6	11	4	42	29	4	3	14	26	48	34	21st	3rd	
2nd Division															
1934/35	42	14	2	5	55	25	8	2	11	34	43	48	6th	4th	
1935/36	42	13	5	3	56	27	7	1	13	32	52	46	8th	5th	
1936/37	42	11	3	7	45	23	11	2	8	35	33	49	4th	3rd	
1937/38	42	12	4	5	38	18	2	4	15	13	40	36	19th	3rd	
1938/39	42	13	3	5	44	21	5	5	9	17	27	46	9th	5th	
1946/47	42	11	4	6	60	32	8	6	7	35	30	48	5th	S-F	
1947/48	42	18	1	2	46	13	6	7	8	26	28	56	2nd	3rd	
1st Division															
1948/49	42	12	5	4	35	29	8	7	6	35	27	52	4th	3rd	
1949/50	42	14	4	3	49	23	5	8	8	28	32	50	5th	4th	
1950/51	42	10	6	5	36	22	8	6	7	26	31	49	4th	W	
1951/52	42	12	4	5	62	28	6	5	10	36	45	45	8th	W	
1952/53	42	9	4	7	34	33	5	4	12	25	37	37	16th	4th	
1953/54	42	9	2	10	43	40	5	8	8	29	37	38	15th	5th	
1954/55	42	12	5	4	53	27	5	4	12	36	50	43	8th	W	
1955/56	42	12	4	5	49	24	5	3	13	36	46	41	11th	6th	

Year	P	Home					Away					Pts	Pos	Cup Comps FA	Lge
		W	D	L	F	A	W	D	L	F	A				
1956/57	42	10	5	6	43	31	4	3	14	24	56	36	17th	4th	
1957/58	42	6	4	11	38	42	6	4	11	35	39	32	19th	4th	
1958/59	42	11	3	7	40	29	6	4	11	40	51	41	11th	3rd	
1959/60	42	10	5	6	42	32	8	3	10	40	46	44	8th	3rd	
1960/61	42	7	7	7	51	49	4	3	14	35	60	32	21st	6th	1st

2nd Division

Year	P	Home					Away					Pts	Pos	Cup Comps FA	Lge
		W	D	L	F	A	W	D	L	F	A				
1961/62	42	10	5	6	40	27	5	4	12	24	31	39	11th	3rd	2nd
1962/63	42	11	8	2	48	23	7	3	11	31	36	47	7th	4th	2nd
1963/64	42	14	2	5	49	26	6	3	12	25	43	45	8th	3rd	3rd
1964/65	42	16	4	1	50	16	8	5	8	31	29	57	1st	3rd	2nd

1st Division

Year	P	Home					Away					Pts	Pos	Cup Comps FA	Lge
		W	D	L	F	A	W	D	L	F	A				
1965/66	42	10	5	6	26	20	4	4	13	24	43	37	15th	4th	2nd
1966/67	42	9	5	7	24	27	3	4	14	15	54	33	20th	4th	2nd
1967/68	42	12	7	2	38	20	1	8	12	16	47	41	10th	3rd	3rd
1968/69	42	12	7	2	40	20	3	7	11	21	35	44	9th	4th	3rd
1969/70	42	14	2	5	42	16	3	11	7	15	19	47	7th	3rd	2nd
1970/71	42	9	9	3	27	16	5	4	12	17	30	41	12th	3rd	3rd
1971/72	42	10	6	5	30	18	5	5	11	19	34	41	11th	3rd	3rd
1972/73	42	12	6	3	35	19	5	7	9	25	32	45	9th	4th	3rd
1973/74	42	9	6	6	28	21	4	6	11	21	27	38	15th	F	3rd
1974/75	42	12	4	5	39	23	3	5	13	20	49	39	15th	4th	5th
1975/76	42	11	4	6	51	26	4	5	12	20	36	39	15th	6th	F
1976/77	42	14	6	1	40	15	4	7	10	24	34	49	5th	4th	4th
1977/78	42	4	6	11	26	37	2	4	15	16	41	22	21st	4th	2nd

Year	P	Home						Away					Pts	Pos	Cup Comps FA	Lge
		W	D	L	F	A		W	D	L	F	A				
2nd Division																
1978/79 42	42	13	3	5	35	24		4	5	12	16	31	42	8th	4th	2nd
1979/80 42	42	13	6	2	35	19		2	8	11	18	30	44	9th	3rd	2nd
1980/81 42	42	11	7	3	22	13		3	7	11	8	32	42	11th	5th	2nd
3 points for a win																
1981/82 42	42	14	4	3	30	14		4	4	13	22	36	62	9th	4th	2nd
1982/83 42	42	13	6	2	43	21		5	7	9	32	32	67	5th	4th	2nd
1983/84 42	42	16	2	3	51	18		8	6	7	34	35	80	3rd	3rd	2nd
1st Division																
1984/85 42	42	11	4	6	33	26		2	9	10	22	44	52	14th	3rd	3rd
1985/86 42	42	12	5	4	46	31		5	7	9	21	41	63	11th	3rd	3rd
1986/87 42	42	10	4	7	33	29		2	7	12	14	36	47	17th	5th	2nd
1987/88 40	40	9	6	5	32	23		5	8	7	23	30	56	8th	5th	3rd
1988/89 38	38	3	6	10	19	28		4	4	11	13	35	31	20th	3rd	2nd
2nd Division																
1989/90 46	46	17	4	2	51	26		5	10	8	29	29	80	3rd*	5th	3rd
Play Offs: Lost 0-2 on aggregate to Sunderland																
1990/91 46	46	8	10	5	24	22		6	7	10	25	34	59	11th	4th	2nd
1991/92 46	46	9	8	6	38	30		4	5	14	28	54	52	20th	3rd	3rd
1st Division																
1992/93 46	46	16	6	1	58	15		13	3	7	34	23	96	1st	5th	3rd
FA Carling Premiership																
1993/94 42	42	14	4	3	51	14		9	4	8	31	27	77	3rd	4th	3rd